Power Plays
How International Institutions Reshape Coercive Diplomacy

Coercive diplomacy – the use of threats and assurances to alter another state's behavior – is indispensable to international relations. Most scholarship has focused on whether and when states are able to use coercive methods to achieve their desired results. However, employing game-theoretic tools, statistical modeling, and detailed case study analysis, *Power Plays* builds and tests a theory that explains how states develop strategies of coercive diplomacy, how their targets shield themselves from these efforts, and the implications for interstate relations. Focusing on the World Trade Organization, *Power Plays* argues that coercive diplomacy often precludes cooperation due to fears of exploitation but that international institutions can solve these problems by convincing states to eschew certain tools for coercive purposes. Yet by constraining the use of some instruments of coercion, institutions cause states to rely on alternative tools, reducing the effectiveness of coercive diplomacy.

Allison Carnegie is an assistant professor of political science at Columbia University. She received a joint PhD in political science and economics from Yale University and was a Postdoctoral Research Fellow at Princeton University from 2013 to 2014. Her work has been published in the *American Political Science Review*, the *American Journal of Political Science*, *Political Analysis*, and the *Election Law Journal*, among other outlets. Carnegie has been awarded the Provost's Grant from Columbia University, along with fellowships from the Bradley, Falk, Ethel Boies Morgan, and Kaufman foundations. Her essay on foreign aid delivery won the Global Development Network's Next Horizons Essay Contest, which was cosponsored by the Bill and Melinda Gates Foundation.

Power Plays

How International Institutions Reshape Coercive Diplomacy

ALLISON CARNEGIE
Columbia University

CAMBRIDGE
UNIVERSITY PRESS

University Printing House, Cambridge CB2 8BS, United Kingdom

One Liberty Plaza, 20th Floor, New York, NY 10006, USA

477 Williamstown Road, Port Melbourne, VIC 3207, Australia

314-321, 3rd Floor, Plot 3, Splendor Forum, Jasola District Centre, New Delhi - 110025, India

103 Penang Road, #05-06/07, Visioncrest Commercial, Singapore 238467

Cambridge University Press is part of the University of Cambridge.

It furthers the University's mission by disseminating knowledge in the pursuit of education, learning and research at the highest international levels of excellence.

www.cambridge.org
Information on this title: www.cambridge.org/9781107121812

© Allison Carnegie 2015

This publication is in copyright. Subject to statutory exception and to the provisions of relevant collective licensing agreements, no reproduction of any part may take place without the written permission of Cambridge University Press.

First published 2015

A catalogue record for this publication is available from the British Library

Library of Congress Cataloging in Publication data
Carnegie, Allison.
Power plays : how international institutions reshape coercive diplomacy / Allison Carnegie.
  pages cm
Includes bibliographical references and index.
ISBN 978-1-107-12181-2 (hardback)
1. International agencies. 2. Non-state actors (International relations) 3. World Trade Organization. 4. Diplomacy. I. Title.
JZ4839.C384   2015
341.2–dc23   2015012677

ISBN 978-1-107-12181-2 Hardback
ISBN 978-1-107-54750-6 Paperback

Cambridge University Press has no responsibility for the persistence or accuracy of URLs for external or third-party internet websites referred to in this publication, and does not guarantee that any content on such websites is, or will remain, accurate or appropriate.

Contents

Figures		*page* vii
Tables		ix
Acknowledgments		xi
1	Introduction	1
	1.1 The Argument in Brief	2
	1.2 Coercive Diplomacy and International Trade	4
	1.3 WTO Reduces Political Hold-up Problems	6
	1.4 Coercive Diplomacy's Displacement and Reduced Effectiveness	9
	1.5 Broader Theoretical Context	9
	1.6 Scope: Institutional Variation	12
	1.7 Method and Plan of the Book	16
2	Theoretical Framework	19
	2.1 Assumptions and Key Concepts	20
	2.2 A Model of Coercive Diplomacy	30
	2.3 Solving the Model	34
	2.4 Appendix: Model Extensions	39
3	Bilateral Agreements and State Similarity	46
	3.1 Hold-up Problems in the Absence of Institutions	47
	3.2 Preference Programs	53
	3.3 Statistical Tests of Coercive Diplomacy	60
4	WTO Membership as a Commitment Strategy	69
	4.1 The WTO and Coercive Diplomacy	71
	4.2 China's WTO Experience	73

		Page
	4.3 Statistical Tests of the WTO and the Reduction of Hold-up Problems	77
	4.4 Testing the Causal Mechanism	80
5	Coercive Diplomacy in Comparative Perspective	89
	5.1 Saudi Arabia, India, and Pakistan	91
	5.2 Nepal, India, and Bangladesh	94
	5.3 Japan, the United States, and India	97
	5.4 Mexico, the United States, and Cuba	101
	5.5 Taiwan, the United States, and China	103
6	Agreements and the Displacement of Coercion	109
	6.1 Instruments of Coercion	110
	6.2 The EU and WTO-Induced Policy Substitution	112
	6.3 Statistical Tests of the WTO and Policy Substitution	116
7	Reduced Effectiveness of Coercion: Evidence from the United States	129
	7.1 WTO Entry and U.S. Influence	130
	7.2 Russia: The Magnitsky Act and Human Rights	131
	7.3 China: The China Commission and Rights Violations	136
	7.4 Vietnam: The Human Rights Act	142
	7.5 Cambodia: Foreign Aid, Visas, and Freedom	146
	7.6 Romania: Accession Agreements and Political Reforms	149
8	Conclusion	155
	8.1 Hold-up at Accession	156
	8.2 Implications for International Relations	158
	8.3 Implications for Welfare	160
Bibliography		165
Index		185

Figures

3.1 Percentage of GSP Investigations.	*page* 63
3.2 Effects of GSP and Dissimilarity on the Percentage of Exports Under GSP.	66
4.1 Effects of WTO on Logged Imports.	82
6.1 Effects of WTO and Human Rights on Logged Imports and Logged Aid.	124
6.2 Years Under GSP Investigation Before and After WTO Entry.	126

Tables

3.1	Effect of GSP and Dissimilarity on the Percentage of Exports Under GSP	*page* 65
4.1	Effect of WTO and Dissimilarity on Logged Imports	81
4.2	Effect of WTO and Contract Intensity on Logged Imports	84
4.3	Effect of WTO on Fixed Capital Investment	85
6.1	Effect of WTO and Human Rights on Logged Imports	120
6.2	Effect of WTO and Human Rights on Logged Foreign Aid	123
6.3	Effect of WTO on GSP Human Rights Investigations	127
7.1	Human Rights Before and After WTO Entry	153

Acknowledgments

This book began in 2009 as a research paper, evolving gradually over the course of my academic studies. As such, it has benefited from almost everyone with whom I have interacted professionally, so I have incurred considerable intellectual and personal debts. First and foremost, I was fortunate to have an exceptionally generous dissertation committee as a graduate student at Yale University. I would like to express my profound appreciation to these three scholars, who guided and helped to shape my thinking and work throughout my graduate studies. Ken Scheve served as an inspiration and intellectual role model and has been an invaluable mentor, teacher, and friend. Ken pushed me to be the best version of myself as a scholar, and I hope that I can someday be the kind of advisor that he has been for me. Giovanni Maggi provided generous and enormously helpful feedback on my dissertation and always supplied a unique and insightful perspective on many topics. Thad Dunning also provided invaluable comments and feedback, along with critical suggestions and advice along the way.

I have benefited greatly from the support of other mentors during graduate school, as well. I am particularly grateful to Susan Hyde for encouragement and guidance throughout my studies and to Don Green for helping me learn how to conduct rigorous research in political science. I also wish to thank Mike Ting for encouraging my nascent interest in political science and for his willingness to work with me as a research assistant prior to graduate school.

After graduate school, I needed some time to reflect and work on turning my dissertation into a book manuscript. The Niehaus Center at Princeton University provided the perfect opportunity to do just that. I am very grateful to Helen Milner and the Niehaus Center for this funding and support. I am also thankful for the friendship, advice, and camaraderie of fellow postdoctoral students at Princeton, including Austin Carson, Julia Gray, Jeff Kucik, Don Leonard, Nimah Mazaheri, Thomas Zeitzoff, and Boliang Zhu.

In addition to their support for my postdoctoral studies, Helen Milner and the Niehaus Center sponsored a remarkable book conference at Princeton in spring 2014. David Singer and Susan Hyde traveled to Princeton solely to attend the conference. Along with Joanne Gowa, Christina Davis, and Bob Keohane, they read the entire manuscript and spent a whole day providing enormously valuable and extensive feedback. I am extremely grateful for this unbelievably enriching experience.

I completed my book as an assistant professor of political science at Columbia University and would like to thank my new colleagues for welcoming me into this community. I would be hard-pressed to find a more engaging and interesting group of scholars with whom to work. I would like to thank my students at Columbia for their infectious energy and spirit and for asking compelling questions about the material as I finished this work. I am also grateful to Claire Mairead Hill for exceptional research assistance.

Along the way, I encountered many policy makers and practitioners who generously shared their knowledge and experiences with me in the process of researching my book, including Jane Armitage, David Black, Raj Desai, Donald Eiss, Gisella Gori, Peter Harrold, Mark Helmke, Altin Ilirjani, Carlos Felipe Jaramillo, Louise Kantrow, Monica Kladakis, Frances Lovemore, Andrew Natsios, and Michael Skol. I was also fortunate to engage with many political scientists who read portions of the book, shared their ideas with me, and inspired me. I would like to thank David Baldwin, Quintin Beazer, Marc Busch, Austin Carson, David Carter, Tom Christensen, Allan Dafoe, Alex Debs, Simone Dietrich, Julia Gray, Bobby Gulotty, James Hollyer, Greg Huber, David Lake, Nikolay Marinov, Helen Milner, David Moss, Irfan Nooruddin, Krzysztof Pelc, Paul Poast, Dani Rodrik, Peter Rosendorff, Cyrus Samii, Anne-Marie Slaughter, Mike Tomz, Jim Vreeland, and Meredith Wilf for excellent comments and helpful conversations. Peter Aronow provided especially generous support and advice on many portions on the manuscript.

Additionally, I received insightful feedback after presenting early versions of this project at the 2012–13 APSA conference, the 2012–13 IPES conference, the Yale Tools of International Pressure Conference, and seminars at Columbia, Emory, Georgetown, Harvard, Princeton, Stanford, the University of Chicago, the University of Illinois, the University of Indiana, and Yale University. Furthermore, I received generous funding from the Bradley, Ethel Boies Morgan, Falk, Yale University, and J. Jacqueline and Roger B. Kaufman fellowships. Three anonymous reviewers also contributed a number of excellent suggestions that greatly improved the book. I am particularly appreciative of my editor at Cambridge University Press, Robert Dreesen, for guiding the manuscript through the publication process expertly and enthusiastically. Of course, I am solely responsible for any errors that appear in the book.

Finally, I am thankful for the friends and family who provided love and support through this process. Friends who kept me sane during graduate school include Kaeli Andersen, Peter Aronow, Cameron Ballard-Rosa, Erica de Bruin,

Acknowledgments

Andreas Dzemski, Nikhar Gaikwad, Adi Greif, Ben Jones, Bonny Lin, Xiaobo Liu, Lucy Martin, and Dawn Teele. I would like to thank my mom, my dad, and my sister Jen for unflagging encouragement and love and for giving me the confidence to pursue my dreams. I would also like to thank my in-laws Lynn, Jerry, Jerry, Britt, and Karin – I couldn't ask for a kinder or more supportive family. Most of all, I thank Charlie Carnegie, to whom this book is dedicated. He is a constant source of love, inspiration, creativity, and fun and has always believed in me.

1

Introduction

In 1876, the United States signed a trade agreement with the Kingdom of Hawaii which eliminated high U.S. sugar tariffs. Hawaii responded by ramping up sugar production for export to the United States, so much so that these exports increased fivefold from 21 million pounds in 1876 to 114 million pounds in 1883. Boosting sugar production required a large investment: sugar producers adopted new sugar-processing technologies, bought government and private land, undertook large-scale irrigation projects, and invested in fertilizers. The Hawaiian government signed the treaty expecting other markets for its sugar exports to open up soon thereafter. However, when the treaty expired in 1883, Hawaii had no viable alternative export market.[1] Thus, during negotiations over the treaty's renewal, the United States demanded exclusive rights to Pearl Harbor; otherwise, the United States threatened to reinstate the high sugar tariff. The Hawaiian government conceded.

Almost 140 years later, this type of pressure remains a widespread phenomenon. Consider several recent examples: the European Union (EU) threatened not to renew trade agreements with Mongolia, Sri Lanka, Vietnam, and Nepal unless they improved their human rights records; the United States warned that it would not renew trade agreements with China, Vietnam, Cambodia, Romania, and Russia until they made political concessions; and China refused to renew many of its trade agreements unless its partners supported its "one China" policy.[2] Indeed, incentives to renege on agreements abound as the intermingling of political and economic arrangements offers many opportunities for states to coerce their partners into making foreign policy concessions.

---

[1] For a full account of this case, see Croix and Grandy (1997) and Kuykendall (1953). Note that Australia had become a sugar exporter and the Canadian population was too small to serve as a substitute (Croix and Grandy 1997). Additionally, Continental Europe had begun producing large quantities of beet sugar as a substitute for imported cane sugar (Rolph 1917).

[2] See Dumbaugh (2008). China frequently requires its partners to recognize it as the legitimate government of the area encompassing both China and Taiwan.

These examples of coercive diplomacy – the use of threats and assurances in combination to influence another state's behavior – highlight the dangers of cooperating with other states in the international system: states may hold their partners hostage at a later date to extract concessions from them. Yet the possibility that states will be taken advantage of has an unfortunate consequence: states often refuse to cooperate in the first place, preferring to "go it alone" rather than be subjected to extortion. When states cannot promise to refrain from holding their partners hostage, cooperation failures abound, making states worse off than they would be if they could commit to not exercising coercive diplomacy over their partners.

Making this kind of commitment is difficult, however, because coercive diplomacy is such a useful tool. In countless situations, one state seeks a concession from another and therefore turns to coercive diplomacy as the most expedient way to extract it. Coercion has been widely used by many states throughout history, as efforts to promote national interests and obtain political goals without resorting to war preoccupy leaders around the world. Thus, as a result of its ubiquity and centrality in international relations, the exercise of coercive diplomacy is a controversial and hotly debated topic. Yet despite its place at the core of interactions between states, coercive diplomacy is not well understood. When do states attempt to coerce their partners, and what problems does this cause? How do states address these issues, and what are the political and economic consequences of their actions?

This book takes up these questions in detail, examining coercive diplomacy's effects on bilateral interactions and assessing its implications for states' abilities to influence their partners. To date, most analyses of coercive diplomacy have concentrated on understanding whether and when states achieve their desired results by applying coercive methods. However, by employing game-theoretic tools, statistical modeling, and detailed case study analysis, this book builds and tests a theory that explains the mechanisms underlying these dynamics to provide a more complete and nuanced account of coercive diplomacy. With a particular focus on the World Trade Organization, the book argues that the potential for coercive diplomacy creates political hold-up problems – difficulty cooperating due to fears of exploitation – but that international institutions can solve these problems by enabling states to commit to not employing certain tools for coercive purposes. Yet, by limiting states' manipulation of some policies for coercion, institutions cause their members to rely on alternative, often weaker instruments. International institutions thus have the power to enhance cooperation among members, but they do so specifically by diminishing states' abilities to coerce their partners.

1.1 THE ARGUMENT IN BRIEF

My argument rests on the idea that the potential for coercive diplomacy restricts interstate cooperation, as it induces states to reduce otherwise productive investments to avoid providing their partners with political leverage. For example, a state may decide not to build a factory to produce a good for export to a partner state if it worries that, ex post, the partner will threaten to raise tariffs on the good unless the state gives in to additional demands. A state may similarly refuse to accept loans, engage in trade, or permit foreign direct investment if it anticipates that its partner will breach these agreements unless it makes further concessions. These political hold-up problems pervade interstate relations, preventing mutually beneficial exchange.

As a result, states commonly seek credible ways to commit to not extorting concessions from their partners. Membership in international institutions represents one such solution. For example, WTO membership deters states from holding their partners up due to the WTO's strong enforcement capacity. The WTO thus allows members to guarantee that they will not to use their WTO-regulated trade policies to wring concessions from their partners.

However, international institutions do not affect cooperative relations among all states equally; rather, they mostly affect pairs in which one state has the capability and incentive to exercise coercive diplomacy against its partner. In particular, a state that wields more power than its partner is better *able* to extort concessions from that partner, and a state that experiences political tensions with a partner is more *willing* to do so. States with disparate interests and capabilities therefore most often engage in coercive diplomacy and thus find cooperation the most difficult outside of international institutions. Institutions thus reshape relations between these states in particular.

Although international institutions solve political hold-up problems by allowing states to commit to not using certain tools for coercion, members do not simply give up on influencing other states. Instead, they *shift coercion* to an area unregulated by the institution. To be sure, states have many instruments at their disposal, such as trade policies, foreign aid provision, foreign asset treatment, diplomatic measures, and military force. Generally, states select the most effective methods, weighing factors such as public opinion, probabilities of success, monetary costs, potential retaliation, and lobbying by domestic groups. Although the precise calculations vary on a case-by-case basis, these considerations figure in the decisions of virtually all states that seek to shape their partners' behaviors. Membership in international institutions, however, changes the cost-benefit assessment, leading states to craft new ways to coerce their partners. In doing so, international institutions thereby alter the ways that states use power in the international system.

In effect, because members of a particular international institution limit their manipulation of those tools which the institution regulates, they experience fewer political hold-up problems in these areas. At the same time, institutions push coercive behavior into alternative realms that typically offer less potent levers of influence. Removing certain instruments from states' foreign policy tool kits restricts their options for exerting pressure on their partners, resulting in diminished coercive abilities. International institutions thus represent a distinct trade-off for many states: they permit cooperation within the institution but restrict states' leverage over other members.

In the remainder of this introduction, I offer a preliminary account of the argument advanced in this book. The discussion elucidates the key intuitions that ground my argument regarding the effects of political hold-up problems on coercive diplomacy. I begin by depicting the nature of the cooperation problems that occur due to states' desires to extract political concessions from their partners and describing how international institutions can solve these issues. I then explain how coercive tactics change as a result of membership in these institutions and characterize the implications for cooperation and coercive behavior in these areas. After situating my argument in the broader theoretical context and describing its scope conditions, I conclude the chapter with an overview of the book.

1.2 COERCIVE DIPLOMACY AND INTERNATIONAL TRADE

To make this argument, I begin by explaining the nature of coercive diplomacy and highlighting the particular salience of trade as a coercive tool. At its core, coercive diplomacy is an indispensable practice in international affairs in which states seek to alter other states' behaviors. Coercers may offer concessions if a given target complies with their demands or may enact penalties if it fails to do so. Coercive diplomacy thus consists of threats and assurances, either explicit or implicit, and can therefore be considered a form of extortion or blackmail.

When exercising coercive diplomacy, states choose among a variety of instruments, including bilateral foreign aid provision, trade policies, financial regulations, foreign direct investment (FDI), foreign asset treatment, diplomatic maneuvers, military tools, environmental policies, technology sharing, immigration regulations, and intelligence cooperation. How do states select which policies to use? Scholars have shown that states do so based on the tools' associated costs and benefits, which depend on many factors, such as national security concerns, the preferences of domestic groups, potential retaliation, the partner country's likely response, and lobbyists' and constituents' interests. Though all coercers face these types of considerations, their circumstances and constraints differ such that each state makes a unique calculation when selecting its tactics.

However, while the precise factors involved in adopting a specific policy vary by state, trade-policy manipulation represents a particularly salient and widely used tactic because of its universal importance and primacy in the international system. Moreover, scholars have long recognized that trade can serve as a key tool of extortion (Baldwin 1985; Hirschman 1969) and have linked trade to economic growth, political power, military capabilities, and even state survival. I therefore maintain a focus on trade as an especially potent instrument of coercion.

Because states often rely on trade as a primary weapon in international relations, the potential for coercive diplomacy can severely disrupt trade relations between states. The dynamics between the United States and Hawaii discussed previously highlight the danger of opening to international trade: a state may be taken advantage of by a trading partner if the profitability of its investments depends on its partner's continued cooperation. To avoid becoming targets of coercive diplomacy, states commonly underinvest in the production of goods that could make them vulnerable to this exploitation. For instance, a state less optimistic than Hawaii would have anticipated the United States's opportunistic behavior and underinvested in sugar production.[3]

Yet, although scholars have long acknowledged that trade can be used for political leverage when the target of such pressure cannot costlessly shift trade elsewhere,[4] it is less well recognized that this possibility leads to underinvestment: the expectation that a partner will either discontinue or threaten to discontinue an agreement to extract political concessions often leads states to refuse to invest and trade with the partner ex ante. Because this trade would be mutually beneficial absent the possibility that a state would be held up for concessions, the decision to refrain from trading represents a market failure. For example, prior to Taiwan's 2002 WTO accession, it restricted economic exchange with China out of fear that such exchange would provide China with political leverage. Similarly, before Mexico joined the institution in 1986, it frequently sought to reduce its vulnerability to the United States's coercive efforts through limitations on trade and investment. Nepal also tried to curb trade with India prior to its 2004 WTO entry because of India's frequent threats to disrupt this trade unless Nepal provided political concessions. I discuss these examples extensively in Chapter 5.

Nonetheless, the linkage of disparate foreign policy issues need not always lead to political hold-up problems. In fact, sometimes bargaining over multiple items helps states to cooperate when it allows them to reach agreements more easily (Davis 2004; Martin 1994; Poast 2012). Political hold-up problems, by contrast, occur when states do not settle such issues jointly. Rather, states fear that once they reach a deal, one side will renege at a later date to extract additional concessions. If an investment's profitability depends on its partner's willingness to stick to the agreement, these concerns may render states unable to cooperate.[5] Thus, unlike haggling over many areas at once, which makes

---

[3] Although the Hawaiian government was aware that it could be held up when it signed the initial agreement, it hoped that it could open other markets for its sugar by the time the treaty was renewed. Charles de Varigny, the Kingdom of Hawaii's foreign minister, explained, "Seven years [the length of time before the treaty's renewal] would give us time to establish our sugar production on a solid basis. After all, we would have an opportunity through similar negotiations to open up other markets" (Croix and Grandy 1997, 177).

[4] See Hirschman (1969, 13) and Keohane and Nye (1977, 211). Keohane and Nye (1977, 19) argue that this occurs primarily under conditions of "asymmetrical interdependence," which I discuss further in Chapter 2.

[5] This argument builds from Hirschman's (1969) observation that political leverage from trade interdependence requires that the target of coercion face a cost to switching trade partners.

states better off by facilitating agreements, political hold-up problems make states worse off by depressing cooperation because of worries that it will lead to extortion.

Furthermore, these cooperation problems do not affect all states equally because some states are more vulnerable to these pressures than others. First, a state that is much stronger than its partner is better able to engage in coercive diplomacy. When a state wields more power than its partner does, it can afford to make threats and assurances that will convince its partner to provide concessions. Second, states face greater incentives to exercise coercive diplomacy when they have more dissimilar policy goals. If a state wants to garner support for a particular policy, it has little reason to coerce states that already share the same views, but it may threaten to renege on commitments to bully dissidents into adopting its preferred course of action.

As an example of a state extorting concessions from another state once it became more powerful than its partner, consider the relations between West Germany and Poland in 1950. West Germany wanted Poland to allow German family members who had been left behind in Eastern Europe to reunite with their families. Instead, Poland passed the Law on Citizenship, which required Germans in Poland to become Polish citizens. However, West Germany had a trade agreement with Poland that it could use as ransom (Spaulding 1997, 378). It therefore waited until the Polish economy had weakened and Poland had become dependent on the trade agreement to obtain German import credit to make up for critical shortages. It then demanded emigration concessions as a condition of renewing the treaty; failing those concessions, it would terminate its cooperation. Because Poland relied on the trade agreement, it complained about extortion but allowed ten thousand people to return to West Germany (Spaulding 1997, 382).

Relatedly, interactions between the United States and former Communist countries provide examples in which states that experienced political tensions had difficulties cooperating. The United States frequently used its trade policies to try to elicit improvements in many of these states' human rights records but had little incentive to do so with those nations that already respected rights (Pregelj 2005). Coercive diplomacy is therefore most prevalent between asymmetric pairs of states that differ in terms of capabilities and political views.

1.3 WTO REDUCES POLITICAL HOLD-UP PROBLEMS

Owing to political hold-up problems' endemic nature in the international arena, states seek out ways to preempt them. International institutions provide a potential solution, as they can tie states' hands with respect to the policies they govern. Furthermore, because trade represents a key coercive tool and causes especially detrimental hold-up problems, the institution that regulates it plays a critically important role in the international system. Therefore, I pay particular attention to the WTO, the primary multilateral institution that governs trade relations among its members. Note that the WTO was created in 1995 to replace the General Agreement on Tariffs and Trade (GATT), the institution that had served this function prior to 1995. Throughout the book, I use the term WTO to refer to both the GATT and the WTO, unless otherwise specified. In my theoretical framework, I treat these institutions in the same manner because they both can solve political hold-up problems in the trade domain, although I discuss their differences in the next chapter.

Established after World War II, the WTO represents one of the oldest international institutions and is considered a success story in terms of liberalizing trade among its members.[6] Part of the WTO's ability to do so stems from its rule-based approach and emphasis on reciprocity, transparency, and nondiscrimination between states. The institution requires all members to agree to provide each other with the same low MFN tariff rates, such that WTO members may not discriminate by offering some members better tariff treatment than others (although several exceptions to these rules exist, as I explain in Chapter 4).

For example, consider the GATT's impact on India's relations with Nepal. In 1989, Nepal's economy essentially shut down. Unemployment rose dramatically: many went hungry, and protests erupted in the streets. Domestic chaos ensued. What sparked this massive upheaval? Nepal's largest trading partner, India, had imposed an economic blockade on Nepal to pressure it to stop buying weapons from India's historic rival, China. After a year of hardship, turmoil, and political turnover, Nepal finally gave in to India's demands, and trade was restored. India thus succeeded in extracting concessions from Nepal by wielding its trade policies as a coercive tool.

Because India manipulated its trade relations with Nepal for political purposes, it presented Nepal with a dilemma: on one hand, international trade lay at the heart of Nepal's national development, economic growth, and prosperity. Thus, Nepal placed extreme importance on trade relations with India. On the other hand, this trade represented a potent weapon, as even states with the best intentions are often unable to refrain from using trade for extortion. Nepal's trade with India therefore provided India with a tool of coercion, but limiting trade with India to reduce this risk would have harmed Nepal's opportunities for growth and progress. Nepal was caught between two dismal alternatives. Nepal sought a third option, however. Its experience with India led it to apply for GATT membership, because joining the institution would mean that India would have to play by a set of established rules when determining its trade policies toward Nepal. GATT membership thus represented a potential way out of Nepal's predicament.

Nepal's experience was far from exceptional; states throughout history have proven unable to resist the temptation to use trade arrangements for coercive diplomacy. Consequently, many states curb trade with their partners when

---

[6] Although see Gowa and Kim (2005) and Rose (2004).

they fear that it will be employed against them in the future. However, international institutions offer states an escape from this bind by allowing them to tie their own hands and those of their partners due to the institutions' effective enforcement capabilities. Once states join these institutions, they can therefore cooperate in the areas overseen by the institutions whenever mutual benefits occur, rather than cooperate only with states where mutual trust to uphold agreements exists.

Furthermore, because political hold-up problems impact certain pairs of states more than others, and international institutions help to solve these problems, these institutions benefit some pairs of states in particular. Specifically, because states with large power disparities and political tensions have the most difficulty cooperating outside of the institution, these states reap the greatest gains from institutional membership within the domains the institutions govern.[7]

International institutions thus help some states overcome the danger of extortion by increasing the penalty associated with violating agreements. They do so by providing clear rules accompanied by transparent and impartial dispute adjudication to enable observers to learn whether members have violated their agreements. Members may thereby develop reputations as cooperators or violators, which allows other states to make informed decisions about future cooperation (Maggi 1999). Unlike bilateral arrangements, international institutions permit treaty violations to tarnish members' reputations in both international and domestic arenas. Enhancing these actors' abilities to identify defectors also permits them to penalize states that breach agreements. Institutions therefore enable multilateral punishments, which can increase the cost of violating agreements to the point that states no longer find such violations beneficial (Keohane 1984). Furthermore, once states become accustomed to operating within an international framework, norms for compliance may be created (Acharya and Johnston 2007, 37).

In particular, the WTO's dispute settlement system enforces members' commitments by adjudicating disagreements. Industries with interests in states' compliance with the WTO's laws identify potential violations, after which their government decides whether to take their complaints to the WTO. Once a state initiates a case against another, the two parties begin consultations. If they cannot reach an agreement, a panel consisting of three expert judges chosen from other member states adjudicates the dispute.[8] This process resolves

---

[7] An implication of my theory is that adversaries trade less than allies absent the WTO. This is also an implication of Gowa's (1995) important work; however, rather than being caused by political hold-up problems, Gowa (1995) argues that trading with adversaries causes security externalities. The two theories' implications diverge regarding the role of institutions, as I argue that the WTO boosts trade for nonallies in particular by resolving hold-up problems, whereas Gowa's (1995) argument implies that the WTO magnifies trade for allies. This is discussed further in Chapter 4.

[8] Under the GATT, panel adoption could be blocked, as discussed in Chapter 2.

Introduction

uncertainties about the law and allows states to develop reputations for compliance (Davis 2012; Maggi 1999). By enforcing long-term trade agreements, the WTO therefore allows states to commit to not using their trade policies as tools of coercive diplomacy, increasing trade and investment for states that might be tempted to do so otherwise.[9]

1.4 COERCIVE DIPLOMACY'S DISPLACEMENT AND REDUCED EFFECTIVENESS

Members of international institutions do not simply give up on exercising coercive diplomacy, however. Instead, states seek to influence their partners using tools that these institutions do not govern. For instance, while the WTO curbs its members' abilities to punish other members by raising tariffs on their goods,[10] they may instead threaten to reduce foreign aid, freeze assets, restrict visas, reduce intelligence cooperation, limit loans, or recall ambassadors if their partners do not comply and offer assurances in these areas if their partners meet their demands.

However, because states frequently select trade as a primary instrument of coercive diplomacy, restricting the use of this instrument generally renders efforts to influence their partners less effective. Indeed, although many doubt trade sanctions' efficacy, I show that trade-based threats and assurances tend to be more effective than most alternative policy instruments. Thus, although the WTO increases overall economic cooperation, doing so often comes at the expense of efforts to coerce other states.

1.5 BROADER THEORETICAL CONTEXT

This book explores foreign policy motivations for protection that are often overlooked because of a divorce between research on trade policy and research on coercive diplomacy. By bringing together concepts from each of these fields, I develop new insights into interstate relations. Specifically, I show how sanctions and other coercive measures cause political hold-up problems, often preventing trade and investment, and explore many unexpected implications of this observation. I demonstrate that incorporating political hold-up problems into the study of coercive diplomacy permits the understanding of many facets of international relations, suggesting the substantive value and theoretical potential of doing so.

---

[9] The WTO itself has no capacity for coercive diplomacy, as it merely enforces mutually agreed upon rules, allowing me to isolate my argument from the possibility that WTO membership causes states to practice coercive diplomacy through the institution.

[10] Several exceptions to this rule exist, as I discuss in detail in Chapter 4; however, I note that they are limited and do not allow WTO members much leeway for trade policy manipulation.

Furthermore, in addition to its contribution to the scholarly literature, this book engages with policy debates over the practice of coercive diplomacy in international relations. Questions regarding the use of coercive methods have become intertwined with disputes over membership in international institutions, as many policy makers worry about sacrificing foreign policy autonomy to these international bodies. At the same time, in an era of rapid globalization, states seek to engage with international institutions to participate in multilateral economic and political transactions that enhance growth, stability, and prosperity. Thus, a more complete understanding of how coercive diplomacy shapes relations between states, particularly in the context of international institutions, is called for.

My argument builds on the large body of literature known as contract theory, which was developed primarily in the field of economics to investigate how economic actors construct contractual arrangements (Bolton and Dewatripont 2005). Hold-up problems between firms represent a key concept in this domain and occur primarily when a firm must make a highly irreversible investment whose profitability depends on another firm's cooperation. In such a case, underinvestment may occur because the firm worries that once it invests, the other firm will confiscate the gains from the investment (Tirole 1988, 25). Typically, firms solve these problems either by writing an enforceable contract beforehand to ensure that the investor will benefit from its investment or through vertical integration, whereby the same firm owns the entire supply chain.

Similarly, the large literature on the politics of foreign direct investment (FDI) suggests that investors refrain from investing in countries that might subsequently violate their property rights or extract concessions. When investors have immobile assets, they cannot make credible threats to relocate, so that once they invest, the bargaining power shifts to the host country. Even when governments seek more FDI and thus have a long-term incentive to stick to the terms of the deal, they face a "time-inconsistency problem" whereby the short-term benefits of violating the agreement may outweigh the long-term costs. If investors anticipate that once the investment is made, the government will change the terms of the deal, they do not invest in the first place.[11] However, this problem may be ameliorated by bilateral investment treaties and other agreements and by domestic host-country characteristics such as democratic institutions and strong property rights laws, which can help to tie the government's hands (Büthe and Milner 2008b; Jensen 2003; Tobin and Rose-Ackerman 2011).

I build on these insights by investigating hold-up problems between governments rather than between firms, or governments and firms, which presents special complications to solving these issues. As a result of the considerable difficulty states experience in enforcing their contracts along with the pervasive links between international economics and politics, these political hold-up

---

[11] This is known as the "obsolescing bargain."

problems are both common and tough to solve. I argue that states frequently hold economic interactions hostage to political demands and that these tactics create underinvestment problems as states seek to avoid extortion. This is important because, since coercive diplomacy represents an indispensable aspect of foreign policy, political hold-up problems feature in diverse areas of international relations.

However, despite the plethora of scholarship on coercive diplomacy and sanctions, scholars have not systematically explored the impact of political hold-up problems on this practice or how these dynamics impact trade policy making. Instead, early investigations focus on describing and categorizing this phenomenon (Baldwin 1985; George 1991; Hirschman 1969), while more recent work has asked when coercive diplomacy achieves its aims (Drezner 1999; Hufbauer et al. 2007) or fails and leads to war.[12] Similarly, scholars have examined the effect of domestic institutions on states' abilities to coerce their partners. For example, some claim that democracies incur greater audience costs when they make a threat and then withdraw it. Because they are less likely to back down, their threats are more credible, and coercive diplomacy is more effective (Schultz 2001, 161–247). Critics of this argument point out that autocracies also face audience costs (Weeks 2008, 2012), and still others maintain that audience costs do not matter much regardless of a state's regime type (Downes and Sechser 2012; Snyder and Borghard 2011).

In addition, few scholars have studied coercive diplomacy in the context of international institutions. Most closely related to this topic is the body of work examining global horse trading within these institutions (Dreher, Sturm, and Vreeland 2009; Dreher and Sturm 2012; Dreher and Vreeland 2014; Kuziemko and Werker 2006) along with that investigating when states use multilateral forums for coercion (Martin 1993; Thompson 2006). However, neither these studies nor those of foreign policy substitution more generally[13] consider how states incorporate institutions into their overall coercive strategies.

Similarly, existing theories of international institutions lack a systematic account of their impact on coercive diplomacy and sanctions. Instead, this literature often focuses on whether international institutions enhance cooperation at all. While realists claim that institutions merely codify prevailing power structures and therefore do little to alter the balance of power in the international system (Grieco 1988; Mearsheimer 1994), neoliberals and constructivists respond by arguing that international institutions commonly foster cooperative behavior. Neoliberals assert that institutions help to solve collective action problems, reduce transaction costs, and alleviate information asymmetries (Keohane 1984; Krasner 1983). In a similar vein, constructivists typically believe that they facilitate the development of norms and standards of behavior (Finnemore and Sikkink 1998; Ruggie 1992).

---

[12] See DiCicco and Levy (1999), Huth (1999), and Powell (2002) for reviews of this literature.
[13] See Art (2003) for an overview.

Outside of these broad paradigms, other work on international institutions' effects tends to ask whether institutions achieve their stated goals. For example, scholars have explored the WTO's effects on trade,[14] the policy area that the WTO is designed to regulate. They offer a variety of theories about when and in what manner the WTO increases trade cooperation. In particular, scholars have shown that the WTO and other trade institutions can resolve a terms-of-trade prisoner's dilemma, whereby governments of large countries have short-term incentives to set tariffs at inefficiently high levels because of their abilities to pass some of these costs on to their trading partners (Bagwell and Staiger 1999). More generally, this work demonstrates that institutions can allow countries to avoid terminating cooperation in response to domestic political pressures and other time-inconsistency problems (Büthe and Milner 2008a; Maggi and Rodriguez-Clare 1998; Mansfield and Pevehouse 2008).[15] Relatedly, some scholars have developed interesting accounts of the ways in which hold-up problems influence institutional design.[16] Although these theories offer important insights, they do not typically delve into the impact of these institutions, once built, on the exercise of coercive diplomacy.

1.6 SCOPE: INSTITUTIONAL VARIATION

Although I maintain a focus on the WTO to fix ideas, other institutions can also solve political hold-up problems and thus can alter strategies of coercive diplomacy. In fact, this framework is readily extendable to other trade, financial, diplomatic, and security institutions. International institutions differ greatly, however, and the extent to which a particular institution affects states in the manner predicted by the theory depends on its specific characteristics, including its structure and the nature of the investments that fall under its purview. When investments are relationship-specific and institutions are designed to capably enforce agreements, these institutions can solve political hold-up problems and thereby alter the tactics and efficacy of coercive diplomacy.

Nature of Investment

Whether international institutions affect coercive diplomacy depends on whether they solve political hold-up problems, which occur when investments

---

[14] See Rose (2009) for an overview.
[15] See Ikenberry (2009) for an explanation of institutional creation, Davis and Meunier (2011) for an application to trade and conflict, Christensen (2011) for an application to alliances, and Wallander (2000) for a theory about NATO.
[16] See Cooley and Spruyt (2009, 148), Gowa and Mansfield (2004), Goldstein and Gowa (2002), Lake (2009, 135–6), Lake (1999, 63, 271), Martin (1992), McLaren (1997), Rector (2009, 32–62), and Yarbrough and Yarbrough (1992, 111–33). Additionally, McLaren (1997) argues that the potential for hold-up problems can have perverse effects on the design of agreements. In contrast, I focus on the effect of long-term agreements on investment behavior, arguing that these agreements can remedy political hold-up problems.

are relationship-specific. Just as political hold-up problems in the trade domain reduce trade and investment, political hold-up problems in nontrade areas cause low levels of cooperation as well. Because relationship-specific investments abound in many settings, political hold-up problems do too, creating a role for international institutions in areas outside of trade. To provide a sense of the these problems' endemic nature, I detail their prevalence in several alternative policy domains: alliances, financial transactions, and foreign aid allocation.[17]

Alliances
Bilateral alliances are often plagued by hold-up problems, as these commitments often require sticky investments that rely on the alliance's continuation. For instance, security cooperation frequently entails joint military training, joint participation in exercises, military equipment purchases for use within the alliance, and shared intelligence communication. Once a state has made these investments, its partner can threaten to renege on the alliance agreement to extract further concessions.[18] Even though it would be better for both states to commit to the alliance ex ante, it is generally too tempting for a state with the ability and incentive to hold up its partner to refrain from doing so ex post.

For instance, Davis (2009) describes a 1902 alliance agreement between Britain and Japan that necessitated relationship-specific investments that enabled Britain to hold Japan up for economic concessions. The alliance treaty committed both parties to adopting a neutral stance if one nation went to war and to fight on the same side if a third party intervened in the war. In renewing the alliance in 1905, the two states strengthened their commitments to each other, agreeing to come to each other's aid in a war against a single power and to defend India. This necessitated relationship-specific investments; Britain altered its naval deployment and land support in India, becoming reliant on Japan for assistance, and moved five battleships to China. Britain also allowed Japan to annex Korea, permitted Japan's increasingly aggressive trade policies, and provided Japan with technology transfers due to the alliance's assurances. Britain and Japan then engaged in negotiations over a trade agreement in 1910, during which Britain warned that implementing Japan's preferred tariff schedules would damage their alliance. In effect, Britain held the alliance hostage to gain concessions in the trade realm, stating that the alliance served as a "very powerful lever in the Diet" (Davis 2009, 171). Japan therefore acquiesced to Britain's demands, reducing tariffs on major British exports such as textiles, iron, and steel goods, even though this decreased national revenue.

---

[17] Hold-up problems in the area of unilateral preference programs are depicted in Chapter 3.
[18] Although see Gowa and Mansfield (2004) for an argument that alliances can solve time-inconsistency problems. See Lake (1999) for an analysis of how these investments can influence alliances' structures.

Financial Transactions
The politicization of financial instruments can also lead to underinvestment. Consider, for instance, the treatment of foreign assets. Many countries invest considerable assets in their partners' financial institutions, which are frequently highly irreversible. Furthermore, these partners often threaten to render such assets inaccessible or worthless to gain political influence. As a result of the political strings attached to the treatment of their assets, states may hesitate to invest if they fear that additional concessions will be demanded of them once they do so. For instance, it was precisely this worry that led Russia to exit the United States's Export-Import Bank in 1998 (Steil and Litan 2006, 54–56). Additionally, since the 2001 terrorist attacks, the United States has imposed financial sanctions on states that it believes sponsor terrorism. Many states have declined to invest with the United States as a result (Steil and Litan 2006, 36–43).

Similarly, hold-up problems occur in the area of loans. For example, during the 1904 Russo-Japanese War, Germany assured Russia that it would observe a policy of "benevolent neutrality" and promised Russia that it would extend loans for resources needed for the war (Spaulding 1997, 82). Germany's guarantees encouraged Russia to shift its military resources from its European border to its eastern border, leaving Russia vulnerable to Germany. Once Russia did so, Germany saw the opportunity to hold Russia up by demanding new trade concessions and threatening to renege on its agreement if Russia did not provide them. Because of its dependence on Germany, Russia was forced to give in to Germany's requests, as the representative sent to renegotiate the treaty on Russia's behalf "had received instructions to bring the parley to a peaceful end at any price" (Spaulding 1997, 83). Thus, after Russia made large investments whose profitability depended on the continuation of its deal with Germany, Germany used the threat of reneging on its loan commitments and military guarantees to obtain extra benefits.

Foreign Aid Allocation
Foreign aid can also lead to political hold-up problems when it necessitates highly irreversible investments whose benefits depend on continued aid flows that cannot be attained from another source. Consistent funding is sometimes necessary to ensure an investment's profitability, as receiving aid can cause citizens to relocate, begin businesses, and build homes and can lead governments to construct health care facilities, establish schools, and commission factories. Without sustained funding, these investments can become inoperable. Carlsson, Somolekae, and Van de Walle (1997, 220) document many such occurrences in Africa: roads and utilities funded by aid fell into disrepair; schools lacked teachers and supplies; and vehicles for agriculture broke down without spare parts. Similarly, Araral (2005, 3) describes the specific case of irrigation in which budget shortfalls, often caused by conditionality, led to "inefficient, unreliable and inequitable water service; chronic underinvestment in maintenance;

rapid deterioration of infrastructure; and reaction in service areas with adverse impacts on cropping intensities and productivity." Furthermore, the reliance on aid to maintain investments has political repercussions. For instance, systems that fall short of the government's promises cause dissatisfaction, which can imperil political survival (Vermillion et al. 2005).

Fears that aid disruptions will render investments worthless are widespread, particularly because other funding sources are frequently unavailable due to recipients' inabilities to borrow from international market-based lenders and domestic capital markets (Araral 2005). Buss and Gardner (2005, 15) note that because sanctions can undo aid's benefits, governments and investors often refuse to invest at all. For example, Buss and Gardner (2005, 28) cite a particular case in which, due to sanctions, many programs "suddenly terminated when aid stopped, unraveling many positive benefits. Once aid started up again, programs had to regain what was lost before they could move forward. This was disastrous because many development projects, even in the best of circumstances, take years to mature and produce results.... Capacity created in Government or among NGOs dissipated. At the same time, the Government was unwilling or unable to continue programs." Because investing may therefore leave governments worse off than not investing (Wallner 2003), they sometimes view aid as windfall profits rather than as funding for long-term investments (Aghion et al. 2010; Bulir and Hamann 2006). Rather than investing in projects that make them vulnerable to coercion, governments may use aid for short-term political payoffs, such as providing political patronage (Lensink and Morrissey 2000), to obtain support without remaining dependent on the donor for political survival.

Enforcement Mechanism

In addition to the nature of the investment, the framework's applicability also depends on a given international institution's ability to enforce its members' commitments. Only institutions that possess strong enforcement capabilities can assure their members that the tools they regulate will not be used for coercion. To illustrate, consider the variety of institutions that regulate international trade. Multilateral institutions that focus on trade relations have multiplied in recent years. Examples include multiparty trade agreements such as the North American Free Trade Agreement, customs unions, and other regional groupings. However, considerable variation in trade institutions' enforcement capabilities exists, such that some institutions can more capably prevent political hold-up problems than others.

For example, much more than just a trade-governing body, the EU features a highly evolved dispute settlement mechanism and governs relationship-specific investments (Baldwin 1995), which allows it to promote cooperation among its members. The EU includes many economically dissimilar states that have a history of political tensions: precisely those that would experience political hold-up problems outside of the EU. The EU mitigates these problems through its strong enforcement capabilities, as violations of EU laws can cause penalties and a diminished reputation in the eyes of other EU member states.[19] Furthermore, the pairs of states that have benefited the most from the union have arguably been the asymmetric pairs. For example, Germany gained a large export market from smaller members, while small states received cheap imports and low interest rates.[20] Finally, as a consequence of losing leverage over its members using tools such as trade, the EU created other levers of influence such as conditional funding (Levitz and Pop-Eleches 2010).

By contrast, the Southern Common Market (MERCOSUR), a customs union among Latin American nations, has exhibited both lax enforcement and implementation and has functioned mainly as a weak alliance between states. Although MERCOSUR members have reduced their tariffs, this was primarily because of unilateral changes rather than membership in the institution (Acharya and Johnston 2007, 121–27). MERCOSUR therefore has done little to increase trade and investment by solving political hold-up problems.

Other institutions recognize this logic and have therefore strengthened their enforcement capacities over time to better mitigate hold-up problems. For example, the Association of Southeast Asian Nations (ASEAN), which includes a free trade area consisting of ten Southeast Asian states, initially garnered few economic benefits for its members. Many members suffered from political mistrust stemming from historical and cultural factors, which created incentives to hold each other up for concessions and led to reduced investment and trade. Yet the free trade area, which had the potential to solve such problems, featured a very weak enforcement mechanism that led members to renege on their commitments to liberalize trade (Acharya and Johnston 2007, 34). Owing to the minimal benefits generated by the institution, in 1990 the group agreed to a strict enforcement system patterned after that of the WTO (Acharya and Johnston 2007, 56). Afterward, trade increased greatly, as hold-up problems were likely alleviated.[21]

1.7 METHOD AND PLAN OF THE BOOK

This book uses a multimethod approach to investigate the practice of coercive diplomacy in international relations. The following chapters develop a game-theoretic model that formally lays out the argument, present statistical analyses of data on interactions between almost all countries over more than sixty years, and provide in-depth qualitative examinations of these dynamics.

---

[19] See Stone Sweet (2010) for an overview. See Cooley and Spruyt (2009) for an interesting analysis of incomplete contracting's role in the setup and functioning of the EU.
[20] See "Eurozone Crisis: if Greece Goes, Germany's Prosperity Goes with It," *The Guardian*, May 26, 2012.
[21] Calculated using data from Liu (2009).

Introduction

I begin by describing the theoretical argument in detail in Chapter 2. Using the concepts discussed earlier to motivate the setup and assumptions, I present a game-theoretic model in which one state, the Coercer, attempts to influence its partner, the Target. The model examines the factors that determine whether political hold-up problems affect these states, finding that international institutions can be particularly beneficial in these cases. It also considers which tools the Coercer selects, both when the states are members of an international institution and when they are not. The model's objective is to understand how political hold-up problems affect the states' strategies and their resulting implications for the states' economic and political relations. The chapter works up to a series of empirical predictions that distinguish my argument from alternative possibilities.

Explaining the effects of political hold-up problems on coercive diplomacy is this book's central ambition, and the remaining chapters investigate this core idea in detail. Chapter 3 shows that, in the absence of an international trade institution, dissimilar states frequently rely on trade policy manipulation for coercive purposes. These states can more easily take advantage of their weaker partners, and they have greater incentives to extort concessions from partners with politically divergent views. This chapter demonstrates that because political hold-up problems plague relations between asymmetric states, the extension of bilateral trade preferences stimulates trade and investment between similar states in particular. By contrast, dissimilar states underinvest owing to concerns that their preferences will be rescinded, and thus they experience fewer benefits from the agreements.

Chapter 4 then substantiates the claim that international institutions can help to solve political hold-up problems. The chapter shows that WTO membership increases trade most for asymmetric states by allowing them to commit to specific trade policies and preventing them from manipulating their tariffs to exercise coercive diplomacy. These results are particularly surprising because standard trade theory predicts that WTO membership will create the largest increase in trade for pairs of states that engage in the most trade outside of the WTO, implying that similar states should reap the biggest benefits from membership (Bagwell and Staiger 1999). This chapter also supplies evidence of the causal mechanism by demonstrating that the WTO boosts trade flows most in industries in which hold-up problems are most prevalent. It concludes that WTO membership leads states to coerce their dissimilar partners using trade policy less frequently than they did before.

Chapter 5 provides a series of examples to show that political hold-up problems impacted many countries over a long span of time and that international institutions helped to resolve these issues. The objective of this analysis is to demonstrate that the mechanisms through which the WTO facilitates trade cooperation match the theoretical account developed in Chapter 2. To do so, this chapter pairs WTO members with both similar and dissimilar partner states. It then shows that WTO accession boosted trade between dissimilar partners because of the alleviation of hold-up problems, while having little impact on interactions between similar states, as expected.

After Chapter 5 establishes that international institutions can solve political hold-up problems, Chapter 6 takes an in-depth look at these institutions' effects on the tools states select for coercion. In so doing, it provides evidence for the contention that these bodies cause states to gravitate toward alternative instruments. Using detailed examples coupled with a systematic analysis, I show that WTO membership leads states to employ tariffs less frequently – and other tools more often – in their efforts to coerce their partners. In particular, I demonstrate that once states join the WTO, their trade flows become less correlated with political tensions, while other policies, such as foreign aid allocation and unilateral preference program eligibility, become more responsive to these political issues.

Chapter 7 then investigates an additional observable implication of the model: WTO membership reduces its members' capacities to engage in coercive diplomacy. I explore this hypothesis by analyzing the economic and political interactions between a particular state and each of its most dissimilar trading partners. Specifically, I look at all contentious debates in the U.S. Congress over other states' WTO accessions to demonstrate that in each case, Congress worried about losing the ability to use tariff policies for leverage and consequently created alternative ways to pressure the country to make concessions. However, this substitution reduced the United States's ability to coerce these partners, particularly in the area of human rights.

I conclude by discussing additional potential threats to inference, along with the theory's significance for policy and scholarship. I close with important implications that result from the book's central finding: the potential for coercive diplomacy creates political hold-up problems, a situation that international institutions can help solve. Doing so, however, generates policy substitution and reduces states' abilities to exercise coercive diplomacy in international relations.

2

Theoretical Framework

To gain insight into the relationship between political hold-up problems and coercive diplomacy, I develop a formal, game-theoretic model. Although I cannot provide a fully specified account of coercive diplomacy because of the complexity of such an endeavor, this basic model strives to elucidate states' key considerations when they attempt to coerce their partners. In so doing, I generate testable empirical hypotheses, providing the foundation for the empirical analysis conducted in the remainder of the book.

The model features two states, a Coercer and a Target. At the beginning of the game, the Target must decide whether to make an irreversible investment that would allow it to produce a good to export to the Coercer. Next, with some probability, a shock occurs that increases the Coercer's desire to influence the Target's behavior. In the advent of a shock, the Coercer may offer threats and assurances to the Target using some combination of tariff and foreign aid policies in exchange for foreign policy concessions. However, if the states are WTO members, the Coercer cannot alter its tariff policy for these coercive purposes. After it receives the offer, the Target chooses whether to accept it, and the game ends.

This simple model predicts that the Target will not invest when it expects the Coercer to use its tariff opportunistically. This risk is greater when the Coercer wields more power than the Target and when the probability of a shock is high, which occurs when the states have dissimilar policy preferences. However, the states can use WTO membership to circumvent these political hold-up problems because the WTO requires the Coercer to commit to not manipulating its tariff policies to extract concessions. The Coercer can, for example, increase its use of foreign aid instead, although this results in diminished leverage over the Target.

2.1 ASSUMPTIONS AND KEY CONCEPTS

Coercive Diplomacy

A model of coercive diplomacy must necessarily adopt a specific view of the concept, as scholars conceive of coercive diplomacy in different ways. Some scholars believe that coercive diplomacy entails either using military force or threatening to do so (Schultz 2001, 5). Others have expanded the definition to include additional coercive instruments, although these scholars tend to confine coercive attempts to include only threats rather than both threats and assurances. Still others distinguish between deterrence, whereby a state prevents a partner from exhibiting undesirable behavior, and compellance, which occurs when a state seeks to stop or undo an action already undertaken by the Target (Schelling 1966, 78–80). These scholars typically call the latter coercive diplomacy, while the former falls under the umbrella of deterrence theory (George 1991; George, Hall, and Simons 1971).

The disagreement over the definition of coercive diplomacy in part reflects the time period in which this concept was first considered. Theories of coercive diplomacy originated during the Cold War and were motivated in particular by concerns about nuclear deterrence. Following the Cold War, coercive diplomacy remained in the background until the late 1990s and was then adapted to fit the altered security landscape, leading to a broader conception of the idea.

The concept I adopt here follows recent scholarship, as I define coercive diplomacy as "the use of threats and assurances in combination to influence another state's behavior." As David Baldwin points out, threats and assurances represent two sides of the same coin, as do deterrence and compellance (Baldwin 1985, 12–24). Thomas Schelling (1989, 117) argues, "The difference between a threat and a promise, between coercion and compensation, sometimes depends on where the baseline is located." Similarly, Nye (2011, 1) states, "Once compensation becomes an expectation, withholding it for nonperformance can be seen as a punishment – and the threat to do so as coercion."

My broad definition incorporates these insights and tends to be favored by scholars today. For instance, Pape (1996, 4) defines coercive diplomacy as "efforts to change the behavior of a state by manipulating costs and benefits." However "efforts" are not precise enough for my purposes, as I must model what these efforts consist of, so I specify this in my definition by following Christensen (2011), who stipulates that coercive diplomacy consists of the use of both carrots and sticks to alter behavior. Specifically, Christensen (2011, 1) defines coercive diplomacy as "the use of threats and assurances in combination to influence the behavior of real or potential adversaries." Although my definition resembles this one, my theory is not specific to adversaries and thus does not include this term. In all other respects, however, I follow Christensen's conceptualization because it most closely fits the way that coercion is typically regarded in ordinary language, as coercion is not usually characterized as merely a contingent promise. Accordingly, in the model, the Coercer relies on a combination of both carrots and sticks, particularly because employing both represents the most effective method of coercion, as many scholars have noted (Cortright and Lopez 2005; Dorussen 2001; Haass and O'Sullivan 2000).[1]

In the model, the Coercer pays a bribe but never actually implements its threats to the Target because the Target always accepts the Coercer's deal. This comports with the large body of literature on bargaining models, which shows that delay results in waste and inefficiency (Rubinstein 1982). The literature on economic sanctions in particular finds that targets accept coercers' offers; thus, sanctions are not typically imposed. Furthermore, when sanctions *are* enacted, they are less successful in achieving coercers' aims (Drezner 1997; Lacy and Niou 2004; Morgan and Miers 1999; Smith 1995).[2]

Of course, in the real world, threats are sometimes acted upon, typically because coercers face considerable uncertainty over the costs that particular policy concessions impose on their targets. The targets may encounter strong domestic constraints, political pressure, adjustment costs, and other costs that the coercer cannot readily observe. To take a concrete example, the level of respect for human rights in a country is determined by a variety of opaque domestic and international factors that have proven difficult for outside observers to discern.[3] Furthermore, coercers cannot simply ask their targets to reveal their costs, as the targets have strong incentives to lie to receive larger bribes. Thus, in reality, coercers sometimes make threats and give assurances that are not strong enough to change their targets' actions, after which coercers implement their threatened punishments.[4] This scenario is easily incorporated into the model and is shown in the appendix for interested readers; the only difference in the outcome is that the Coercer offers a deal based on the expected costs and benefits and the deal sometimes fails to motivate the Target to make the requested concession.

Relationship Specificity, Dependence, and Underinvestment

In the model, trade and investment lead to political hold-up problems when investments are relationship-specific. Relationship specificity presents special concerns with which economic actors must contend, a situation that is well

---

[1] Furthermore, my definition highlights my focus on state behavior. Although this framework could potentially apply to nonstate actors, states are international institutions' primary members. Because I am interested in the role of these institutions in the development of strategies of coercive diplomacy, I limit the analysis to state actors.
[2] This selection bias may partially explain other, more pessimistic views of sanctions' efficacy (Pape 1997).
[3] See Davenport (2000, 18), Goodliffe and Hawkins (2006), Poe, Tate, and Keith (1999), Rejali (2009, 15), and Vreeland (2008).
[4] Alternatively, commitment difficulties and the indivisibility of disputed issues also may contribute to the implementation of sanctions.

recognized in theories of international trade. Whereas standard trade theory assumes that markets are perfectly competitive and that constant returns to scale characterize production – such that the unit cost does not change with output – "new trade theory" acknowledges that this is not always true. Instead, production frequently exhibits increasing returns to scale – such that the average cost of production falls as output grows. Thus, while standard trade theory assumes free market entry, new trade theory accounts for the fact that production often requires fixed costs. Although the type of investments required to produce a good varies by industry, most industries require some "sticky" investments. For instance, investments in labor, technology, equipment, land, infrastructure, transportation, advertising, research and development, machinery, and training can all be difficult to reverse once undertaken.

Not all fixed investments are relationship-specific, however; if a country can export a good to other partners that maintain low enough tariffs to justify the investment's cost, then the exporter need not rely on a particular partner's cooperation to benefit from the investment. For example, in 1906, Austria-Hungary and Serbia engaged in a dispute now known as the Pig War, in which Austria-Hungary imposed a customs blockade on pork from Serbia due to Serbia's efforts to increase ties to Bulgaria and France. Because pork represented Serbia's main export and was sold primarily to Austria, Austria expected Serbia to capitulate to its demands. However, Serbia easily found other markets for its pork, and Austria's efforts failed (Glenny 2012, Chapter 4). In this case, because substitute markets were readily available, investments in the pork industry were not relationship-specific.

However, if a state finds that switching trading partners is too costly to make the investment worthwhile, the state may require a particular partner's cooperation. Finding a viable alternative market can be difficult for three primary reasons. First, existing infrastructure may only allow trade with a specific partner. Oil and natural gas pipelines represent common examples of this phenomenon. For instance, in 1940, the Allies placed an oil embargo on Spain, lifting it only after Spain agreed to ensure its neutrality during World War II (Caruana and Rockoff 2003). Similarly, in 1985, the United States used its monopsony power over Libya's oil to threaten to halt imports unless Libya made concessions in the area of counterterrorism (O'Leary 1985).

Second, substituting by using an alternative market can be infeasible when a particular partner pays more favorable prices than other potential partners. Sometimes this occurs when one state deliberately seeks leverage over its partner by offering below-market prices so that the state invests and trades above the level dictated by purely economic considerations. For instance, during the Cold War, the USSR supported Finland's otherwise uncompetitive metals industry, threatening to reduce this assistance unless Finland backed some aspects of its foreign policy and did not discriminate against Communists in Finland's government (Allen 1959).

Third, investments are relationship-specific when the good produced is demanded primarily by a particular market. This can occur both when goods are homogenous, meaning that a good remains identical no matter where it is produced, or heterogeneous, meaning that it differs depending on where it is produced. When goods are heterogeneous, they may be created for a particular market. For instance, cars may be manufactured to meet a particular state's especially stringent emissions standards. Alternatively, when goods are homogenous, their production can still require relationship-specific investments when their main buyers are large states, which often hold some monopsony power. In other words, even if consumers do not care which state their bananas come from, if the United States were the major purchaser of those bananas, then banana producers would not be able to easily find an alternative market. Any investments made in the banana industry, such as in land, fertilizer, labor, irrigation, farm roads, land clearing and preparation, farm machinery, and chemicals, would thus be relationship-specific because their profitability would require the United States's continued purchase of the bananas (at or above a particular price).

Once a country invests in producing a good that requires trade with a certain partner to be profitable, that country becomes dependent on its partner and becomes vulnerable to extortion. Although the problem potentially affects a variety of countries, small countries in particular tend to rely on larger countries as their main trading partners. For instance, the United States typically serves as the primary trading partner for many states in Central and South America; India represents the biggest trading partner for Sri Lanka, Nepal, and Bangladesh; China represents the largest partner of many East Asian states and many others; Britain, France, and Spain are often the main partners of their former colonies; and Russia trades disproportionately with many Eastern European states. In these cases, the larger state may use this trade dependence for extortion.[5]

For example, the Philippines depends on China to purchase many of its exports, which consist primarily of electronic products but also of many other goods such as bananas. In fact, China serves as the Philippines's main market for bananas, which require large, irreversible investments (Philippines Statistics Authority 2013). An estimated 35 billion pesos are invested in the Philippines's banana industry for infrastructure, planting, and distribution.[6] Banana plants are planted many months before the bananas are harvested, requiring investments in land, pesticides, the plants themselves, and labor. Then the produce must be refrigerated and shipped, which requires further investment. The Philippines relies on exporting to China to recoup these investments' costs; China possesses a large market for which no other market can serve as a viable

---

[5] Even if both countries make relationship-specific investments, a situation called a "bilateral monopoly" (Tirole 1988), the large state typically faces a much smaller cost from the agreement's termination and therefore can hold up the weaker state more easily than the weaker state can hold it up.

[6] See Cruz, John Dela. "Philippine Banana Production and Exporting." *Manila Trade*. August 22, 2013.

substitute, and shipping to other markets is too expensive. For instance, shipping to the United States and the Middle East takes weeks, whereas shipping to China takes a few days.[7]

China has used the Philippines's dependence on its markets for extortion. On May 9, 2012, China announced that it would begin inspecting banana and pineapple shipments. China then started impounding banana-carrying ships from the Philippines, which led to spoilage of the fruit and reduced profits for Philippine banana growers. The president of the Pilipino Banana Growers and Exporters Association, an influential lobbying group, stated that China's actions could threaten two hundred thousand jobs that were particularly concentrated on Mindanao Island. Widespread speculation emerged that the move was intended to pressure the Philippines to make political concessions regarding the disputed Spratly Islands, particularly due to its Department of Agriculture's assertion that the type of pest that China claimed to have found in the bananas does not occur in bananas.[8] However, the incident received considerable international attention and caused speculation that the Philippines would initiate a WTO dispute.[9] In response, China resumed its banana imports on May 23, 2012, just two weeks after the policy's introduction.[10]

States that are vulnerable to such scenarios may reduce trade and investment with particular partners to avoid extortion. Because this trade would be mutually beneficial absent the potential for coercion, this underinvestment represents a market failure. For example, in retaliation for meeting with the Dali Lama, China suspended imports from Mongolia for one day. Mongolia sells 90 percent of its exports to China and worried that China could cut off trade for a longer time period in the future. Mongolia therefore intensified efforts to reduce its dependence on China, banning some Chinese investment in Mongolia and reducing bilateral trade, although it incurred significant costs in doing so.[11]

As a more extended example, consider relations between the United States and Canada. Canada's main exports to the United States include vehicles, machinery, electrical equipment, natural gas, oil, plastics, fertilizer, wood pulp, and timber (CIA World Factbook 2014). Each of these industries requires large investments that are difficult to reverse. For instance, investments in technology and infrastructure, including pipelines, factories, roads, and railways, are required. Furthermore, one in seven Canadian jobs depends on trade with the United States (CIA World Factbook 2014) and typically necessitates search costs, training, and education. To take one case in particular, Canada's

[7] Ibid.
[8] See "China's Banana Diplomacy with the Philippines," *Stratfor*, May 17, 2012.
[9] See Shi Qiaolin, "Philippine, Chinese Analysts on South China Sea Row," *Caixin Online Opinion Commentaries Philippine*, May 31, 2012.
[10] See Czeriza Valencia, "Phl Bananas Cleared for Export to US," *Philippine Star*, May 23, 2012.
[11] See Associated Press, "Mongolia Finds China Can Be Too Close for Comfort," December 9, 2012.

softwood lumber industry depends heavily on trade with the United States, which serves as its largest export market. This trade entails many highly irreversible investments in thousands of workers, roads for hauling, sawmills, land, and specialized logging railways and vessels. Pulp and paper demand high-speed machines, chemicals, and other capital-intensive inputs in particular (Minnes 2006). Canada thus remains highly dependent on the U.S. market, a state of affairs that has contributed to many disputes between the two countries, such as those over the price of Canadian lumber exports (Ritchie 1997).

Because lumber and other exports to the United States figure so importantly in Canada's economy, many in Canada fear that the United States will use this trade to extract political concessions, but membership in the WTO has deterred the United States from doing so. A recent analysis of the United States's policies toward Canada concludes,

The real fear... is that the Americans will somehow shut the borders to trade with Canada if our foreign, military, immigration, and criminal justice policies do not please our southern neighbors.... [Therefore], Canada has an interest in maintaining strong international instruments to review trade barriers. For example, Canada has engaged in successful litigation over softwood lumber before panels for the General Agreement on Tariffs and Trade, the North American Free Trade Agreement, and, most recently, the World Trade Organization. This litigation provides a direct and constructive means to fight linkage and trade retaliation. (Roach 2003, 165)

Owing to these dispute resolution mechanisms, investment in the lumber industry increased, as political hold-up problems were alleviated (Simpson 2007).

Although the preceding examples detailed political hold-up problems related to exports, this logic pertains to imports as well. For instance, China produces 85 percent of the world's rare earth minerals and holds half of the world's known reserves. Rare earth minerals consist of seventeen elements that exist in low concentrations and are costly to mine. Many industries use them, including those manufacturing wind turbines, electronics, electric cars, and clean energy technology. Each industry requires irreversible investments in technology, capital, and infrastructure.[12] Because states that produce many goods in these industries rely on Chinese imports, China has been able to exploit its power for political purposes.

For instance, in response to Japan's arrest and detention of a Chinese boat captain in September 2010, China implemented an export ban on rare earth materials to Japan. Although the Chinese government denied that the ban was directed against Japan, many observers and other Chinese government officials disagreed (Reilly 2012).[13] In targeting the highly sensitive and influential Japanese electronics industry, China's export ban had a large effect

---

[12] See Zhou Xin and Koh Gui Qing, "China May Not Issue New 2011 Rare Earths Export Quota: Report," Reuters, December 30, 2010.

[13] Because the ban disrupted trade with the United States and the EU as well, the United States, the EU, and Japan brought the issue to the WTO, and a WTO panel was formed on July 23,

on Japan, inciting widespread outrage. Furthermore, the ban caused political hold-up problems, as Japan subsequently sought to reduce its investment and consumption in sectors that use rare earths. Japan announced that its goal was to decrease its consumption of rare earths by 30 percent over the following two years.[14] As this example demonstrates, political hold-up problems are common regarding both exports and imports, often diminishing overall bilateral trade.

WTO Enables Commitment

In modeling these dynamics, I make several simplifying assumptions, some more important than others. Before presenting the model, I flag one of its key assumptions: I assume that members cannot deviate from their WTO commitments, as doing so is too costly. While members do sometimes bend or break their agreements in actuality, the assumption's crucial aspect is that WTO membership increases the penalty associated with doing so. For the purposes of this simple model, I thus assume that WTO members never break their commitments, although in the appendix I show that similar results are obtained when I relax this constraint by making it costly for members to break their commitments rather than impossible.

This assumption's validity rests on a large body of literature that documents the ways in which WTO membership increases the penalties associated with breaking agreements. The WTO accomplishes this through multiple mechanisms, including fostering the development of norms for compliance (Johnston 2002), creating incentives to maintain rules that other states obey (Hudec 2002; Jackson 1997; Kovenock and Thursby 1992), generating systemic incentives for cooperation, allowing members to develop reputations for compliance (Maggi 1999), and increasing domestic pressures and political cover for adhering to agreements (Allee and Huth 2006; Gaubatz 1996; Mansfield, Milner, and Rosendorff 2002; Staiger and Tabellini 1999). The ability to establish reputations for cooperation may be particularly important, as it motivates states to adhere to the law to gain continued cooperation in the future (Tomz 2007, 223–27). If countries frequently violate agreements, their partners may withdraw trade concessions, exhibit reluctance to enter agreements, or become less cooperative in related areas (Maggi 1999).

These mechanisms operate in particular through the WTO's sophisticated dispute resolution system, which has evolved over time. Under the GATT, potential violations of its laws were typically identified by industries or other groups that had a stake in adherence to these regulations, after which the government decided whether to bring the cases to the GATT's dispute settlement

---

2012. See Joe McDonald, "China Rare Earths Producer Suspends Output," Associated Press, September 24, 2010.

[14] See Reuters, "Japan to Slash Use of a Heavy Rare Earth as China Tightens Grip," February 8, 2012.

system. Once one party initiated a complaint against another, the two parties began consultations. If they could not reach an agreement, the complainant could request a panel consisting of three expert judges chosen from and nominated by the member states, rendering the panelists much more impartial than the parties to the dispute.[15] Third parties could also participate if they had a "substantial interest" in the outcome. The respondent country could block the panel's formation, although this occurred infrequently. This system was strengthened with the WTO's creation, as the blocking of panels and panel reports is no longer allowed, unilateral sanctions are permitted, an Appellate Body exists, and strict timetables are enforced. Furthermore, after it reaches a decision, the court can authorize retaliation against the offending party, after which it monitors compliance with the ruling. If issues with compliance arise, a compliance panel may be formed or retaliation may be authorized. Under both the GATT and the WTO, participants thus receive "a guarantee for the right to negotiate, a common standard for evaluating outcomes, the option for several countries to join a dispute, and incentives for states to change a policy found to violate trade rules" (Davis 2006).

The system's enforcement capacities are also facilitated by its promotion of transparency and impartiality. The GATT (and subsequently the WTO) required states to issue notification of changes to trade policies that would affect other members. Moreover, countries had the right to learn disputes' outcomes. Transparency was enhanced further in 1988, as the GATT began to regularly monitor compliance with international law through trade policy reviews, which the WTO now conducts every two years for the biggest traders (the United States, the EU, China, and Japan), every four years for the next sixteen biggest traders, and every six years for the smallest traders.[16]

As a result, although the WTO strengthened the system, both GATT and WTO enforcement mechanisms have been shown to be quite effective. Examples abound in which the WTO helped to bring states into compliance, even in cases brought by weak states against powerful states (Busch and Reinhardt 2003, 2004; Davis 2006; Wilson 2007).[17] Often, threatening to initiate a WTO dispute leads to compliance with WTO law. For example, Japan threatened to file a case against the United States in 1995 in response to U.S. threats regarding Japanese automobiles. After the filing, the United States backed down (Davis 2012, 205). In addition, stock prices respond to WTO rulings, indicating that investors anticipate compliance (Busch, Raciborski, and Reinhardt 2009), as exemplified by the movement in Chiquita Bananas's stock price after the WTO ruled that the EU had to lower tariffs on these items.

---

[15] Under the GATT, panels of five judges were sometimes formed.
[16] Although note that states may review the reports before they are published.
[17] Busch, Raciborski, and Reinhardt (2009) show that large WTO members reduce protectionist practices against small WTO members in particular.

Indeed, government officials also seem to believe that the WTO can enable their partners to commit to agreements. Consider the U.S. Congress's discussion of the potential benefits of Russia's 2012 WTO accession. Congressman Levin expected Russia's entry to help the United States because "now that they're in the WTO...when they violate the requirements, there's a dispute settlement system that can be enforced."[18] Similarly, Representative Howard Berman argued that, without the constraints imposed by the WTO, "we have no idea how Russia will treat our U.S. exports and we will have no way to hold them accountable."[19] Senator Rob Portman stated, "By joining [the WTO], Russia agrees to abide by a certain set of common rules, and when they break those rules, other countries can then take them to court and help hold their feet to the fire."[20] WTO membership thus imposes high costs for deviating from WTO agreements, which is reflected in the model's assumptions.

Additional Simplifications: Domestic Politics

Any formal model must make simplifying assumptions to remain tractable, and thus in this model I abstract from many domestic political dynamics that underlie states' policy-making decisions. The model is state-centric, not because domestic politics are unimportant, but because they do not much alter the basic outlines of the story told here. Instead, domestic considerations change the ways in which this account is manifested in particular states or pairs of states. In this section, I briefly highlight several areas in which domestic politics figure importantly in the outcomes. Although this by no means represents an exhaustive list, it provides a sense of the ways in which domestic considerations play a crucial, albeit behind-the-scenes, role in the theory.

First, although I argue that international institutions lead states to adopt alternative coercive tools, the particular instruments they select depend in part on domestic considerations in both the coercer and recipient states. Consider, for example, how the domestic ramifications associated with altering trade and aid policies may differ. In some cases, a donor may easily cut foreign aid if doing so hurts few people in the donor country. The donor may even save money from the drop in expenditures. However, it may be more complicated for a coercer state to restrict trade with a target if this harms domestic actors in the coercer state. In such a case, using trade for coercive purposes may require the donor to subordinate domestic economic and political interests in favor of its foreign

---

[18] See "Providing for Consideration of H.R. 6156, Russia and Moldova Jackson-Vanik Repeal and Sergei Magnitsky Rule of Law Accountability Act of 2012," *Congressional Record*, Vol. 158, No. 146, November 15, 2012, p. H6383.

[19] See "Russia and Moldova Jackson-Vanir Repeal and Sergei Magnitsky Rule of Law Accountability Act of 2012," House of Representatives, *Congressional Record*, Vol., 158, No. 155, November 16, 2012, p. S7443.

[20] Ibid., S7443.

policy goals. Alternatively, however, foreign aid may be difficult to cut because it may benefit strong domestic interests in the donor state. Economic aid has been shown to assist capital owners in capital-intensive donor countries; food aid helps agricultural groups; military aid benefits the defense industry, and so on (Milner and Tingley 2010). When there is strong domestic support for maintaining foreign aid flows, then other instruments may prove less costly for the donor to employ.

Other domestic considerations matter to the coercer as well. For instance, Milner and Tingley (2012) show that in the United States, the degree of congressional influence relative to that of the president, as well as ideological factors, help to determine whether the United States selects particular foreign policy tools to use for coercion. Similarly, other scholars argue that whereas states administer sanctions for security reasons, interest-group lobbying activities shape the particular form they take (Hiscox 2009; Kaempfer and Lowenberg 1988). Some sanctions may also be viewed as more legitimate than others or carry symbolic importance to the public more generally (Baldwin 1971).

In addition, domestic politics contributes to determining both whether a target state is vulnerable to coercion and which tool is most effective. In particular, sanctions are often selected based on whether they are likely to work, which depends on the domestic politics in the target state (Kaempfer, Lowenberg, and Mertens 2004). When a state is susceptible to coercion, domestic politics then shapes which tools will lead that state to make concessions. For instance, if foreign aid is given directly to state leaders, whereas the benefits from trade (or the costs of forgone trade) accrue mainly to domestic actors such as consumers and business owners, then a recipient may be most susceptible to coercion via aid cuts. Alternatively, if the recipient receives little aid from the coercer, or has many alternative donors to draw from, yet relies on the coercer's export market, trade may represent a more effective tool.

These considerations, although important, do not affect the basic hypotheses derived from the formal model. The point here is that each potential foreign policy instrument is associated with a variety of costs and benefits, which states weigh when choosing the optimal combination of tools to use for coercion. Joining the WTO simply adds an additional cost to using trade policy for coercion, causing states to select trade policy less frequently and to rely more heavily on other tools. I do not claim that these tools are perfect substitutes, just that each may be used for coercion, and a tool's selection depends in part on the costs associated with its application.

The use of this formal model to study states' strategic considerations when exercising coercive diplomacy thus does not deny the complexity of these domestic considerations. However, the formal model helps to isolate the strategic logic that underpins states' decision-making processes. Rather than attempt to capture every aspect of states' foreign policy calculations, I instead highlight their most pertinent features to develop general, testable hypotheses.

2.2 A MODEL OF COERCIVE DIPLOMACY

The model consists of interactions between two states, a Coercer (C) and a Target (T), which are denoted by superscripts. The Target may produce a good that is demanded by the Coercer but not by the Target's domestic population. If the Target produces the good, it exports it to the Coercer. The good's specific characteristics are unimportant; it could be any item, such as food, machinery, chemicals, minerals, vehicles, or weapons. All that matters is that the Coercer demands the good and that the Target would like to sell it.

The amount of the good that the Target exports depends on the Coercer's import tariff, τ, which is a tax placed on the Target's good. The Coercer may choose to set the tariff at any level up to the prohibitive tariff beyond which it is not profitable for the Target to export the good.[21] States face many considerations when selecting their tariff levels. For example, higher tariffs often provide an easier way for the government to collect revenue when it lacks bureaucratic capacity (Kaldor 1962) and frequently help domestic industries that produce similar goods. Furthermore, positive tariffs typically benefit large states due to these states' abilities to pass off some of the tariffs' costs onto other states (Bagwell and Staiger 2002, 3). Yet even small states frequently desire positive tariffs, as they often argue that tariffs allow them to protect new industries that cannot yet compete effectively absent this protection (Chang 2002, 39, 53)[22] or pursue a strategy that emphasizes domestic production over foreign imports, known as import substitution (Baer 1972). However, higher tariffs also raise prices for consumers, can harm industries that use the good as an input in their production processes, and result in an overall net welfare loss according to standard economic theory. It is not necessary to specify these considerations explicitly; instead, I model both the Coercer's and Target's utilities over the good using a function that is sufficiently general to allow for the many reasons states desire positive tariffs.

Because the amount of the good available for export and consumption depends on the tariff, it is convenient to denote the countries' utilities over the good as functions of the tariff. Furthermore, the utility that each state receives from the tariff depends on that state's total capabilities. When states have large capabilities, they care less about a single tariff, as it represents a small fraction of their resources. For instance, when states possess an advanced military, a large population, and plentiful sources of energy, they may rely on their own resources or take them through military force. Thus, the utility function captures the idea that the greater a state's capabilities, the less it requires exchange with a particular partner (Krasner 1976).

---

[21] An export tax or subsidy could be modeled equivalently, but I focus on tariffs for simplicity, as is standard.

[22] Note that most economists recommend against this practice.

Formally, each state's utility over the tariff is a function of its total capabilities π, or $\Omega^k(\tau, \pi^k)$, where $k = \{C, T\}$. $\Omega^C(\tau, \pi^C)$ is assumed to have an interior maximum with respect to τ of τ^N, which is the noncooperative tariff. Furthermore, $\Omega^T(\tau, \pi^T)$ is assumed to be concave in τ and monotonically decreasing in τ so that the Target prefers a lower tariff, all else being equal.[23] Because states care less about a single tariff when they have more power, the cross partial derivative for the Coercer, $\frac{d^2\Omega^C(\tau, \pi^C)}{d\tau d\pi^C}$, is negative and the cross partial for the Target, $\frac{d^2\Omega^T(\tau, \pi^T)}{d\tau d\pi^T}$, is positive.

If the two states are not WTO members (or if one state is a member and the other is not, and thus WTO laws do not govern trade between the two states), then they begin the game with a tariff rate that was set as part of a cooperative agreement, such as a comprehensive trade agreement, which is not modeled here. This agreement could be modeled explicitly, but this is unnecessary and thus remains in the background to reduce notation and complexity. The tariff is either equal to or lower than the Coercer's ideal tariff level, because both states would be worse off if it were set higher than this level. Although the tariff on the traded good could be modeled as the Nash equilibrium tariff, the model's purpose is to understand cooperation's potential dangers; thus, it is more interesting to consider a cooperative tariff.

By contrast, if the two states are WTO members, the Coercer must provide the Target with the tariff rate that was agreed upon within the context of the WTO negotiations. This is known as the most-favored-nation (MFN) tariff rate, τ^{MFN}. In this case, the game begins with the tariff set at the MFN level.

At the beginning of the game, the Target decides whether to undertake a costly investment, $i \in \{0, 1\}$, that allows it to produce the good to export to the Coercer. If the Target invests, it incurs cost i, such that i represents both the investment decision and investment's cost. Although it may seem strange for the tariff to be set before the good is produced, this timing represents in reduced form the intuition of a dynamic model in which investment is made periodically to sustain the industry, such that the countries' commitments to future policies influence current investment levels. The timing is meant to capture the idea that without periodic investment, the industry would collapse. The interpretation should not literally be that countries bargain over tariffs before any good is produced.

The investment could be of any type; for example, it could include items needed to produce the good, such as new factories, technology, training, or equipment, or infrastructure necessary to transport the good, such as roads, pipelines, or ports. The investment's crucial feature is that it is relationship-specific; the investment's profitability depends on the Coercer's continued cooperation with the Target. In the model, this occurs by construction because only

---

[23] Although a state's optimal tariffs depend on its market power in standard economic theory, a state always prefers that its trading partners maintain lower tariffs on its goods.

two countries exist. Consequently, the Coercer must maintain a low tariff for the investment to be profitable for the Target, because if the tariff were too high, the Target would not benefit enough to justify the investment's cost. Although investments are not always relationship-specific in reality, the model captures important and frequently encountered situations in international exchange, as explained previously.

As is standard in models of hold-up problems, I assume that parties cannot contract over the Target's investment decision, because the investment cannot be verified (Fudenberg and Tirole 1991). For example, suppose the Target agrees to invest in its agricultural sector. If the Target fails to invest, the Coercer may observe low agricultural output but cannot tell if the low output results from low investment or, say, adverse weather conditions.

Next, after the Target decides whether to invest, a disagreement forms between the two countries with probability p. The particular nature of the dispute is unimportant; it could arise in diverse areas, including territory, human rights, environmental policies, extradition, immigration, arms transfers, military intervention, transnational crime, terrorism, or drug policies. The necessary feature is that the states' preferences over the handling or outcome of the issue differ.

Importantly, however, the probability with which a disagreement arises depends on the relationship between the Coercer and the Target. The more dissimilar the states' political views, the greater propensity for a difference of opinion to form. To see this, consider several examples. Suppose protests occur in a given state. If that state responds with repression and violence, it could draw in another state that places strong emphasis on respect for human rights. Historically, this has happened on many occasions, as states that respond to shocks by violating human rights tend to incur the wrath of states that promote respect for rights, such as the United States and the EU. Or a state that begins a military build-up might prompt a dispute with its adversaries. Friction occurs for many reasons, but it is, in general, more likely between two politically asymmetric states.[24]

If a disagreement breaks out, the Coercer may offer the Target a take-it-or-leave-it deal to settle the dispute. In particular, the Coercer seeks a foreign policy concession $f \in \{0, 1\}$ from the Target, where $f = 1$ means that the concession has been made. For instance, if the Target violates human rights, the Coercer may seek increased respect for rights. If the Target engages in a conflict, the Coercer may demand that it cease hostilities. If the Target holds a

---

[24] Note that p could also be modeled as a function of trade levels or WTO membership. This would not alter the basic outcome of the game. For example, a more dynamic game could be modeled in which trade in one period influences p in the next period. In such a case, conflict would be ever greater for asymmetric states as the game progressed, which would merely exacerbate the dynamics identified here. Alternatively, if p were greater for non-WTO members, the basic outcome would not be a effected because p does not influence tariff levels for WTO members, as explained further later.

fraudulent election, the Coercer may request a recount. However, the Target's ability to make the concession desired by the Coercer is constrained. The cost for compliance can include any reason that the Target dislikes making the concession such as domestic actors' disapproval, adjustment costs, or negative economic impacts.

The Coercer has two policy tools at its disposal to offer as compensation. In reality, of course, the Coercer may have many policy instruments to draw from, such as foreign aid, trade policies, military force, loans, diplomacy, visas, or foreign assets. However, I only consider two polices, because doing so has the benefit of simplicity without sacrificing any of the model's central insights.

The first policy instrument available to the Coercer is the tariff on the good exported by the Target. The Coercer may offer a lower tariff level than the one previously agreed upon prior to the start of the game in exchange for the Target's compliance and may threaten to raise the tariff level if the Target does not provide the policy concession. However, if the two states are WTO members, the Coercer loses this power, as it must maintain the MFN tariff level, as explained previously.[25]

The second policy instrument could be any tool, but to fix ideas, I refer to it as foreign aid, denoted α. Variable α is very general, however, and represents any form of foreign assistance, such as military aid, loans, grants, security guarantees, intelligence sharing, or other concessions. The initial level of α was agreed upon by the states prior to the game in a bargain over both aid and the tariff that is not modeled here.[26] As with the tariff, the Coercer can offer additional aid in exchange for compliance, in excess of the amount that was agreed upon prior to the start of the game. The Coercer may also threaten to reduce the aid allocated to the Target if concessions are not forthcoming. The Coercer may thus provide any amount of aid, from no aid up to the maximum amount of available resources.

Like the tariff, aid is more valuable to a country when the country possesses fewer capabilities. For instance, a country with a relatively stronger military, a larger population, and greater energy resources can more easily find the means to provide for itself and will not mind relinquishing aid as much as a country with fewer capabilities, because such assistance represents a smaller fraction of its wealth. Utility over aid is thus modeled as $g^T(\alpha, \pi^T)$ for the Target and $g^C(\alpha, \pi^C)$ for the Coercer, where $g(\cdot)$ is increasing in α. Reflecting this logic

---

[25] Of course, WTO members could in reality give additional tariff concessions through trade agreements or trade preference programs, although there exist many restrictions to doing so and the benefits are typically relatively small. For instance, trade agreements are generally costly and time consuming to negotiate, and preference programs may not be used to discriminate between similar recipients. However, these complications are not modeled here without loss of generality. Furthermore, although some areas remain outside of the WTO's purview, the model's purpose is to unpack the WTO's impact, and thus I ignore this nuance.

[26] If the states are WTO members, the initial level of α is set at the Coercer's preferred level.

formally, the cross partial derivatives for the Coercer and Target, $\frac{d^2 g^k(\alpha,\pi^k)}{d\alpha d\pi^k}$, are negative.

Furthermore, although the Coercer could in principle offer only assurances, and not threats, doing so often cannot alter the Target's behavior. For instance, when tariffs are already set at low levels, cutting them further does not represent a high inducement, and providing additional aid requires a large cost for the Coercer. A policy of only offering bribes also often faces domestic resistance, because domestic audiences may prefer not to reward an adversary (Lindsay 1986). Furthermore, the coercive diplomacy literature indicates that assurances must be combined with credible threats to be effective (Christensen 2011), as explained earlier. Thus, I focus on cases in which the Coercer uses both.

States therefore care about the tariff, foreign aid, the Target's foreign policies, and the Target's investment. Formally, the Coercer's utility function is $u^C(\tau, f, i, \alpha, \pi^C) = i\Omega^C(\tau, \pi^C) + I(f) - g(\alpha, \pi^C)$, where $I(\cdot)$ is an indicator function that equals 1 if a dispute occurs and 0 if a dispute does not occur. The Target's utility function is $u^T(\tau, f, i, \alpha, \pi^T) = i\Omega^T(\tau, \pi^T) - i - f + g(\alpha, \pi^T)$. Notice that I have set the cost of the Target's foreign policy concession equal to 1. Attaching a specific value is useful for concreteness and does not alter the outcome, because what matters are the parameters' relative values.

After the Coercer makes its offer, the Target chooses whether to accept, and if it does, the states fulfill the bargain's terms. Because the states make a static exchange in which the Target provides a concession in return for specific rewards, there is no scope for deviation. If the Target does not accept, the Coercer selects its preferred tariff and foreign aid allocation. Thus the timing is as follows:

1. The Target chooses whether to invest.
2. A dispute breaks out with probability p.
3. If desired, the Coercer selects a combination of threats and assurances using τ and α to offer the Target in exchange for f.
4. The Target chooses f and the Coercer chooses τ and α.

With all of the game's pieces in place, I now solve the model.

2.3 SOLVING THE MODEL

I proceed using backward induction; that is, I analyze the states' behavior at the game's end and move backward to the game's beginning. Because states are forward looking, they make choices based on their likely consequences. Thus, to determine their actions in the beginning of the game, I first consider the implications of those actions. Formally, the solution concept used here is subgame perfect Nash equilibrium.

In essence, I solve two forms of the game: one in which both states are WTO members and thus have no strategic choice of the tariff, and one in which at least one state is not a WTO member so that the tariff decision is strategic. Suppose first that either one state or neither state is a WTO member. If no dispute occurs, at the end of the game, the states maintain whatever arrangement was in place prior to the start of the game. Because there exists no reason for the Coercer to demand a concession, the agreement continues uninterrupted.

If a dispute occurs, however, the Coercer offers the Target a deal. If the Target takes the deal, the Target and the Coercer exchange the Target's foreign policy concession for the Coercer's bribe. If the Target refuses the deal, both states enter into the noncooperative solution – the policies that they would most favor if they chose them individually rather than as part of a cooperative arrangement. The Target does not make the foreign policy concession, because it prefers not to. The Coercer implements the tariff level that it favors, $\tau = \tau^N$, and does not provide foreign aid because doing so is costly.

Given this outcome, consider the threats that the Coercer makes to the Target. Both states know that if the Target refuses the deal, the Coercer will impose the tariff and aid policies that it prefers unilaterally. Thus, any other threat would not be credible. The Coercer therefore threatens to terminate the tariff and aid levels agreed to prior to the start of the game and to institute the noncooperative tariff and aid levels instead.

Now consider the assurances the Coercer offers to the Target in exchange for the foreign policy concession. The Coercer does not provide any bribes above the bare minimum required to convince the Target to make the concession. Why incur an extra cost without obtaining any extra benefit? Thus, the Coercer selects the combination of tariff concessions and aid provision that it most prefers, subject to the condition that it offers just enough to convince the Target to concede.

Suppose for now that the Coercer is able and willing to make a deal that the Target would accept, though I return to the case in which this does not hold later. If the Target did not invest earlier in the game, it does not export the good to the Coercer, and so the tariff level remains irrelevant. In this case, the Coercer simply provides enough aid to compensate the Target for making concessions, or it chooses α to satisfy $g^T(0, \pi^T) = g^T(\alpha, \pi^T) - 1$, because the foreign policy concession's cost is 1. If the Target invested, the Coercer selects the aid, tariff, and foreign policy levels that it most prefers subject to the constraint that the Target will then agree to the deal. Formally, the Coercer solves the following problem: $\max_{\tau, f, \alpha} \Omega^C(\tau, \pi^C) + f - g^C(\alpha, \pi^C)$ subject to $\Omega^T(\tau, \pi^T) - f + g^T(\alpha, \pi^T) \geq \Omega^T(\tau^N, \pi^T) + g^T(0, \pi^T)$.[27]

Taking the derivatives, $\Omega^C_\tau(\tau, \pi^C) = -\Omega^T_\tau(\tau, \pi^T)$ and $g^C_\alpha(\alpha, \pi^C) = g^T_\alpha(\alpha, \pi^T)$. Furthermore, because the Coercer possesses all of the bargaining power, it offers the Target a deal that satisfies the Target's constraint with equality, or

---

[27] $\alpha \geq 0$ is also a constraint, as the Coercer will not extract aid.

$g^T(\alpha, \pi^T) = 1 + \Omega^T(\tau^N, \pi^T) - \Omega^T(\tau, \pi^T) + g^T(0, \pi^T)$. The solution, denoted τ^*, f^*, and α^*, thus satisfies these three equations.

Of course, there may not exist a deal that would make the Coercer better off and satisfy the Target's constraint. The Coercer would be better off when $\Omega^C(\tau, \pi^C) + f - g^C(\alpha, \pi^C) \geq \Omega^C(\tau^{eff}, \pi^C) - g^C(0, \pi^C)$, where τ^{eff} is the tariff level agreed to prior to the start of the game (the effective tariff). Combining the two constraints by substituting for f, a deal is possible when $\Omega^T(\tau, \pi^T) - \Omega^T(\tau^N, \pi^T) + g^T(\alpha, \pi^T) - g^T(0, \pi^T) + \Omega^C(\tau, \pi^C) - \Omega^C(\tau^{eff}, \pi^C) - g^C(\alpha, \pi^C) + g^C(0, \pi^C) \geq 0$. Thus, the more the Coercer cares about giving up aid and reducing the tariff, the less likely this equation is to hold, and the more the Target desires aid and a lower tariff, the more likely it is to hold. Because of the assumptions on the cross partial derivatives, when π^C is large relative to π^T, the Coercer cares less about the tariff and aid than the Target does, and therefore coercive diplomacy is more likely to occur.

Now suppose both states are WTO members. In this case, the Coercer solves the preceding problem, but maintains $\tau = \tau^{MFN}$ in accordance with WTO laws. Regardless of the Target's investment decision, the optimal level of aid if a dispute occurs, denoted α^{WTO}, therefore satisfies $g^T(0, \pi^T) = g^T(\alpha^{WTO}, \pi^T) - 1$. Comparing the Coercer's offer when the states are WTO members versus when they are not, α^{WTO} is bigger than α^* as long as $\Omega^T(\tau^N, \pi^T) < \Omega^T(\tau^*, \pi^T)$, which always holds. This suggests the following proposition:[28]

Proposition 1. *Joint WTO membership decreases the Coercer's use of τ and increases its use of α to extract foreign policy concessions.*

Investment Decision

Having established the offer that the Coercer makes to the Target in the event of a dispute, I now determine whether the Target undertakes the investment at the beginning of the game. The Target decides to invest if its likely payoff from doing so is greater than its likely payoff from failing to do so. I thus turn to a comparison of these payoffs.

Suppose that a dispute occurs. In that case, if the Target invested, the Coercer makes an offer that represents the bare minimum required to convince the Target to make the concession. This offer therefore provides the Target with a payoff equal to the payoff it receives if it does not take the deal, which represents the payoff from the Coercer's optimal tariff level and no aid. Formally, the Coercer chooses tariff and aid levels such that $g^T(0, \pi^T) = g^T(\alpha^{WTO}, \pi^T) - 1$ and $\tau = \tau^{MFN}$ if both states are WTO members and $\Omega^T(\tau^*, \pi^T) - 1 + g^T(\alpha^*, \pi^T) = \Omega^T(\tau^N, \pi^T) + g^T(0, \pi^T)$ otherwise. If the Target did not invest, the Coercer's offer provides the Target with aid that

---

[28] If a deal that satisfies both constraints does not exist, the WTO has no effect on α because $\alpha = 0$ regardless; thus, this proposition holds on average.

satisfies $g^T(0, \pi^T) = g^T(\alpha^*, \pi^T) - 1$, and the tariff does not matter because no good was produced. Thus, regardless of the Target's investment decision, the Coercer gives the Target an offer equal to the Target's cost of undertaking the foreign policy concessions. In other words, the total value of concessions offered to the Target equals 1 either way. Importantly, however, if the Target invested, it incurred a cost of -1, *which is not accounted for in the deal* because the investment happened in the past. Therefore, if a dispute occurs, the Target is made worse off if it invested previously.[29]

Suppose a dispute does not occur. If the Target invested, it receives utility from trading with the Coercer at the previously agreed-upon tariff level if at least one state is not a WTO member and at the MFN tariff level if both are WTO members. If the Target did not invest, it does not obtain this utility. It collects the previously agreed-upon foreign aid either way. Thus, in this case, the Target is worse off if it did not invest previously.

Because a dispute occurs probabilistically, the Target decides to invest if the expected benefit from doing so is greater than the expected benefit from not doing so. Recall that the previously agreed-upon tariff and aid levels are denoted τ^{eff} and α^{eff}. The Target invests when $p(-1) + (1-p)[\Omega^T(\tau^{eff}, \pi^T) + g^T(\alpha^{eff}, \pi^T) - 1] \geq p(0) + (1-p)(g^T(\alpha^{eff}, \pi^T))$, or $-1 + (1-p)\Omega^T(\tau^{eff}, \pi^T) \geq 0$. When p is larger, this equation is less likely to hold and the Target is less likely to invest. However, when both states are WTO members, the Target receives τ^{MFN} regardless. In that case, the Target invests when $p(-1 + \Omega^T(\tau^{MFN}, \pi^T) + g^T(0, \pi^T)) + (1-p)[\Omega^T(\tau^{MFN}, \pi^T) + g^T(\alpha^{eff}, \pi^T) - 1] \geq p(+g^T(0, \pi^T)) + (1-p)(g^T(\alpha^{eff}), \pi^T)$, or, simplifying, when $\Omega^T(\tau^{MFN}, \pi^T) - 1 \geq 0$, which always holds.

Thus, the investment is always profitable for the Target when both states are WTO members. Absent the WTO, the investment is only worthwhile when p is not too large. Because p is larger when states are more politically dissimilar, these states experience underinvestment and trade outside of the WTO. This suggests the following two propositions:

Proposition 2. *Outside of the WTO, politically similar states trade and invest more than politically dissimilar states.*

Proposition 3. *Joint WTO membership increases trade and investment for politically dissimilar states.*

Furthermore, recall that when the Coercer has few capabilities and the Target has many, the Coercer is less likely to be able to exercise coercive diplomacy. In this case, the Target invests because the tariff level remains unchanged

---

[29] This finding comports with the idea that once an irreversible investment is undertaken, known as a "sunk cost," this cost will not factor into future decisions. Ex ante, however, the cost will influence the Target's investment decision.

regardless of whether a dispute occurs. If the Coercer can exercise coercive diplomacy, the Target may not invest, as shown earlier.

If both states are WTO members, however, the investment is always profitable for the Target, as explained previously. Therefore, joint WTO membership increases investment specifically when the Coercer is able to exercise diplomacy, which occurs when it is more powerful and the Target is weaker.

Furthermore, note that I have modeled the effect of coercive diplomacy using an import tariff. However, an equivalent model could feature the Coercer limiting the export of a good that the Target requires or placing an export tax on such a good unless the Target makes concessions. In that case, the Target underinvests in sectors or industries that require the good as an input. Joint WTO membership should thus boost trade and investment most for pairs of states with dissimilar capabilities, or different values of π. This logic suggests the following two propositions:

Proposition 4. *Outside of the WTO, states with similar capabilities trade and invest more than states with dissimilar capabilities.*

Proposition 5. *Joint WTO membership increases trade and investment for states with dissimilar capabilities.*

Note that, if the Target does not invest, the Target's payoff equals the outcome under investment and joint WTO membership. Thus, this prediction holds on average, although it does not strictly hold for some pairs of states.

Efficacy of Coercion

To consider the impact of joint WTO membership on the efficacy of the Coercer's attempts to extract concessions from the Target, I introduce a slight modification to the model. In particular, I relax the assumption that f is a binary decision and instead assume that $f \in [0, \bar{f}]$, where $\bar{f}$ represents the maximum concessions the Target could make. For instance, if the Coercer demands a transition to democracy, $\bar{f}$ represents a full transition. The Coercer now solves the following problem: $\max_{\tau, f, \alpha} \Omega^C(\tau, \pi^C) + f - g^C(\alpha, \pi^C)$ subject to $\Omega^T(\tau, \pi^T) - f + g^T(\alpha, \pi^T) \geq \Omega^T(\tau^N, \pi^T) + g^T(0, \pi^T)$. Taking the derivative with respect to f, τ, and α and solving, it is apparent that the Coercer chooses α^* and τ^* that satisfy $g_\alpha^C(\alpha, \pi^C) = g_\alpha^T(\alpha, \pi^T)$ and $\Omega_\tau^C(\tau, \pi^C) = -\Omega_\tau^T(\tau, \pi^T)$. Combining this result with the Target's constraint, which holds with equality, yields the solution.

However, if the Coercer and Target are WTO members, the Coercer solves the same problem, but $\tau = \tau^{MFN}$. In this case, the equilibrium condition for aid becomes $g_\alpha^C(\alpha, \pi^C) = g_\alpha^T(\alpha, \pi^T)$. Comparing this condition to the prior one, α^* is the same regardless of whether both states are WTO members. Furthermore, using the Target's constraint, it is clear that when at least one state is not a member, $f = \Omega^T(\tau^*, \pi^T) - \Omega^T(\tau^N, \pi^T) + g^T(\alpha^*, \pi^T) - g^T(0, \pi^T)$,

Theoretical Framework 39

whereas when both are WTO members, $f = g^T(\alpha^*, \pi^T) - g^T(0, \pi^T)$. Because $\Omega^T(\tau^*, \pi^T) \geq \Omega^T(\tau^N, \pi^T)$, the Target makes greater foreign policy concessions when one or both states are not WTO members.[30]

Proposition 6. *The Coercer extracts more foreign policy concessions from the Target when one or both of these states are not WTO members.*

With this in mind, the next four chapters empirically evaluate the model's predictions using a mix of quantitative and qualitative approaches. Taken together, the evidence overwhelmingly supports the claims derived from the model. In the absence of international institutions, states consistently underinvest in relations with their dissimilar partners due to political hold-up problems. Once they join these institutions, hold-up problems are resolved in the areas the institutions govern but are displaced into domains outside the institutions' purviews, reducing their members' coercive powers.

2.4 APPENDIX: MODEL EXTENSIONS

Extension 1: Deviation from WTO Commitments

Having solved for the equilibria of the basic model, I now relax the assumption that the Coercer cannot deviate from its WTO commitments. As before, if a disagreement breaks out, the Coercer may offer the Target a take-it-or-leave-it deal to settle the dispute. The Coercer has the same two policy tools at its disposal to offer as compensation. However, the Coercer may now choose to deviate from its WTO agreements by offering a lower tariff or by raising the tariff, although doing so incurs a cost. This cost may arise from retaliation, the loss of domestic and international reputation, or other factors and is captured in the model using the notation $K = \{0, c\}$, where $K = 0$ if no deviation occurs and $K = c$ if the Coercer deviates. The Coercer's utility function is now $u^C(\tau, f, i, \alpha, \pi^C) = i\Omega^C(\tau, \pi^C) + I(f) - g(\alpha, \pi^C) - K$, where $I(\cdot)$ is an indicator function that equals 1 if a dispute occurs and 0 if a dispute does not occur. The Target's utility function is unchanged.

I again proceed using backward induction. Suppose that either one state or neither state is a WTO member. The outcome is the same as before; that is, the Coercer selects the combination of tariff concessions and aid provision that it most prefers, subject to the condition that it offers just enough to convince the Target to concede. Suppose the Coercer is able and willing to make a deal that the Target would accept. If the Target did not invest earlier in the game, the Coercer again simply provides enough aid to compensate the Target for making concessions, or it chooses α to satisfy $g^T(0, \pi^T) = g^T(\alpha, \pi^T) - 1$, because the foreign policy concession's cost is 1. If the Target invested, the Coercer selects the aid, tariff, and foreign policy levels that it most prefers

---
[30] Again, if no deal is possible, the WTO has no effect, so that the proposition holds on average.

subject to the constraint that the Target will then agree to the deal. Formally, the Coercer solves the following problem: $\max_{\tau, f, \alpha} \Omega^C(\tau, \pi^C) + f - g^C(\alpha, \pi^C)$ subject to $\Omega^T(\tau, \pi^T) - f + g^T(\alpha, \pi^T) \geq \Omega^T(\tau^N, \pi^T) + g^T(0, \pi^T)$. The solution to this problem is identical to that shown in the basic game. Of course, there may not exist a deal that would satisfy both the Coercer's and the Target's constraints. However, as before, when π^C is large relative to π^T, the Coercer cares less about the tariff and aid than the Target does, and therefore coercive diplomacy is more likely to occur.

Now suppose both states are WTO members. In this case, the Coercer has two options. First, it can solve the preceding problem but maintain $\tau = \tau^{MFN}$ in accordance with the WTO's laws. Regardless of the Target's investment decision, the optimal level of aid if a dispute occurs, denoted α^{WTO}, satisfies $g^T(0, \pi^T) = g^T(\alpha^{WTO}, \pi^T) - 1$. Comparing the Coercer's offer when the states are WTO members versus when they are not, α^{WTO} is bigger than α^* as long as $\Omega^T(\tau^N, \pi^T) < \Omega^T(\tau^*, \pi^T)$, which always holds. So far, the solution is unchanged.

However, the Coercer can also deviate from the WTO's rules at cost c. In this case, the Coercer solves the following problem: $\max_{\tau, f, \alpha} \Omega^C(\tau, \pi^C) + f - g^C(\alpha, \pi^C) - c$ subject to $\Omega^T(\tau, \pi^T) - f + g^T(\alpha, \pi^T) \geq \Omega^T(\tau^N, \pi^T) + g^T(0, \pi^T)$. Because the only addition to the maximization problem is the constant c, this solution is the same as that from the non-WTO case.

The Coercer therefore compares its utility from deviating from its WTO agreements to its utility from sticking with its WTO commitments and chooses whichever option maximizes its utility. Formally, it deviates when $\Omega^C(\tau^*, \pi^C) + 1 - g^C(\alpha^*, \pi^C) - c \geq \Omega^C(\tau^{MFN}, \pi^C) + 1 - g^C(\alpha^{WTO}, \pi^C)$. Thus, imperfect compliance leads the Coercer to sometimes violate its WTO agreements, but as long as it does not violate them all of the time, joint WTO membership increases the Coercer's use of aid for coercion and decreases its use of the tariff on average, in accordance with Proposition 1.

Having established the offer that the Coercer makes to the Target in the event of a dispute, I now determine whether the Target undertakes the investment at the beginning of the game. Suppose that a dispute occurs. If the Target invested, the Coercer makes an offer that represents the bare minimum required to convince the Target to make the concession. This offer therefore provides the Target with a payoff equal to the payoff it obtains if it does not take the deal, which represents the payoff from receiving the Coercer's optimal tariff level and no aid. Formally, the Coercer chooses tariff and aid levels such that $g^T(0, \pi^T) = g^T(\alpha^{WTO}, \pi^T) - 1$ and $\tau = \tau^{MFN}$ if both states are WTO members and the Coercer has complied with the WTO's rules, and $\Omega^T(\tau^*, \pi^T) - 1 + g^T(\alpha^*, \pi^T) = \Omega^T(\tau^N, \pi^T) + g^T(0, \pi^T)$ otherwise. If the Target did not invest, the Coercer's offer provides the Target with aid that satisfies $g^T(0, \pi^T) = g^T(\alpha^*, \pi^T) - 1$, and the tariff does not matter because no good was produced. Thus, regardless of the Target's investment decision, the Coercer gives the Target an offer equal to the Target's cost of undertaking the foreign policy concessions.

Theoretical Framework

The result is the same as before if a dispute does not occur. If the Target invested, it receives utility from trading with the Coercer at the previously agreed-upon tariff level if one or both of the states are not WTO members and at the MFN tariff level if both are WTO members. If the Target did not invest, it does not obtain this utility. It collects the previously agreed-upon foreign aid either way. Thus, in this case, the Target is worse off if it did not invest previously.

Because a dispute occurs probabilistically, the Target decides to invest if the expected benefit from doing so is greater than the expected benefit from not doing so. Recall that the previously agreed-upon tariff and aid levels are denoted τ^{eff} and α^{eff}. The Target invests when $p(-1) + (1-p)[\Omega^T(\tau^{eff}, \pi^T) + g^T(\alpha^{eff}, \pi^T) - 1] \geq p(0) + (1-p)(g^T(\alpha^{eff}, \pi^T))$, or $-1 + (1-p)\Omega^T(\tau^{eff}, \pi^T) \geq 0$. When p is larger, this equation is less likely to hold, and the Target is less likely to invest.

However, when both states are WTO members, the Target receives τ^{MFN} as long as the Coercer complies with its agreements. Because the Target can anticipate whether the Coercer will comply, if the Coercer will do so, the Target invests when $p(-1 + \Omega^T(\tau^{MFN}, \pi^T) + g^T(0, \pi^T)) + (1-p)[\Omega^T(\tau^{MFN}, \pi^T) + g^T(\alpha^{eff}, \pi^T) - 1] \geq p(+g^T(0, \pi^T)) + (1-p)(g^T(\alpha^{eff}), \pi^T)$, or, simplifying, when $\Omega^T(\tau^{MFN}, \pi^T) - 1 \geq 0$, which always holds. If the Coercer will not comply, the Target invests when $p(-1) + (1-p)[\Omega^T(\tau^{MFN}, \pi^T) + g^T(\alpha^{eff}, \pi^T) - 1] \geq p(0) + (1-p)(g^T(\alpha^{eff}, \pi^T))$, or $-1 + (1-p)\Omega^T(\tau^{MFN}, \pi^T) \geq 0$. Thus, investment is profitable for the Target when both states are WTO members and the Coercer complies. Absent the WTO, or absent compliance, the investment is only worthwhile when p is not too large. Because p is larger when the states are more politically dissimilar, these states experience underinvestment and trade outside of the WTO, or in the face of noncompliance. Propositions 2 and 3 thus continue to hold on average.

Furthermore, recall that when the Coercer has few capabilities and the Target has many, the Coercer is less likely to be able to exercise coercive diplomacy. In this case, the Target invests, whereas if the Coercer can exercise coercive diplomacy, the Target may not invest, as shown earlier. If both states are WTO members, however, the investment is always profitable for the Target if the Coercer complies with its WTO agreements, as explained previously. Therefore, joint WTO membership tends to increase investment when the Coercer is able to exercise coercive diplomacy, which occurs when it is more powerful and the Target is weaker. This logic suggests that Propositions 4 and 5 continue to hold on average.

Finally, to consider the impact of joint WTO membership on the efficacy of the Coercer's attempts to extract concessions from the Target, I again relax the assumption that f is a binary decision and instead assume that $f \in [0, \bar{f}]$, where $\bar{f}$ represents the maximum concessions the Target could make. The Coercer now solves the following problem: $\max_{\tau, f, \alpha} \Omega^C(\tau, \pi^C) + f - g^C(\alpha, \pi^C)$ subject to $\Omega^T(\tau, \pi^T) - f + g^T(\alpha, \pi^T) \geq \Omega^T(\tau^N, \pi^T) + g^T(0, \pi^T)$. Taking the derivative with respect to f, τ, and α and solving, it is apparent that the

Coercer chooses α^* and τ^* to satisfy $g_\alpha^C(\alpha, \pi^C) = g_\alpha^T(\alpha, \pi^T)$ and $\Omega_\tau^C(\tau, \pi^C) = -\Omega_\tau^T(\tau, \pi^T)$.

However, if the Coercer and Target are WTO members and the Coercer complies with its agreements, the Coercer solves the same problem, but $\tau = \tau^{MFN}$. In this case, the equilibrium condition becomes $g_\alpha^C(\alpha, \pi^C) = g_\alpha^T(\alpha, \pi^T)$. Comparing this condition to the previous one, α^* is the same regardless of whether the the states are WTO members and regardless of compliance. Furthermore, using the Target's constraint, it is clear that when one or both of the states are not WTO members or when the Coercer does not comply, $f = \Omega^T(\tau^*, \pi^T) - +\Omega^T(\tau^N, \pi^T) + g^T(\alpha^*, \pi^T) - g^T(0, \pi^T)$, whereas when they are WTO members and the Coercer complies, $f = g^T(\alpha^*, \pi^T) - g^T(0, \pi^T)$. Because $\Omega^T(\tau^*, \pi^T) \geq +\Omega^T(\tau^N, \pi^T)$, the Target makes greater foreign policy concessions when one or both of the states are not WTO members, so that Proposition 6 continues to hold on average.

Extension 2: Uncertainty over the Target's Costs

The setup of this extension is identical to the basic model, with one added twist: if a disagreement breaks out, the Coercer may offer the Target a take-it-or-leave-it deal to settle the dispute, but now the Coercer is uncertain of the cost of the foreign policy concession to the Target. Specifically, the Target may face either a low cost or a high cost to making the concession and is the low-cost type with probability q. To simplify the problem, I assign arbitrary numerical values to the cost parameters, such that the low-cost type faces a cost of -1 while the high-cost type faces a cost of -1.5. Now, if the Target is the low-cost type, its utility function is $u^T(\tau, f, i, \alpha, \pi^T) = i\Omega^T(\tau, \pi^T) - i - f + g(\alpha, \pi^T)$, whereas if it is the high-cost type, its utility function is $u^T(\tau, f, i, \alpha, \pi^T) = i\Omega^T(\tau, \pi^T) - i - 1.5f + g(\alpha, \pi^T)$.

Suppose that either one state or neither state is a WTO member. If no dispute occurred, at the end of the game, the states maintain whatever arrangement was in place prior to the start of the game. If a dispute occurred, however, the Coercer offers the Target a deal. If the Target takes the deal, the Target and the Coercer exchange the Target's foreign policy concession for the Coercer's bribe. If the Target refuses the deal, both states enter into the noncooperative arrangement so that the Coercer imposes the tariff and aid policies that it prefers unilaterally.

Now consider the assurances the Coercer offers to the Target in exchange for the foreign policy concession. The Coercer prefers not to provide any bribes above the bare minimum required to convince the Target to make the concession. However, the Coercer is not sure how much it costs the Target to do so. Thus, the Coercer selects the combination of tariff concessions and aid provision that it most prefers, factoring in the probability that the Target is the low-cost type.

Suppose that the Coercer is able and willing to make a deal that either type of Target would accept. If the Target did not invest earlier in the game, the tariff level remains irrelevant. In this case, the Coercer tries to provide enough aid to compensate the Target for making concessions. It chooses α to satisfy either $g^T(0, \pi^T) = g^T(\alpha, \pi^T) - 1$, because the foreign policy concession's cost is 1 for the low-cost type, or $g^T(0, \pi^T) = g^T(\alpha, \pi^T) - 1.5$, because the cost is 1.5 for the high-cost type. It does not make sense to provide any other value because offering a value somewhere in between would overpay the low type and still would not convince the high type to concede, whereas a value greater than the latter amount would overpay both types. The Coercer selects the value based on the probability that the Target is the low type, and the Coercer's utility. Denote the value of α needed to satisfy the low type's budget constraint α^{lt} and the value needed to satisfy the high type's budget constraint α^{ht}. The Coercer then chooses the former amount when $q[f - g^C(\alpha^{lt}, \pi^C)] + (1-q)[-g^C(0, \pi^C)] \geq f - g^C(\alpha^{ht}, \pi^C)$.

If the Target invested, the Coercer compares the aid, tariff, and foreign policy levels that it most prefers subject to the constraint that the low type of Target will then agree to the deal it secures when the high type would agree, taking into account the probability of each scenario. Formally, the Coercer solves the following problem: $\max_{\tau, f, \alpha} \Omega^C(\tau, \pi^C) + f - g^C(\alpha, \pi^C)$ subject to $\Omega^T(\tau, \pi^T) - f + g^T(\alpha, \pi^T) \geq \Omega^T(\tau^N, \pi^T) + g^T(0, \pi^T)$. The derivation is the same as that shown previously, and the budget constraint holds with equality. The solution, denoted τ^{lt}, f^{lt}, and α^{lt}, thus satisfies the three equations. The Coercer then compares its utility under this solution to its utility under the solution that solves the following problem: $\max_{\tau, f, \alpha} \Omega^C(\tau, \pi^C) + f - g^C(\alpha, \pi^C)$ subject to $\Omega^T(\tau, \pi^T) - 1.5f + g^T(\alpha, \pi^T) \geq \Omega^T(\tau^N, \pi^T) + g^T(0, \pi^T)$. Taking the derivatives results in the following equations: $g_\alpha^C(\alpha, \pi^C) = \frac{2}{3} g_\alpha^T(\alpha, \pi^T)$ and $\Omega_\tau^C(\tau, \pi^C) = -\frac{2}{3} \Omega_\tau^T(\tau, \pi^T)$. The Target's constraint again holds with equality. With three equations and three unknowns, the solution, denoted τ^{ht}, f^{ht}, and α^{ht}, can be determined.

The Coercer chooses the solution that solves the first maximization problem rather than that which solves the second when $q[\Omega^C(\tau^{lt}, \pi^C) + f^{lt} - g^C(\alpha^{lt}, \pi^C)] + (1-q)[\Omega^C(\tau^N, \pi^C) - g^C(0, \pi^C)] \geq \Omega^C(\tau^{ht}, \pi^C) + f - g^C(\alpha^{ht}, \pi^C)$. Of course, a deal may not exist that satisfies both the Coercer's and the Target's constraints. Combining the two constraints by substituting for f, a low-cost deal is possible when $\Omega^T(\tau^{lt}, \pi^T) - \Omega^T(\tau^N, \pi^T) + g^T(\alpha^{lt}, \pi^T) - g^T(0, \pi^T) + \Omega^C(\tau^{lt}, \pi^C) - \Omega^C(\tau^{eff}, \pi^C) - g^C(\alpha^{lt}, \pi^C) + g^C(0, \pi^C) \geq 0$. A high-cost deal is possible when $\Omega^T(\tau^{ht}, \pi^T) - \Omega^T(\tau^N, \pi^T) + g^T(\alpha^{ht}, \pi^T) - g^T(0, \pi^T) + \Omega^C(\tau^{ht}, \pi^C) - \Omega^C(\tau^{eff}, \pi^C) - g^C(\alpha^{ht}, \pi^C) + g^C(0, \pi^C) \geq 0$. In either case, the more the Coercer cares about giving up aid and reducing the tariff, the less likely the equation is to hold, and the more the Target desires aid and a lower tariff, the more likely it is to hold. Because of the assumptions on the cross-partial derivatives, when π^C is large relative to π^T, the Coercer cares less about the tariff and aid than the Target does, and therefore coercive diplomacy is more likely to occur.

Now suppose both states are WTO members. In this case, the Coercer solves the preceding problem but maintains $\tau = \tau^{MFN}$ in accordance with

WTO laws. Regardless of the Target's investment decision, the optimal level of aid if a dispute occurs, denoted either $\alpha^{WTO_l t}$ or $\alpha^{WTO_b t}$, therefore either satisfies $g^T(0, \pi^T) = g^T(\alpha^{WTO_l t}, \pi^T) - 1$ or $g^T(0, \pi^T) = g^T(\alpha^{WTO_b t}, \pi^T) - 1.5$. The Coercer selects the amount that satisfies only the low-cost type when $q[f - g^C(\alpha^{WTO_l t}, \pi^C)] + (1 - q)[-g^C(0, \pi^C)] \geq f - g^C(\alpha^{WTO_b t}, \pi^C)$.

Comparing the Coercer's offer when both states are WTO members versus when they are not, $\alpha^{WTO_l t}$ is bigger than α^{lt} as long as $\Omega^T(\tau^N, \pi^T) < \Omega^T(\tau^{lt}, \pi^T)$, and similarly $\alpha^{WTO_b t}$ is bigger than α^{ht} as long as $\Omega^T(\tau^N, \pi^T) < \Omega^T(\tau^{ht}, \pi^T)$, both of which always hold. Thus, Proposition 1 continues to hold on average.

Now consider the Target's investment decision. Suppose first that a dispute occurs. In that case, if the Target invested, the Coercer either provides a total value of concessions equal to 1 or 1.5 based on its calculations presented previously. Importantly however, if the Target invested, it incurred a cost of -1, which is not accounted for in the deal because the investment happened in the past. Looked at ex ante, the Target thus ends up with a total utility of either -1 or -0.5. Thus, if a dispute occurs, the Target is made worse off if it invested previously. If a dispute does not occur, the Target is worse off if it did not invest previously, just as in the basic model.

Because a dispute occurs probabilistically, the Target decides to invest if the expected benefit from doing so is greater than the expected benefit from not doing so. Recall that the previously agreed-upon tariff and aid levels are denoted τ^{eff} and α^{eff}. The Target knows in advance whether the Coercer will offer it a deal valued at either 1 or 1.5, because it has complete information about the Coercer's calculation. If the Coercer offers it a deal valued at 1, the Target invests when $p(-1) + (1 - p)[\Omega^T(\tau^{eff}, \pi^T) + g^T(\alpha^{eff}, \pi^T) - 1] \geq p(0) + (1 - p)(g^T(\alpha^{eff}, \pi^T))$. If the Coercer offers a deal valued at 1.5, it invests when $p(-.5) + (1 - p)[\Omega^T(\tau^{eff}, \pi^T) + g^T(\alpha^{eff}, \pi^T) - 1] \geq p(0) + (1 - p)(g^T(\alpha^{eff}, \pi^T))$. In either case, when p is larger, the equation is less likely to hold and the Target is less likely to invest. However, when both states are WTO members, the Target receives τ^{MFN} regardless. In that case, the Target invests when $\Omega^T(\tau^{MFN}, \pi^T) - 1 \geq 0$, which always holds. Thus, investment is always profitable for the Target when both states are WTO members; otherwise, the investment is only worthwhile when p is not too large, which occurs when the states are not too politically dissimilar. Thus, Propositions 2 and 3 continue to hold on average.

Furthermore, just as in the basic model, when the Coercer has few capabilities and the Target has many, the Coercer is less likely to be able to exercise coercive diplomacy. In this case, the Target invests because the tariff level remains unchanged regardless of whether a dispute occurs. If the Coercer can exercise coercive diplomacy, the Target may not invest, as shown earlier. If both states are WTO members, however, the investment is always profitable for the Target, as explained previously. Therefore, joint WTO membership increases investment specifically when the Coercer is able to exercise diplomacy, which

Theoretical Framework

occurs when it is more powerful and the Target is weaker. Recalling that an equivalent model could feature the Coercer limiting the export of a good that the Target requires or placing an export tax on such a good unless the Target makes concessions, Propositions 4 and 5 continue to hold on average.

Finally, as in the basic model, to consider the impact of joint WTO membership on the efficacy of the Coercer's attempts to extract concessions from the Target, I assume that $f \in [0, \bar{f}]$, where $\bar{f}$ represents the maximum concessions the Target could make. The Coercer now solves the following problem: $\max_{\tau, f, \alpha} \Omega^C(\tau, \pi^C) + f - g^C(\alpha, \pi^C)$ subject to $\Omega^T(\tau, \pi^T) - f + g^T(\alpha, \pi^T) \geq \Omega^T(\tau^N, \pi^T) + g^T(0, \pi^T)$. Taking the derivative with respect to f, τ, and α and solving, it is apparent that the Coercer chooses α^{lt} and τ^{lt} that satisfy $g_\alpha^C(\alpha, \pi^C) = g_\alpha^T(\alpha, \pi^T)$ and $\Omega_\tau^C(\tau, \pi^C) = -\Omega_\tau^T(\tau, \pi^T)$. With two equations and two unknowns, the aid and tariff levels can be solved for and then plugged back into the Target's constraint to find the level of foreign policy concessions made by the Target.

The Coercer then solves the following similar problem: $\max_{\tau, f, \alpha} \Omega^C(\tau, \pi^C) + f - g^C(\alpha, \pi^C)$ subject to $\Omega^T(\tau, \pi^T) - 1.5f + g^T(\alpha, \pi^T) \geq \Omega^T(\tau^N, \pi^T) + g^T(0, \pi^T)$. Taking the derivative with respect to f, τ, and α and solving, it is apparent that the Coercer chooses α^{ht} and τ^{ht} to satisfy $g_\alpha^C(\alpha, \pi^C) = \frac{2}{3} g_\alpha^T(\alpha, \pi^T)$ and $\Omega_\tau^C(\tau, \pi^C) = -\frac{2}{3} \Omega_\tau^T(\tau, \pi^T)$. Again, all three parameters can be solved for. The Coercer chooses the solution that solves the first problem when $q[\Omega^C(\tau^{lt}, \pi^C) + f^{lt} - g^C(\alpha^{lt}, \pi^C)] + (1-q)[\Omega^C(\tau^N, \pi^C) - g^C(0, \pi^C)] \geq \Omega^C(\tau^{ht}, \pi^C) + f - g^C(\alpha^{ht}, \pi^C)$.

However, if the Coercer and Target are WTO members, the Coercer solves the same problems, but $\tau = \tau^{MFN}$. In this case, the equilibrium condition becomes $g_\alpha^C(\alpha, \pi^C) = g_\alpha^T(\alpha, \pi^T)$ for the low type and $g_\alpha^C(\alpha, \pi^C) = \frac{2}{3} g_\alpha^T(\alpha, \pi^T)$ for the high type. Comparing these conditions to the prior ones, the aid levels are identical regardless of whether the states are WTO members. Furthermore, using the Target's constraint, it is clear that when one or both of the the states are not WTO members, either $f = \Omega^T(\tau^{lt}, \pi^T) - \Omega^T(\tau^N, \pi^T) + g^T(\alpha^{lt}, \pi^T) - g^T(0, \pi^T)$, or $f = \frac{2}{3}[\Omega^T(\tau^{lt}, \pi^T) - \Omega^T(\tau^N, \pi^T) + g^T(\alpha^{lt}, \pi^T) - g^T(0, \pi^T)]$, whereas when both are WTO members, either $f = g^T(\alpha^*, \pi^T) - g^T(0, \pi^T)$ or $f = \frac{2}{3}[g^T(\alpha^*, \pi^T) - g^T(0, \pi^T)]$. Because both $\Omega^T(\tau^{lt}, \pi^T) \geq +\Omega^T(\tau^N, \pi^T)$, and $\Omega^T(\tau^{ht}, \pi^T) \geq +\Omega^T(\tau^N, \pi^T)$, the Target makes greater foreign policy concessions when one or both of the states are not WTO members. Proposition 6 thus continues to hold on average.

3

Bilateral Agreements and State Similarity

NATIONS KEEP AGREEMENTS, KEEP THEIR TREATIES SO LONG AS THEY CONTINUE TO DO THEM GOOD.

Linus Pauling[1]

In 1976 the United States and Mexico discussed the construction of a natural gas pipeline that had the potential to improve both countries' welfare through gains from trade. However, Mexico expressed concerns that once the pipeline was built, the United States could violate the agreement's terms to extract political concessions from Mexico (Grayson 1981, 37–49). For example, the United States might threaten to curb imports or even seize the pipeline unless Mexico met its demands. The two states therefore failed to reach an agreement at the time.

Such political hold-up problems pervade relations between many states in the absence of international institutions. When states trust each other not to use trade for coercion, economic cooperation can occur. However, when they worry that their partner will use the cooperative arrangement to exercise coercive diplomacy, as Mexico feared the United States would, they avoid engaging in bilateral trade and investment.

These suspicions exist between two types of states in particular: those with dissimilar capabilities and those with dissimilar policy preferences. Consider the impact of asymmetric power on bilateral trade and investment. When one country possesses much stronger capabilities than another, it is typically much more difficult to coerce than the weaker state because it relies on cooperation with the weaker state much less than the weaker state depends on cooperation with it. For example, if a weak state invests in trade relations with a strong

---

[1] *Meet the Press*, May 11, 1958. The statement was made regarding a nuclear test ban treaty between the U.S. and the Soviet Union.

state, it may incur a large cost from the investment but reap little reward, because the strong state can then use the cooperative arrangement to coerce the weak state to make concessions. By contrast, the weak state is generally unable to hold up the strong state, because the strong state places a lower value on the bilateral arrangement. Because weak states anticipate powerful states' attempts to use agreements for coercive diplomacy, they frequently fail to undertake investments whose profitability requires cooperation with their stronger partners.

Now consider the effect of dissimilar policy preferences on the prevalence of hold-up problems. Asymmetric foreign policy interests indicate that states are more likely to espouse views and prefer actions contrary to their partners' wishes. These states worry that once they invest, situations will arise in which their dissimilar partners will seek to use the arrangements for coercion. They thus underinvest in relationship-specific goods, and cooperation remains low.

The previous chapter modeled these dynamics, deriving specific predictions about both the distribution of benefits from trade and the effects of international institutions. In this chapter, I focus on the former set of predictions, showing that outside of international institutions, similar states engage in higher levels of trade because asymmetric states remain vulnerable to coercive diplomacy. I first depict the pervasive nature of political hold-up problems in international relations and the strategies that targets of coercion adopt as a result. I then explain why targets respond to the potential for coercion through underinvestment by detailing an example in which a large state, Germany, was able to hold up small, politically dissimilar states for foreign policy concessions. I next discuss the political hold-up problems that result from the potential for coercive diplomacy, focusing in particular on the domain of preference programs. Finally, I demonstrate through a systematic empirical analysis that extending trade preferences most stimulates trade and investment between states with similar capabilities and compatible political interests. These include allies and those with similar regime types, because these states do not typically suffer from political hold-up problems. By contrast, less powerful recipients, nonallies, and states with dissimilar regimes underinvest and thus receive a smaller increase in trade from these agreements.

3.1 HOLD-UP PROBLEMS IN THE ABSENCE OF INSTITUTIONS

Bilateral trade can serve as a dangerous weapon – once one partner becomes dependent on this trade's continuation, the other partner can exploit that dependence by demanding additional concessions (Hirschman 1969, 41–48). Because states anticipate that they might be held up, they fail to enter into these arrangements in the first place – the political hold-up problem. Trade thus tends to occur between states that trust each other not to extort concessions from one another. If states can strike deals with their partners over the treatment of goods requiring relationship-specific investments and stick to the agreements, they achieve mutual benefits. However, states typically cannot commit to maintaining their ends of the bargains. Thus, states underinvest, and both parties are worse off than they would be if they could guarantee that neither would use the trading relationship for coercive diplomacy.

Underinvestment due to political hold-up problems occurs among states that lack access to an effective enforcement mechanism. In a bilateral context, states generally face low costs from deviating from agreements because the international community has difficulty both learning about potential violations and adjudicating between parties to the disputes. If one country claims that a breach has occurred, while another asserts that it has not, third parties may have no way to discern the truth without an impartial dispute settlement procedure. In such a case, the only punishment available for a possible infraction may be the penalty one party to the agreement can apply to the other.

Consider a historical example in which states initially planned not to trade when one party feared the other might use the agreement for political leverage (though they relented when they discovered that using the agreement for leverage was not possible): in 1892 Germany selected Russia as a trading partner partially due to Germany's interest in using trade as a political lever. Germany wanted to ensure that Russia's foreign policies remained favorable to Germany despite the lack of a formal alliance between them. Initial discussions focused on "the political side of the treaty," which would create "a strong, powerful, new wire to Russia" (Spaulding 1997, 43). At first, Russia hesitated to cooperate with Germany due to the potential for coercion. However, as both Germany and Russia came to realize, such a treaty could not be used for political leverage because Germany did not have the capability to do so. Specifically, Germany would need the ability to raise tariffs on Russia's goods to use the agreement to extract political concessions. However, Germany's export and import controls were too weak; customs could not verify the origins of German imports and therefore could not assign different tariffs to goods based on the country of origin. To extort concessions from Russia, Germany would have to credibly threaten to raise tariffs on all imports rather than on only Russian imports, which would have been highly costly. Therefore, "the practical impossibility of placing Russia on less-favorable footing than Germany's other trade partners helped force the passage of [the] treaty in 1894" (Spaulding 1997, 43).

As a more recent example, consider trade in energy resources between Russia and many Eastern European states, particularly prior to Russia's WTO accession. Russia consistently manipulated its tariffs on oil and gas to try to extract political concessions from Eastern European states to gain their political allegiance and to influence elections (Bruce 2005, 7–18). In response, many states attempted to decrease domestic consumption by, among other efforts, reducing investments in industries likely to use energy-intensive goods.[2]

---

[2] See "Ukraine's Quest for Energy Diversification," *Stratfor*, November 29, 2012.

More generally, states sometimes chose autarky before the advent of other solutions such as WTO membership. For instance, between 1860 and 1880, states maintained an extensive web of bilateral trade treaties throughout Europe. However, these treaties provided no multilateral enforcement mechanism and, as a result, were subject to political hold-up problems. Indeed, many economists have shown that the agreements did little to liberalize trade, as they were signed primarily in the 1860s, during which time trade liberalization actually declined (Accominotti and Flandreau 2008). Many treaties involved very shallow commitments, and consequently, the breadth of integration remained low (Bordo, Eichengreen, and Irwin 1999). Furthermore, owing to the poor enforcement of the treaties, many states reneged on their commitments, which often led to tariff wars (Irwin 1993). Similarly, after World War I, states turned inward, minimizing trade by enacting high levels of protection in part to reduce their dependence on foreign markets (Knorr and Trager 1977, 46–54).

Bilateral solutions to hold-up problems, which allow investment to occur when it otherwise would not due to fears of extortion, may sometimes serve as alternatives to autarky. However, while a variety of these methods can address hold-up problems, many also increase the risk of moral hazard (Yarbrough and Yarbrough 1992, 70–80). Furthermore, political hold-up problems between governments rather than firms or individuals introduce additional complications (Adelman 1970; Rodrik and Zeckhauser 1988). Firm-level hold-up problems occur in an environment in which investments are observable by the firm but unverifiable by a court. In such a setting, many remedies to hold-up problems exist (such as "renegotiation-proof" contracts, common ownership, and allocation of property rights); however, they require enforceable contracts. When parties include sovereign nations, contracts frequently do not meet this requirement, as governments cannot be compelled by a court to take actions contrary to their interests.

Suppose, for example, that a state would like to make an investment whose profitability depends on the enforcement of an agreement with a partner state. One potential solution to the enforceability problem is for the state to offer some form of collateral such as a sum of money to be paid if it violates the contract. However, if the state later breaches the agreement, how can its partner force it to relinquish the collateral? Even if the state places the collateral in a third party's control, how can its partner demonstrate that a contract violation has occurred? Without an impartial, powerful arbitration system, the partner state may be unable to prove its case and to collect payment.

FDI represents another potential solution. If one state worries that its partner will renege on the agreement, the partner could undertake the investment's cost in exchange for its gains. Although sometimes available, this solution frequently remains out of reach; risks such as political instability or weak rule of law frequently deter investment, particularly in weak states that suffer most from hold-up problems. Furthermore, states often restrict FDI inflows if they view foreign ownership as an impingement on their sovereignty or if they want to prevent a foreign state from reaping all of the investment's benefits. This concern is especially salient between politically dissimilar states, which need this remedy most due to their susceptibility to hold-up problems. Many sectors are also not conducive to FDI, and foreign entities may lack the necessary expertise or resources.[3]

Alternatively, states may choose to solve political hold-up problems through military means. For instance, if a small state refuses to cooperate with a large state, the large state may use its military resources to force the small state to do so. For example, the historically widespread practice of colonization may have been encouraged, in part, by weaker states' hesitation to accede to their more powerful partners' demands (Cooley and Spruyt 2009, 103). Similarly, Europe and the United States compelled China and Japan to open their markets, demanding that China sign the Treaty of Nanking in 1842 after Britain defeated it in the Opium Wars. The treaty elicited many trade concessions from China without obliging Britain to provide any in return (Ouchterlony 1844, 450–52). States may thus use their military to ensure that markets remain open, facilitating investment.

Hostile military take-overs can incur high costs, however, as the aggressor state must expend many resources in such an endeavor. States may therefore select a more inexpensive type of integration instead, such as a political union or federation (Rector 2009, 10) or a more informal form of subordination (Lake 2009, 138–40). This option often appears unattractive to states, however, because they may be unwilling to relinquish sovereignty. For example, a large group of Arab states discussed improving cooperation by forming a federation in 1944 but quickly rejected the idea as they viewed the proposition as a threat to their autonomy (Acharya and Johnston 2007, 189). Furthermore, states may renege on such an arrangement because of enforcement problems (Lake 2009).[4]

States thus frequently experience great difficulty in solving political hold-up problems on a bilateral basis. As a result, they typically underinvest in trade relations with their partners; otherwise, they risk becoming vulnerable to their partners' attempts to exercise coercive diplomacy.

The Example of Germany

To illustrate why asymmetric states hesitate to engage in bilateral trade and investment, I consider a historical case in which Germany used its bilateral agreements with dissimilar Eastern European states as instruments of coercive diplomacy. This example is particularly appropriate because it revises and extends the main case analyzed in Hirschman's (1969) pioneering book, which

---

[3] See Blonigen (2005) for an overview.
[4] Lake (2009) also identifies great power rivalries and democratic political systems as constraints on dominant states.

the argument advanced here builds from. I then provide evidence that fears of such opportunistic behavior also drive asymmetric states to underinvest more generally.

In the early 1900s, many Eastern European countries invested heavily in their agricultural sectors, making them dependent on agricultural exports for revenue by the end of World War I. While Germany served as one of their largest export markets, the danger of potential extortion did not slow their investments because Germany had little incentive to try to influence their foreign policies during this period (Hehn 2005, 100–101). Furthermore, these states failed to anticipate the subsequent events that would dramatically increase their vulnerability to Germany's opportunistic behavior. First, the Great Depression hit Eastern European economies hard, intensifying their dependence on Germany's export market. Next, Adolf Hitler's unexpected election heightened Germany's interest in influencing Eastern European states' foreign policies (Hehn 2005, 120–23).[5] At the time, Hitler did not have much electoral support, and Eastern European states did not foresee his rise to power when they decided to invest in their agriculture sectors (Tooze 2006, 39).

Hitler's surprise election enabled him to hold up many Eastern European countries because of their considerable investments in goods whose profitability relied on access to the German market. Germany sought increased political influence in Eastern Europe to ensure that the region went along with Germany's political goals. For example, economic czar and Reichsbank director Schacht spoke of using Germany's "import monopoly" for political control (Hehn 2005, 102) and, as Foreign Office official Ritter put it, "to attempt the creation of a secure foothold" in the area (Hehn 2005, 104). To achieve both goals, Germany actively worked to increase Eastern Europe's dependence on its markets and became each Eastern European country's most important trading partner. (Yugoslavia, which traded most with Italy, was the exception.) Germany placed imports under central control, and because Hitler became completely focused on conquest, influence over these states took on paramount importance (Tooze 2006, 197–98). Eastern European states thus produced over and above what they would have absent the receipt of preferential treatment from Germany, thereby relying on this treatment's continuation.

Germany's annexation of Austria on March 11, 1938, further increased Eastern Europe's dependence on Germany because Austria had been the second most important importer of Eastern Europe's goods. Afterward, the share of Hungary's total exports that went to Germany rose from 26 to 44 percent, and the share of Yugoslavia's exports that went to Germany increased from 32 to 43 percent (Tooze 2006, 247). The *Economist* stated in 1938 that "Germany's penetration of Central and South-Eastern Europe has assumed, with

---

[5] Prior to Hitler's election to the position of German chancellor in 1933, Gustav Stresemann served as chancellor. Stresemann led the German People's Party and held more moderate views than did Hitler.

the incorporation of Austria, the character of a drive towards a self-sufficient Central and Southeastern Europe under the political and economic tutelage of Great Germany. And Italy emerges as being four or five times more economically dependent on Greater Germany than is Great Germany upon her. The political and strategic implications need no emphasis" (Hehn 2005, 180).

To enhance its ability to extract concessions, Germany then demanded the creation of clearinghouses with the Eastern European countries, or bilateral trade agreements whereby Germany's purchases were credited against offset purchases from Germany's markets. In practice, Germany's exports to a recipient could only be paid for by Germany's imports from that state. Germany compelled Eastern European countries to agree with the new arrangement, as they otherwise faced losing trade ties with Germany and could not easily have found other markets. Once the clearinghouses were set up, Germany began importing very high volumes of raw materials from Eastern European states. These states thus could not simply sell their goods to other markets because they were not competitive, so Eastern European states depended on access to Germany's market (Basch 1944, 68).

Once these states became reliant on trade with Germany, Germany began demanding political concessions under the threat of reduced trade. For instance, in 1934, Germany convinced Poland to sign a nonaggression pact despite Poland's alarm at Germany's increasing militarism. The nonaggression pact "was a serious blow at the French defensive system in Eastern Europe which rested on the Polish alliance" (Carr 1979, 395). Additionally, because Eastern European states were "already dependent on Germany economically... they tried to make their peace with Fascism; Yugoslavia came to terms with Italy and Bulgaria in 1937 while Romania disengaged herself from the French alliance as quickly as possible" (Carr 1979, 400). Furthermore, Yugoslavia became so vulnerable to Germany that Germany managed to "compel a closer alignment to the Axis powers, adherence to the Anti-Comintern Pact and also [to] ... gain control over Yugoslavia's raw materials and foodstuffs" (Hehn 2005, 112). In 1935 the British Foreign Office report concluded that, because Germany "controlled over one half the foreign trade of Bulgaria and Turkey and a high percentage of that of Hungary, Romania, Greece, and Yugoslavia... in the event of any important conflict of opinion between the Great Powers, it would be the German point of view to which these countries would be primarily responsive.... The disadvantage and danger of such a situation to Great Britain and to other Powers is obvious" (Hehn 2005, 182).[6]

However, as expected by the theory, Germany did not hold up all countries equally. Instead, it held up politically and economically dissimilar economies more severely because it had a greater ability to take advantage of small states and more incentive to hold up states that did not already accommodate

---

[6] Of course, other factors contributed to this as well, such as Britain's unwillingness to commit to a defense pact.

its actions. For example, it continued to provide more consistent, favorable trade treatment to its allies, because these states already supported Germany, and to large states, which were not as susceptible to extortion (Tooze 2006, 188). Germany was therefore able to use a surprise election, unexpected economic changes, and the annexation of Austria to hold up its dissimilar partners in Eastern Europe for closer foreign policy alignments.

3.2 PREFERENCE PROGRAMS

Just as Germany provided especially favorable trade treatment to Eastern European states to ensure that these states relied on Germany's market, modern preference programs can create conditions under which the profitability of recipients' investments depend on the programs' continuation. These programs, which place lower tariffs on many goods from developing countries if those countries fulfill certain requirements, frequently serve as coercive tools, and thus represent a particularly salient arena in which to test the theory. However, although Germany's coercive behavior caught Eastern European states by surprise because of the particular conditions described, states typically anticipate this behavior and therefore underinvest to reduce their vulnerability to coercion in a bilateral setting, as I show subsequently.

While condoned by the WTO under the enabling clause, these preference programs operate largely outside of the WTO's purview. Instead, domestic legislation initiates preference programs by specifying a variety of goods that receive reduced tariffs for countries that meet political and economic eligibility criteria. For example, the United States passed the Andean Trade Preference Act in 1991, which provides trade benefits to all Andean countries in exchange for significant progress in the reduction of drug trafficking. The United States also initiated the Caribbean Basin Trade and Partnership Act in 1984 (now the Caribbean Basin Initiative) and the African Growth and Opportunity Act in 2000, both of which lower tariffs in return for respect for workers' rights and child labor restraints. The EU, too, offers many such programs, such as its Cotonou Agreements, which extend trade and aid to recipients that qualify.

Although many preference programs exist, I focus the analysis on a particular program – the Generalized System of Preferences (GSP) – along with related programs as described later. As the oldest and largest trade preference program, GSP represents an ideal setting in which to test the theory. Furthermore, GSP status is more comparable across recipients than is participation in many other agreements such as regional trade agreements (RTAs). While RTAs vary considerably in breadth and depth, the GSP benefits offered by a particular state are typically much more congruent, making comparisons of the programs' effects more appropriate. Additionally, although many view GSP programs as unilateral in nature, they actually entail ongoing bilateral negotiations over the extent to which the donor lowers tariffs for a particular state and the precise behavior a recipient must exhibit to remain eligible. The GSP bargain thus mirrors the dynamics of the model presented in Chapter 2: the donor, which would be called the Coercer in the context of the model, offers lower tariff rates to the recipient, or the Target, in exchange for foreign policy concessions such as human rights improvements. GSP programs thus offer a particularly clear test of the theory.[7]

My examination of the distribution of benefits from preference programs stands in contrast to existing literature, which focuses on the programs' average effects (Aiello, Cardamone, and Agostino 2010; Herz and Wagner 2011; Lederman and Özden 2004; Nilsson 2002, 2007; Özden and Reinhardt 2005; Sapir and Lundberg 1984; Subramanian and Wei 2007; Tomz, Goldstein, and Rivers 2007; Verdeja 2006).[8] Scholars typically find that these programs confer small but positive economic benefits and have identified many factors inhibiting states from realizing larger gains. Early critiques point out that preference programs may encourage specialization where no comparative advantage exists, generate high administrative costs, and diminish enthusiasm for multilateral trade liberalization (Johnson 1967; Patterson 1965). Later work suggests that many preference schemes fail to cover products that become too competitive (Devault 1996), lead to new nontariff barriers (Brenton 2003; Clark and Zarrilli 1992), cause trade diversion (Borchert 2009), increase terms of trade volatility (Mansfield and Pevehouse 2008), and may provide few advantages beyond already low MFN tariff levels (Ahmad 1978; Stevens and Kennan 2005; Yamazaki 1996). These problems can result in the under-utilization of benefits (Brenton and Manchin 2003; Stevens and Kennan 2005).[9] In addition, several empirical studies have found that preference programs reduce liberalization, as Özden and Reinhardt (2004) show that former recipients have higher export-to-GDP ratios and Özden and Sharma (2006) argue that GSP benefits curtail incentives for exporters to lobby for liberal trade policies.[10]

However, despite the large body of literature examining these programs' average effects, scholars do not typically analyze how the programs function as tools of coercive diplomacy.[11] Additionally, although some scholars argue that the human rights clauses in preferential agreements can help to boost rights in recipient countries (Hafner-Burton 2005, 2009), the literature largely focuses on these programs' economic effects. This emphasis on economics has led scholars to overlook important political dynamics that help to determine the programs' impacts.

---

[7] Although hold-up problems exist in trading relationships more generally, states trade for many reasons, and thus isolating my theory's mechanism represents a challenge in these broader contexts.

[8] See De Benedictis and Salvatici (2011) and Hoekman and Özden (2005) for overviews.

[9] However, some argue that high rates of utilization are achieved under the system (Keck and Lendle 2012).

[10] Other scholars contest this interpretation, arguing that preference programs help countries transition to liberal trade policies before they graduate (Conconi and Perroni 2004).

[11] Though see Hsu (2014).

GSP Benefits and Coercion

GSP programs were instituted internationally in 1968 by the United Nations (UN) Conference on Trade and Development to benefit "the developing countries, including special measures in favour of the least advanced among the developing countries." The programs were expected "(a) to increase their export earnings; (b) to promote their industrialization; and (c) to accelerate their rates of economic growth."[12] This goal has remained at the center of most GSP programs, as "the basic principle behind the various GSP programs worldwide is to provide certain goods originating in developing countries with preferential market access to developed-country markets in the form of lower tariff rates in order to spur economic growth in the poorer countries."[13]

Although most developed countries offer some form of GSP, I concentrate on the United States's GSP program, which includes well over a hundred beneficiary developing countries (BDC) that face no tariffs on about 4,650 tariff lines.[14] I focus on the United States's program for three primary reasons. First, as the most powerful state, the United States represents a clear test of the theory. Second, GSP eligibility across Organization for Economic Cooperation and Development (OECD) members is correlated, as many GSP programs are influenced by "the extent to which other major developed countries are undertaking a comparable effort."[15] The United States's GSP policy thus serves as an important indicator of many other OECD countries' policies (Özden and Reinhardt 2005). Third, the United States explicitly threatens to revoke GSP benefits unless recipients make policy concessions, which ensures that the United States's program closely resembles the model outlined in the previous chapter.

The U.S. GSP program maintains a variety of specific requirements for eligibility: GSP may be revoked if a recipient violates human rights, harbors terrorists, nationalizes U.S. property, or experiences high economic growth. It may also be retracted from individual products if the United States determines that they place too much pressure on U.S. producers. If interested parties believe that a GSP recipient has violated the eligibility criteria, they may file petitions requesting an investigation into that state's eligibility. The American Federation of Labor and Congress of Industrial Organizations (AFL-CIO), the largest federation of unions in the United States, files the majority of these petitions in protest of recipients' poor human rights records.[16] The Office of

---

[12] See "About GSP," presented at the U.N. Conference on Trade and Development, at http://www.unctad.org.
[13] Ibid.
[14] Around one-third of these countries are classified as "least developed" and pay no tariffs on an additional 1,750 lines.
[15] See "US Generalized System of Preferences Guidebook," Office of the United States Trade Representative, Executive Office of the President, Washington, DC, March 1999, 6.
[16] This was calculated using data collected from the Office of the U.S. Trade Representative.

the U.S. Trade Representative then chooses whether to investigate each claim and, if it does so, engages with the recipient to elicit reforms. On the basis of the recipient's subsequent behavior, the United States then decides whether to suspend its GSP benefits (UNCTAD 1998).

The GSP program therefore represents an ongoing bargain between the United States and recipient states, as the United States offers GSP preferences in exchange for concessions from its partners. In fact, many members of the U.S. government emphasize GSP's utility as a tool of coercive diplomacy. For instance, Ambassador Barshefsky testified to the U.S. Congress, "The GSP program has been particularly valuable in furthering intellectual property rights, in furthering worker rights, and in furthering a more open investment regime in GSP beneficiary countries."[17] Furthermore, then U.S. Trade Representative Zoellick testified to Congress, "The threat of loss of GSP... has proven to be an effective point of leverage with some of our trading partners."[18] Similarly, in a cable to the United States, the U.S. ambassador to Brazil stated that Brazil had made improvements "on piracy over the past 18 months, under the threat of U.S. revocation of GSP," and thus the United States "need[s] to keep flexibility on [GSP], as GSP can be a powerful tool."[19]

GSP revocation can serve as an effective instrument of coercive diplomacy, as it not only can cause economic damage but can also harm recipients' reputations, providing an important signal to investors and to the international community. For example, in a cable to the U.S. Trade Representative, the U.S. ambassador to Bangladesh stated, "Factory owners, industrialists and investors... approach the GSP issue with a clear understanding of the stakes involved.... They appreciate that the larger issue of worker's rights in the GSP review is a public-relations liability that may be seized upon by their customers."[20] Similarly, when the United States commenced an investigation of Guatemala's labor practices in 1992, the executive director of the U.S./Guatemala Labor Education Project (U.S./GLEP) stated, "U.S. companies are increasingly being held accountable for the working conditions in the factories and on the plantations from which they purchase goods for the U.S. market.... If Guatemala fails to respect basic worker rights, it will increasingly find U.S. investment going elsewhere and will find ever-increasing efforts to

---

[17] See "Cambodia and Bulgaria MFN Trade Status; Renewal of the GSP Program; and Trade Agency FY 1996 Budgets Hearing before the Subcommittee on International Trade of the Committee on Finance." *Congressional Record*, Dominican Association of Free Zones, 104th Cong., 1st sess, August 1, 1995, 10.

[18] See "Examining the Theft of American Intellectual Property at Home and Abroad," *U.S. Senate, Committee on Foreign Relations*, Hearing, February 12, 2002, 107–457.

[19] See Clifford Sobel, "Bangladesh: Labor-GSP Petition – Stakeholder Views," *Wikileaks*, May 9, 2006, 1.

[20] See ibid., 3.

deny Guatemala access to the U.S. market."[21] In response to the investigation, businesses placed considerable pressure on Guatemala, leading it to reform its labor practices by allowing union recognition and increasing penalties for violations of labor laws.[22]

Similarly, the United States began an investigation into Bangladesh's labor rights practices in 2007, threatening to suspend GSP benefits unless Bangladesh undertook reforms. A leading civil society think tank in Bangladesh testified to the United States that revoking GSP would deter "investors willing to invest in Bangladesh, to the detriment of Bangladesh's and, in the end, Bangladesh's workers' broader interests."[23]

The U.S.-Bangladesh Working Group of the U.S. Chamber of Commerce expressed hope that the issue would be resolved quickly due to concerns over trade and investment between the two states.[24] However, in 2013, a garment factory collapsed in Bangladesh, killing 1,129 workers and resulting in GSP suspension. Three weeks later, Bangladesh implemented many labor law reforms, such as requiring factories to create welfare funds for employees, increasing salaries, and easing requirements for union recognition.[25] These anecdotes suggest that GSP revocation can be highly detrimental to recipients, serving as much more than a symbolic action taken by the United States.[26]

Conditionality Leads to Underinvestment

Bilateral treaties and agreements have the potential to provide economic benefits to signatories owing to their abilities to clarify rules, help elites address

---

[21] See "Challenging Guatemala's Labor Abuses," *Multinational Monitor*, May 1993, 1, http://multinationalmonitor.org.
[22] Ibid.
[23] See "US-GSP Hearing: Submission by CDP," *The Daily Star*, February 3, 2013.
[24] See "GSP Suspension to Harm Workers' Interest: PM," *The Daily Star*, September 27, 2013.
[25] See Steven Greenhouse, "Under Pressure, Bangladesh Adopts New Labor Law," *New York Times*, July 16, 2013.
[26] Note that other states use their GSP programs as instruments of coercion as well. For example, since the EU's GSP program originated in 1971, it has contained a social clause which requires adherence to the International Labor Organization convention, a UN organization that sets international labor standards. Since 1995, GSP can be temporarily withdrawn for reasons including violations of labor and human rights conventions, prison labor, drug trafficking, unfair trading, and violations of fisheries agreements. After investigations into violations of eligibility conditions, GSP was taken away from Burma in 1997 due to the presence of forced labor; Belarus in 2007 due to its prohibition of collective bargaining and freedom of association; Venezuela in 2009 due to its nonratification of the convention against corruption; and Sri Lanka in 2010 for insufficient implementation of the International Covenant on Civil and Political Rights, the Convention on the Rights of the Child, and the Convention against Torture and Other Cruel, Inhuman or Degrading Treatment or Punishment. Other countries that have been investigated under the program on political grounds but have not been sanctioned include Pakistan in 1997 and El Salvador in 2008 (Orbie 2011).

domestic demands, and establish forums for bargaining (Mansfield and Milner 2012, 11–13). However, states may not take full advantage of these treaties or even sign them in the first place if they do not trust their partner to uphold the bargain. For instance, because the United States uses its GSP program to compel compliance with political objectives, many recipients remain unable to realize the program's potential benefits. Instead, recipients underinvest in the production of goods whose profitability relies on remaining eligible for the program. Examples in which fears of GSP revocation led to underinvestment abound. For instance, in 1995, a representative of the Dominican Association of Free Zones testified, "These [GSP] investigations have been a tremendous disincentive to increased investment in the Dominican Republic.... It must be recognized that the fact a country is under investigation and could lose its GSP... has a tremendous chilling effect on increased investment in the country, and while the investigation is underway, it is almost a total bar to investment."[27] The representative went on to describe reforms which the government had undertaken to prevent the loss of GSP, including "the adoption of a New Labor Code in June 1993 (and implementing [those] regulations in October 1993), the establishment of significant new protections for union organizers, the formation of new Labor Courts, the formation of a tripartite (government, business, and labor) Oversight Commission for the free zones, and the appointment of a new, reform-minded Minister of Labor." The representative expressed hope that these adjustments would lead the United States to reduce investigations and spur investment.[28]

The United States recognizes that underinvestment can occur due to the inconsistent application of GSP benefits; according to a U.S. government report, improving the stability of GSP eligibility "would help beneficiaries attract the investment necessary to derive significant development benefits from the programs." The report declared that this predictability remains "important to [the GSP recipients] in making business plans and investment decisions" (U.S. GAO 2008). The report cited the Colombian flower industry as a specific example, explaining that uncertainty over the continued receipt of GSP preferences "made it difficult to attract investment needed to enable them to compete with other international cut-flower producers. They said investors need certainty about preference benefits" (U.S. GAO 2008). As the report highlights, many countries do not take full advantage of GSP benefits (Portela 2012, 156–57), likely as a result of fears that the United States will rescind eligibility.[29]

---

[27] See "Cambodia and Bulgaria MFN Trade Status; Renewal of the GSP Program; and Trade Agency FY 1996 Budgets Hearing before the Subcommittee on International Trade of the Committee on Finance," *Congressional Record*, Dominican Association of Free Zones, 104th Cong., 1st sess., August 1, 1995, 99.

[28] Ibid., 100.

[29] Though many potential explanations for this behavior exist, political hold-up problems represent a particularly likely reason.

Distribution of Benefits

While many states limit investment due to threats of GSP revocation, the frequency with which the United States uses its GSP program as a tool of coercive diplomacy varies by recipient. Because the United States decides whether its eligibility conditions pertain on a case-by-case basis, it often wields GSP eligibility as an instrument to extract political concessions from certain recipients. Specifically, the United States has a reduced ability to do so from larger countries, and a smaller incentive to coerce politically similar countries, from which the United States desires fewer concessions.

In fact, the United States built the ability to target politically asymmetric states with threats of GSP ineligibility into the program from its inception. In 1985 Congress introduced a bill that proposed adding respect for workers' rights as an eligibility condition for GSP status. The bill specified that rights violations would result in automatic suspension from the program. However, the U.S. administration desired greater flexibility in the law's application "depending on larger geopolitical and foreign policy situations" (Compa and Vogt 2000, 203). For instance, many U.S. officials sought to avoid subjecting the United States's longtime ally, Israel, to criticism over its treatment of Palestinians. Congress thus revised the eligibility conditions to allow discretion over the law's administration. The bill's passage led the United States to apply the program's requirements so selectively that human rights organizations and labor unions sued the government in 1990, accusing it of "improperly screen[ing] petitions on the basis of non-statutory factors" and instead selecting petitions on the basis of "foreign policy" (Travis 1992, 184).

Indeed, such inequitable treatment occurs often in practice. For instance, in comments from the government of Thailand to the United States, Thailand emphasized its belief that the United States applies GSP in a discriminatory fashion, stating,

> Trade preferences function best when they are predictable and facilitate long-term investment ... [but] the United States makes GSP country eligibility contingent upon compliance or cooperation with a number of U.S. goals and policies.... Thailand believes these mandatory provisions should be as clear and objective as possible, eliminating the possibility of discrimination and undermining the goals of the GSP.[30]

Furthermore, because Thailand wanted to steer clear of eligibility issues, it emphasized its close ties to the United States, stating, "The Royal Thai Government wishes to underscore that Thailand has been a steadfast ally of the United States and a supporter of U.S. initiatives on a variety of geo-strategic issues.... The Royal Thai Government hopes that the U.S. Congress will

---

[30] See "The U.S. Generalized System of Preferences: Comments of the Royal Thai Government," white paper prepared by the Office of Commercial Affairs, Royal Thai Embassy, Washington, DC, November 2010, 2.

consider this legacy of close U.S.-Thai cooperation as it evaluates... Thailand's role in the program."[31] Similarly, the United States partially suspended Pakistan from the GSP program in 1996 because of workers' rights violations, after which Pakistan exhibited little effort to improve respect for such rights. However, its benefits were reinstated in 2004, most likely as a result of Pakistan's assistance to the United States in Afghanistan and its designation as a "non-NATO ally" that same year (Compa and Vogt 2000).

In sum, the United States uses GSP for coercive diplomacy when it has the ability and incentive to do so. The United States is most capable of retracting benefits from weak states, which it can afford to coerce, and has the greatest motive to threaten politically dissimilar states, which it would most like to influence, such as nonallies and recipients with dissimilar regime types. These dissimilar states are thus most vulnerable to political hold-up problems or, in other words, are least likely to increase investment and trade in response to receiving the program's benefits.

3.3 STATISTICAL TESTS OF COERCIVE DIPLOMACY

The preceding discussion suggests that the GSP program benefits some recipients more than others. International institutions do little to regulate GSP benefits, and therefore political hold-up problems occur when GSP is used for coercive diplomacy. Recipients increase investment and trade in products covered by GSP when they have more confidence in the durability of their GSP eligibility, which is higher when states share more political similarities with the United States. Similar states thus reorient their exports to take advantage of the GSP program's benefits. The data should show that more powerful states and those that are more like the United States politically take advantage of GSP benefits by increasing the share of products they export to the United States under the GSP program. I now test whether this assertion holds systematically across GSP beneficiaries.

Hypotheses and Measures

The formal model's results generate several empirical hypotheses. Recall that the model predicts that outside of an international institution, a state is better able to hold up its asymmetric partners because it incurs a smaller cost from doing so. A powerful state can extend or revoke trade concessions from a weaker partner more easily than it can from another powerful state because the weaker state depends more on those concessions while the powerful state relies less on trade with that partner. Because GSP represents a central tool of coercion, the United States's GSP recipient designation should lead stronger states to take advantage of GSP's benefits most effectively, increasing their share

---

[31] Ibid., 12.

of exports under the GSP program. To operationalize the model's prediction, then, I test the following hypothesis:

Hypothesis 1. *GSP eligibility increases the share of recipients' exports that falls under the program more for states with greater power relative to the United States than for those with less power.*

To measure how much power a state possesses relative to the United States, I use a variable constructed from the Correlates of War's Composite Index of National Capability (CINC) (Singer 1988), a widely used indicator of power (Geller 1993; Reed et al. 2008), which is derived from six variables: iron and steel production, military expenditures, military personnel, primary energy consumption, total population, and urban population.[32] The variable is specified as an indicator of whether the difference in power between the United States and a given state is greater than that of the median difference in the sample.

Furthermore, the model predicts that states with more disparate policy preferences underinvest in industries that receive GSP program benefits to a greater extent than do states with similar preferences because they fear that the investment will allow the United States to use coercive diplomacy to extract concessions. One signal of policy preference similarity is whether an alliance exists between two states. Scholars have long employed this measure to indicate similarity, arguing that alliances "are often the primary expression of a state's foreign policy preferences" (Lai and Reiter 2000, 1). I therefore expect the following:

Hypothesis 2. *GSP eligibility increases the share of recipients' exports that falls under the program more for U.S. allies than for non-U.S. allies.*

To test this hypothesis, the key independent variable is U.S. *Ally*, an indicator of an alliance between the United States and a recipient. An alliance is defined as a defense pact, neutrality or nonaggression treaty, or entente agreement, although alternative measures of this variable are discussed in the robustness checks.[33]

Furthermore, pairs of states with similar regime types tend to have more in common and therefore attempt to coerce each other less than do pairs with dissimilar regime types. For instance, it is well recognized that many democracies, such as the United States and the EU, regularly use coercive measures against nondemocracies, frequently to encourage democratization. Democracies tend to see foreign policy areas in a more similar light, forming clubs such as the OECD[34] and the Organization of American States (OAS) (Legler, Lean, and Boniface 2007, 21–28), both of which restrict their memberships to other likeminded states. Similarly, the EU may impose sanctions to achieve the goals laid

---

[32] Note that the use of capabilities rather than GDP distinguishes this hypothesis from the gravity model.
[33] As before, alliance data come from the ATOP data set (Leeds et al. 2002).
[34] See Crawford (2001, 4–5), Dobbins (2008, 46), Uvin (1993), and Uvin and Biagiotti (1996).

out in Article 21, paragraph 2 of the Treaty on European Union, which include "democracy, the rule of law, the universality and indivisibility of human rights and fundamental freedoms, respect for human dignity, the principles of equality and solidarity, and respect for the principles of the United Nations Charter and international law."

Similarly, nondemocracies may have more in common with each other than with democracies. This can be seen, for instance, by the USSR's efforts to spread Communism in many regions during the Cold War. More generally, scholars have shown that autocrats frequently promote similar regime types in partner states both to enhance domestic legitimacy and to more easily pursue their own foreign policy goals. For instance, scholars have long documented China and Russia's attempts to do so (Bader, Grävingholt, and Kästner 2010). States thus worry that partners with different regime types will coerce them to make additional policy concessions and therefore underinvest in goods for trade with these partners. Under the United States's GSP program, I therefore expect the following:

Hypothesis 3. *GSP eligibility increases the share of recipients' exports that falls under the program more for democracies than for nondemocracies.*

The key independent variable in the examination of this hypothesis is *Democracy*, an indicator of whether the recipient has a democratic form of government as coded by Cheibub, Gandhi, and Vreeland (2010). Again, however, alternative measures are discussed in the robustness checks.[35]

Descriptive Statistics

I have argued that GSP investigations deter investment and trade for dissimilar states in particular, as those represent the primary targets of coercive diplomacy. I thus first explore whether the United States typically selected such states for investigation during the period 1985–2012.[36] The investigation process begins once an interested party petitions the U.S. Trade Representative (USTR), after which the USTR decides whether to conduct an investigation.

---

[35] Note that debate exists over the impact of alliances and regime type similarity on overall trade. Some studies find that allies trade more than nonallies (Gowa and Mansfield 1993; Gowa 1995; Mansfield and Bronson 1997), some disagree (Bliss and Russett 1998; Morrow, Siverson, and Tabares 1998; Souva, Smith, and Rowan 2008; Wolford and Kim 2012), some say "it depends" (Long and Leeds 2006), and others believe alliances have little impact (Copeland 1996; Kastner 2007; Papayoanou 1997). Similarly, some argue that democracies trade more with each other (Bliss and Russett 1998; Morrow, Siverson, and Tabares 1998; Mansfield, Milner, and Rosendorff 2000), whereas others dispute this claim (Dai 2002; Garrett 2000; Kono 2006, 2008; O'Rourke and Taylor 2006). However, by focusing on GSP's impact, under which the United States gives preferential trade treatment to all GSP recipients but then manipulates eligibility for political purposes, I am better able to isolate the mechanism specified in the model.

[36] These data were obtained directly from the USTR and extend back to 1985.

Bilateral Agreements and State Similarity

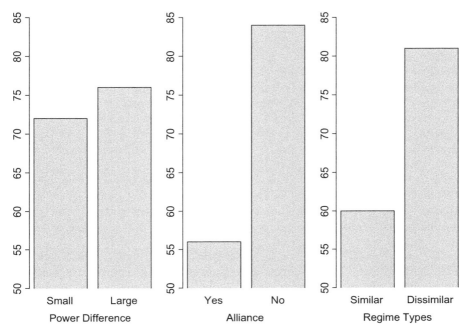

FIGURE 3.1. Percentage of GSP Investigations.

Because the USTR chooses whether to investigate recipient states each year, the dependent variable is an indicator of an investigation's initiation for a particular state in a given year.

The political process favors states that are similar to the United States; thus, I expect the USTR to accept a greater percentage of cases targeting less powerful and politically dissimilar states. Such a finding would indicate that the U.S. government determines the politicized pattern of benefits through a higher approval of petitions against the trade of these asymmetric states. I therefore begin by examining the impact of having smaller capabilities (relative to the rest of the states in the sample), being nonallied with the U.S., and being a nondemocracy on the likelihood of an investigation. Figure 3.1 demonstrates that the United States investigates dissimilar states more frequently than similar states: the USTR accepts petitions in 81 percent of cases involving nondemocracies versus 60 percent for democracies, 84 percent for nonallies versus 56 percent for allies, and 76 percent for weaker states versus 72 percent for stronger states.[37]

---

[37] The countries that have been investigated at least once include Armenia, Bahrain, Bangladesh, Belarus, Benin, Brazil, Burma, Central African Republic, Costa Rica, Dominican Republic, El Salvador, Fiji, Georgia, Guatemala, Haiti, Honduras, Indonesia, Israel, Kazakhstan, Lebanon, Liberia, Malawi, Malaysia, Maldives, Mauritania, Moldova, Nepal, Niger, Oman, Pakistan,

Model

Having presented some descriptive statistics, I now more rigorously investigate whether the GSP program most assists like-minded friends of the United States. I follow Blanchard and Hakobyan (2013) and use a sample that includes all countries that ever received GSP during the period 2002–2009, a total of 164 countries. Blanchard and Hakobyan (2013) chose this period because the GSP program must be renewed in Congress and is sometimes allowed to lapse, creating additional uncertainty over the benefits' continuation, but no such lapses occurred during this time.[38] Furthermore, I use year and country fixed effects, which account for any time-invariant factors that are specific to a given country, such as whether it is landlocked or an island as well as its size and distance from the United States. The year fixed effects account for any factors that are common across countries in a given year. As is standard, I use robust standard errors, clustered by country due to the fact that the same countries are observed over multiple years.

Because the GSP program primarily benefits recipients by providing lower U.S. tariff rates on certain products, recipients should export more products covered by GSP relative to their total exports. The outcome variable is thus the ratio of exports that receive GSP benefits over total exports.[39] Furthermore, overlap exists between GSP treatment and other, smaller benefit programs that the United States maintains for select groups of countries. These include the Caribbean Basin Initiative, the Andean Trade Preference Act, and the African Growth and Opportunity Act. These preference systems function similarly to the GSP program and include most items covered by the GSP program plus additional products; thus, I also include these benefits in the dependent variable.[40]

The inclusion of fixed effects limits potential confounding factors to those that are both country specific and time varying. Thus, I estimate a parsimonious model, controlling for several factors commonly found in gravity models. These include the log of the recipient's GDP, the log of the recipient's GDP per capita, an indicator of WTO membership, and an indicator of an RTA, denoted $\log(GDP)$, $\log(GDPPC)$, *WTO Member*, and *RTA*, respectively.[41] However, I also verify the robustness of the results to a variety of covariate profiles

---

Panama, Paraguay, Peru, Philippines, Poland, Romania, Russia, South Korea, Sri Lanka, Sudan, Swaziland, Syria, Taiwan, Thailand, Turkey, Uganda, Ukraine, and Uzbekistan.

[38] The results are robust to the inclusion of the full sample.
[39] The numerator includes exports that actually obtain GSP treatment, not just those eligible for such treatment. Some eligible products do not use this treatment because the costs of doing so are too high or the benefits are too small.
[40] See Francois, Hoekman, and Manchin (2006) for more detail on these programs. The product-level data used to construct the dependent variable were retrieved from the U.S. International Trade Commission.
[41] A country's economic development partially determines its inclusion in the program; thus, controlling for $\log(GDPPC)$ helps to account for this potential selection issue.

TABLE 3.1. *Effect of GSP and Dissimilarity on the Percentage of Exports Under GSP*

	1	2	3
Lg Power Diff × GSP	0.042		
	(0.084)		
Ally × GSP		0.589***	
		(0.160)	
Democracy × GSP			0.495***
			(0.142)
GSP	0.251	0.056	−0.012
	(0.155)	(0.043)	(0.067)
Large Power Difference	−0.017	0.011	0.009
	(0.063)	(0.078)	(0.078)
Democracy	0.094	0.060	−0.361*
	(0.096)	(0.113)	(0.163)
log(GDP)	−0.914	−1.108	−1.128
	(0.967)	(0.926)	(0.925)
log(GDPPC)	0.480	0.679	0.733
	(0.604)	(0.533)	(0.538)
WTO Member	0.089	0.120	0.022
	(0.110)	(0.092)	(0.127)
RTA	−0.066	−0.024	−0.095
	(0.099)	(0.092)	(0.095)
Constant	17.861	20.884	21.210
	(18.762)	(18.296)	(18.259)
R^2	0.639	0.645	0.643
N	1252	1252	1252

Notes: OLS regression estimates of the effect of GSP on the ratio of imports under GSP to all imports conditional on power, democracy, and alliance status from 2002 to 2009. Unit of observation is the country year. Robust standard errors are clustered by country. * $p < 0.05$, ** $p < 0.01$, *** $p < 0.001$.

discussed further in what follows. Note that *Ally* does not vary over time during the sample period and thus does not appear in the model because it is collinear with the fixed effects.

The results, presented in Table 3.1 and shown graphically in Figure 3.2, show that in general, receiving GSP from the United States increases exports most for states that share more similarities with the United States. The marginal effect for U.S. allies (the coefficient on *Ally X GSP* plus the coefficient on *GSP*) is 0.645 ($p = 0.001$), but is only 0.056 for nonallies. Furthermore, the marginal effect for democracies is 0.483 ($p = 0.000$), whereas for nondemocracies, it is −0.012. Additionally, the marginal effect of GSP for more powerful countries is 0.293 ($p = 0.003$), whereas for less powerful states, it is 0.251. In addition, while the impact of GSP on allies and democracies is precisely estimated, the

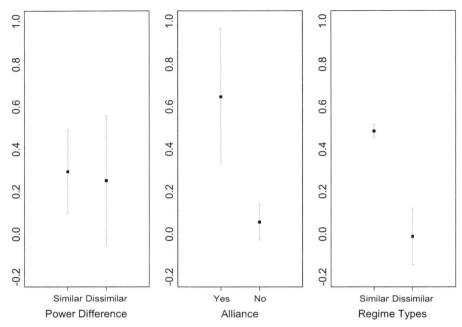

FIGURE 3.2. Effects of GSP and Dissimilarity on the Percentage of Exports Under GSP.

program's effect on weaker states, nonallies, and nondemocracies is not statistically significant, as expected, because these countries should not benefit much from the program. However, it is important to note that the coefficient on *Lg Power Diff* × *GSP*, although positive, is not statistically significant. A likely explanation for this is that all GSP partners are weak relative to the United States, and it is therefore difficult to detect a difference in the effect of the program between states that are slightly more or slightly less weak.

Thus, these results strongly support the contention that states that share political similarities with the United States possess greater abilities to take advantage of GSP benefits because the United States is less likely to use GSP against them as a coercive tool. In contrast, asymmetric states underinvest in the production of products that would benefit from GSP status and thus gain less from the program. Although the results for states with large differences in power are suggestive, they do not provide clear support for the theory, but this is likely due to the overall weakness of GSP recipients relative to the United States. I therefore take care to explore additional evidence for this hypothesis in later chapters.

These results are robust to many alternative specification and coding decisions, although in some cases they are less precisely estimated. Although I do not present the results here, I briefly discuss these alternative models. To ensure that the findings are not driven by particular measures of the key independent variables, I verify the results using alternative measures of power, alliance, and regime type: power is measured using total military personnel (Geller 1993; Reed et al. 2008), alliance is measured using an indicator of an informal alliance with the United States, and regime type is measured using Polity scores.[42] I also show that the findings do not depend on the specific covariate profile or sample by controlling for a variety of other factors that could influence trade flows such as foreign aid and FDI. I then demonstrate that the effects are not due to especially influential dyads by dropping observations for which the residuals are greater than 5 times the standard deviation and observations for which the residuals are greater than 3 times the standard deviation. Furthermore, to ameliorate concerns that the United States provides GSP in response to democratization, I lag the key independent variables in the analysis and find similar results. Next, because RTAs are also bilateral agreements, I include goods that receive more favorable treatment due to these agreements in the construction of the dependent variable. Finally, I subset for those countries in the GSP program rather than using the interaction term approach applied in the main models. This allows me to limit my conclusions to those states that are selected into the program, although the alliance term drops out due to collinearity with the fixed effects.

I also flag two potential concerns that I am only partially able to deal with. First is the possible importance of "multilateral resistance terms," which are country-specific barriers to trade, as described by Anderson and van Wincoop (2003). Although I account for time-invariant barriers by virtue of the fixed effects, I am unable to account for barriers that vary over time apart from controlling for some potential barriers such as income. However, although this represents an unresolved problem in the literature, the relatively small time frame under study minimizes its severity, because these barriers likely do not vary much over this period.

Second, GSP status may be endogenous, although endogeneity represents less of a concern here than in many studies of GSP's effects. While the typical issue is that states might enter the GSP program when they would have increased trade with the United States anyway, in this case powerful states, allies, and democracies would have to enter the program when they would have increased trade in products covered by GSP anyway – a harder claim to argue. However, I should emphasize that although these results comport with the theoretical expectations, it is necessary to be careful when making causal claims based on observational data such as those used here.

In sum, the theory, examples, and empirical tests examined in this chapter attest to the prevalence of political hold-up problems in bilateral settings due to

---

[42] Polity scores are computed from measures of executive recruitment, constraints on executive authority, and political competition and range from −10 to 10 (Marshall et al. 2004).

the frequent use of trade for coercive diplomacy, particularly between dissimilar states. Owing to the economic damage caused by political hold-up problems, states seek ways to commit to not using trade as part of their strategies of coercive diplomacy. International institutions represent one such option, and it is to this possibility that I now turn.

4

WTO Membership as a Commitment Strategy

> UNLESS COMMITMENT IS MADE, THERE ARE ONLY PROMISES AND HOPES.
> *Peter Drucker*[1]

I have shown that states attempt to extort concessions from weaker states with dissimilar interests in bilateral settings because have both the ability and the incentive to do so. As a result, these states invest and trade inefficiently to protect themselves from extortion. To allow trade to flourish, states need to credibly commit to respect their trade agreements. This chapter demonstrates that the WTO allows states to do just this, solving otherwise intractable political hold-up problems by increasing the costs of members reneging on their WTO-regulated commitments. But although it is widely recognized that the WTO can increase cooperation (Keohane 1984), this chapter incorporates the insight that coercive diplomacy causes political hold-up problems to provide a more nuanced view of the institution's role. I demonstrate that WTO membership improves trade cooperation primarily between states that would otherwise suffer from these hold-up problems.

However, WTO membership represents a trade-off for some states: they must relinquish a powerful coercive tool to reap the economic benefits of cooperation. States often elect to do so to obtain these large economic rewards; for example, the United States's desire to tie its own hands has been cited as a motivation for the GATT's creation after World War II (Yarbrough and Yarbrough 1992, 61–65). Furthermore, when the WTO replaced the GATT in 1995, its improved enforcement capacity was in part due to U.S. efforts to prevent itself from violating the institution's laws. The United States had passed domestic legislation called Section 301 in 1974 that allowed it to unilaterally retaliate against any nation that it deemed to have violated a trade agreement.

[1] See Drucker (1974, 128).

It turned to Section 301 with increasing frequency during the 1980s, which reduced other states' willingness to trade with it (Elliott and Bayard 2004; Goldstein and Gowa 2002).[2] Because the United States exercised discretion over what constituted a violation, it could use the act to further its foreign policy preferences. By strengthening the GATT's enforcement capacity, the United States could encourage other states to trade and invest with it more, benefiting the United States economically.

The WTO's power to reduce its members' abilities to use their trade policies for coercion is also evident in a variety of states' WTO accession decisions, as many states enter the WTO to prevent their partners from wielding trade as a coercive tool against them. For example, during India's 1989 economic blockade of Nepal, observers pointed out that India was able to cut off trade because Nepal was not a GATT member and therefore could not enforce its MFN tariff treatment (Garver 1991). This dispute precipitated Nepal's application to join the GATT, as it sought to force India to abide by its rules.[3] I discuss this example further in Chapter 5.

Many states also join the WTO to reassure their partners that they will not use trade against them. For example, a factor in Mexico's and Russia's initial resistance to WTO membership was that they did not want to lose their abilities to wield their oil and natural gas as leverage over other states; however, they ultimately decided to join in part because they believed that the economic benefits associated with membership were great enough to override this concern.[4] Similarly, one reason Saudi Arabia entered the WTO in 2005 was to commit to providing continuous and predictable oil and gas supplies, which it had previously used for coercive purposes.[5]

In sum, because bilateral agreements cause political hold-up problems for frequent targets of coercive diplomacy, states turn to international institutions to help solve these problems. I next explain the WTO's specific provisions governing the use of trade for coercion and then examine WTO membership's impact on a particular state – China – to illustrate the theory. Finally, I evaluate the theory's observable implications systematically, demonstrating that WTO membership increases trade most for asymmetric states by allowing them to commit to specific trade policies. I also substantiate the causal mechanism by verifying that WTO membership provides the largest boost to trade flows in industries where hold-up problems are most prevalent and increases fixed capital investment. Taken in sum, the evidence presented in this chapter provides strong support for the contention that states rely on WTO membership

---

[2] Although a large state such as the United States might not be greatly harmed if a single small state reduced trade with it, many states doing so would cause substantial economic loss.
[3] See Bank (2002, 38–39), Subedi (2006), and United Nations (2003).
[4] See Contreras (2008, 138–39) and Bruce (2005, 20).
[5] See Bradley S. Klapper, "WTO Approves Saudi Arabia Membership Bid," *Washington Post*, November 11, 2005.

to reassure their partners that they will not employ trade to extract political concessions.

4.1 THE WTO AND COERCIVE DIPLOMACY

The WTO limits coercive diplomacy using trade by restricting unilateral discrimination against specific trade partners. Whereas states commonly rely on their trade policies to punish or reward trading partners outside of the institution,[6] WTO members must agree to accord all other members MFN tariff rates.[7] Several exceptions to this rule exist that allow countries to implement additional trade restrictions or enable them to offer concessions beyond those guaranteed by WTO membership.[8] Consider the exceptions that permit additional trade restrictions. These provisions were first agreed to under the GATT but were subsequently incorporated into the WTO; they are thus referred to as articles of the GATT. Although GATT Articles I and XI prohibit discriminatory trade policies, Article XXI contains exceptions to the rule, stating that GATT laws are subordinate to the UN Charter. If the UN votes to sanction a specific country, WTO members may abide by the decision, but, importantly, this exception does not cover *unilateral* action. UN decisions are multilateral

---

[6] A large legal debate exists regarding WTO members' abilities to restrict trade due to concerns such as human rights (Ala'i 2000; Appleton 2000; Bhagwati 1998; Cleveland 2001; Cohn 2000; Howse and Mutua 2000; Lim 2001; Marceau 2002; Petersmann 2000; Qureshi 1998; Stirling 1996). However, I simply claim that the WTO makes discriminating against particular partners more costly. In addition, while the principal supplier rule – which requires a country to negotiate its tariff with exporters that have a "principal supplying interest" in that country's market for the product – may allow some states to benefit more than others (Gowa and Kim 2005), it does not allow ex post renegotiation. States must still abide by MFN rules.

[7] Although leeway in WTO laws allows states to raise tariffs under certain circumstances, the MFN requirement increases the cost associated with doing so. For instance, legal overhang is common, whereby countries do not impose tariffs at the maximum allowed rate. Thus, a state may punish a particular country by increasing tariffs to the maximum rate without violating WTO trade law. However, such a state would have to raise tariffs for all of its trading partners, which constitutes a much more costly action than raising tariffs on a particular partner. Furthermore, such a state could not raise tariffs over the bound rate, which is known to all parties (Pelc 2011). In addition, legal overhang is most common among developing countries, which are the least likely to use trade policy for coercion. Thus, the scope for using trade as a weapon is limited. However, loopholes exist (such as safeguards and antidumping measures), which are often difficult to prove and require the violated party to initiate a WTO dispute. Yet the ability to initiate such a dispute again increases the cost of using tariff policies as a weapon.

[8] Under the GATT, exceptions include the following: Article I:2–4 based on Historical Preferences, Article IV(c) for Cinematographic Films, Article XX for General Exceptions such as those relating to morals or the environment, Article XXIV:3 for Frontier Traffic, Article XXIV:5 for PTAs and Customs Unions, Article XXI for Security Exceptions, the 1979 Enabling Clause, and the Marrakesh Agreement Article IX:3 Waiver. Members rarely use many of these exceptions, such as the security clause, whereas they frequently use others, such as the PTA exception. Similar MFN exceptions exist under the General Agreement for Trade in Services and Trade-Related Aspects of Intellectual Property Rights.

in nature and therefore do not permit individual countries to sanction partners without UN approval (Zagel 2004). Securing approval can be difficult and time consuming, resulting in many instances in which a country would like to administer sanctions but cannot obtain UN agreement.

Article XXI also contains a national security exception that states, "Nothing in this Agreement shall be construed to... prevent any contracting party from taking any action which it considers necessary for the protection of its essential security interests." At first glance, this seems like an extremely permissive exception. Yet countries have been very cautious about invoking the security exception, as they have rarely done so, and these have never led to a binding WTO decision.[9] According to an official with extensive experience in U.S. trade policy, "the bar is high for the national security exemption. If the bar is too low, the [WTO] system falls apart. Countries must believe in a stable, predictable environment."[10] Other scholars attribute the reluctance to use the exception to desires to follow international norms, self-interest, and fears of retaliation (Alford 2011). Thus, although this tool is technically available to justify discriminatory policies, countries must carefully weigh the gains associated with invoking the exception against the risks posed to the WTO as a whole.[11]

GATT Article XX provides other exceptions allowing trade restrictions, condoning deviation from GATT rules in cases involving "the protection of public morals, the protection of human, animal or plant life or health, measures relating to prison labor, and the conservation of exhaustible natural resources." Again, however, these exceptions place strict limits on policy discrimination. For example, a country can invoke the public morals clause, which allows it to decline to import goods that conflict with its society's moral values, such as pornography or gambling. However, it must refuse to import the good from *all* WTO members, which can be very costly, both because of the costs borne by domestic consumers and the anger that such a ban would elicit from its trading partners. Similarly, a country could place restrictions on goods from a country that uses prison labor, but it would have to first prove that prison labor had actually been used and then place restrictions on all other countries that use

---

[9] The United States used the exception to defend its import ban on Czechoslovakia during the GATT's second year; Sweden tried to use it to justify a 1975 import quota on footwear but instead revoked the quota; the EEC, Australia, and Canada used it to defend a 1982 two-month ban on Argentinian goods after Argentina's annexation of the Falkland Islands, although no dispute panel was convened; the United States used it to justify a 1985 trade and transactions ban on Nicaragua, although the panel refused to rule on the dispute; and the United States invoked it to justify the 1996 Helms – Burton Act embargo on Cuba, although the parties reached an agreement and the WTO proceedings were dropped (*Guide to GATT Law and Practice (Analytical Index)* 1995).

[10] U.S. trade policy official, interview by author, February 22, 2012.

[11] I am unaware of any evidence that countries time their WTO accessions such that they enter when this exception (along with Article 35, which allows states to choose not to apply GATT rules to a new entrant) is unlikely to be used against them (Davis and Wilf 2011).

prison labor to produce that good as well. Otherwise, trade protection would constitute "arbitrary and unjustifiable discrimination between countries where the same conditions prevail" (Article XX).[12]

Exceptions also exist that permit preferential trade schemes. Under the enabling clause, countries may grant each other extra concessions in preferential trade agreements and may provide programs such as GSP schemes and EU development agreements, which offer lower tariffs for developing countries (Hafner-Burton 2009, 36, 169–72). Although these types of trade concessions may be conditioned on a partner's policies, such as its human rights record, they frequently provide limited leverage over partner countries because the repeal of the preference program constitutes the maximum penalty that a member can exact unilaterally. In other words, the WTO sets an upper bound on its members' abilities to punish other members, as members can potentially withhold preferential treatment from a partner but must grant MFN status regardless (Jones 2008).[13]

4.2 CHINA'S WTO EXPERIENCE

To illustrate the reduced scope for coercive diplomacy that results from WTO membership, I examine the WTO's impact on the bilateral relations between China and several states with which China has experienced political tension: Japan, Vietnam, Russia, and the United States. In each example, WTO membership allowed China to boost trade and investment with its partners once they, too, joined the WTO, as it either limited China's ability to exercise coercive diplomacy or reduced other states' abilities to use trade for coercion against China.

Japan

China and Japan have a long history of low trade and investment owing to fears of exploitation. After World War II, China consistently manipulated trade with Japan to obtain political concessions. The two states signed four trade

---

[12] Other exceptions to WTO rules in response to industry or economy-wide contingencies exist but remain beyond this discussion's scope. For an overview, see Hoekman and Mavroidis (2007).

[13] Additionally, the criteria given for preference program eligibility cannot discriminate among countries. For instance, the EU offered trade privileges to specific developing countries that showed progress in combating drug trafficking. India, a developing country that was not eligible for the program, disputed the program's administration, arguing that its exclusion represented unlawful discrimination. The EU lost the case and repealed the program (WTO 2012). Similarly, the EU reevaluated its development aid under the Lomé agreements, preferential trade concessions offered to fifty-three EU trading partners that could be suspended for human rights violations, because the program was challenged on the basis that it discriminated among developing countries (Holland 2002). However, this limitation often does not constrain states much in practice because states can frequently define the criteria for program eligibility very narrowly so that they only apply to specific countries.

agreements between 1952 and 1958, and each time their trade agreements were renegotiated, "the PRC [People's Republic of China] leadership exploited Japan's obvious trade hunger to blend economics and politics" (Sayuri 1995, 229) by linking the process to political demands. In particular, China required Japan to cease its recognition of Taiwan and instead to recognize the PRC by, for example, allowing the PRC to establish a permanent trade representative's office in Japan and permitting the trade mission to fly its flag. Indeed, "every move was purposely directed toward one supreme prize: diplomatic recognition" (Sayuri 1995, 245). Furthermore, China cut off trade completely with Japan in 1958, stating that it was doing so to punish Japan for the Nagasaki Flag Incident, during which a Japanese draftsman allegedly pulled down the Chinese flag at a textile fair. Many accounts contend that China refused to restore trade unless the Socialist Party won the upcoming election in Japan, using the trade embargo to try to sway the outcome (Morris 1958). (Although note that this strategy did not succeed, and the Socialist Party did not win the election.) Similarly, Japan chose to recognize Taiwan over the PRC in 1964, which led China to terminate contracts with Japan and to refuse to negotiate new ones (Schaller 1997, 176). In the 1980s, China violated several agreements with Japan, canceling additional contracts with Japanese companies, and made many threats to curb trade unless Japan acceded to its demands. For example, in 1959, China stated that to trade with China, Japan was required "to cease being hostile to China, not to join the conspiracy of admitting two Chinas, and not to obstruct the diplomatic normalization between China and Japan" (Morino 1991, 87).

Indeed, a major worry during the Cold War was that China would use trade for coercion; policy makers voiced concerns such as, "If Japan's steel industry relied on Chinese coking coal, what would prevent Beijing from abruptly cutting off supplies to force a 'serious economic crisis' for political purposes?" (Schaller 1997, 22). They also feared that trade could give China "powerful leverage over Japan" (Schaller 1997, 22) and could allow China to "'choke' off trade 'with a gun at Japan's breast' and say 'now you either come our way or you starve" (Schaller 1997, 105).

Owing to these many irritants, Japan became increasingly wary of investing in and trading with China (Morino 1991; Morris 1958; Wang 1993), so much so that their bilateral trade agreements had little effect on trade (Morino 1991). However, once China joined the WTO (of which Japan was already a member) in 2001, bilateral trade increased dramatically, as China lost its ability to break agreements with Japan for coercive purposes without violating WTO laws. Japan's exports to China in 2002 thus exhibited the highest growth in a decade, which many analysts attribute in large part to China's WTO accession (Sasaki and Koga 2003). The share of Japan's total exports that were purchased by China doubled from 5 percent to 10 percent between 1997 and 2002, and its imports from China rose from 12 percent to 18 percent of total imports over the same time period (Sasaki and Koga 2003). China then replaced the United States as Japan's largest trading partner in 2007.

Furthermore, WTO membership has been shown to effectively govern the trading relationship between the two states (Davis 2012). Although Japan exhibited hesitation to formally file disputes against China in the WTO, it frequently joined them as a third party and was able to resolve trade conflicts informally because of the *option* of resorting to WTO adjudication. For instance, when China instated a new tariff on the Japanese company Fujifilm, Japan threatened to take the case to the WTO, and China lowered the offending tariff in response (Davis 2012, 238–39). More generally, in the wake of many recent political disputes, trade between the two states remained high (Davis and Meunier 2011), as the WTO allowed China to commit to not holding Japan up for concessions.

The United States

The U.S.–Chinese trade relationship was marred by political conflict prior to China's WTO entry, as well. In 1979, the two states signed a bilateral trade agreement that granted China short-term MFN status and was renewed yearly by the United States. With the fall of the USSR, the United States obtained considerable leverage over China (Kissinger 2011, 447–61), both because no other single market was large enough to absorb such a high volume of Chinese goods and because China had acquired a diminished strategic importance (Lilley and Willkie 1994, 127). As a result, after the Tiananmen Square incident increased the salience of differences in human rights policy preferences, the U.S. Congress repeatedly threatened China with tariff increases unless China addressed the United States's concerns regarding human rights, weapons proliferation, and trade (Lilley and Willkie 1994, 24). Accordingly, China made many policy concessions in exchange for low U.S. tariffs from 1990 to 1993: it released 881 Tiananmen prisoners, lifted martial law, provided information on high-profile political prisoners, agreed not to export products made with prison labor, allowed the Red Cross to visit prisoners, sent two human rights delegations to the United States, and gave passports to many families of political exiles (Lilley and Willkie 1994, 86).

Investment in China declined over this period (Walmsley, Hertel, and Ianchovichina 2006), suggesting that hold-up problems persisted between the two states. WTO membership was recognized as a means to increase investment and trade between China and the United States. U.S. senator Wellstone argued, "I think the evidence is pretty clear. [Permanent MFN status will result in] ... more investment."[14] As expected, once China joined the WTO, investment and capital stocks grew dramatically (Walmsley, Hertel, and Ianchovichina 2006), as the United States could no longer use its MFN agreement with China as an instrument of coercive diplomacy.

---

[14] See U.S. Senate, "To Authorize Extension of Nondiscriminatory Treatment to the People's Republic of China," *The Congressional Record*, 105th Cong., March 19, 1998, 4156.

Vietnam

Similarly, consider the clashes between China and Vietnam over political issues such as disputed territorial claims. In response to Vietnam's insistence on ownership of contested territory in 1974, China threatened to cut off economic relations unless Vietnam conceded the territory (Path 2011). When Vietnam did not comply, China severed economic ties with Vietnam as punishment (Path 2011).

Fear of this type of trade interruption affected economic exchange between the two states long afterward. Even once relations normalized in the post – Cold War period, trade and investment remained low, in part due to these political tensions (Womack 2006, 214–45). In 1997, total bilateral trade between the two states was less than $1 billion. Furthermore, "although Vietnam generally welcomed investment in most sectors, China was the exception" (Womack 2006, 216). Once Vietnam joined the WTO in 2007, however, trade increased dramatically, doubling from $10 billion in 2006 to around $20 billion in 2008 (McCornac 2011). Furthermore, trade between the two nations continued to grow despite political tensions over the South China Sea.[15]

Russia

Prior to Russia's 2012 WTO accession, China and Russia viewed bilateral trade warily. For example, for more than a decade, China hesitated to conclude a natural gas agreement with Russia that would require building a pipeline through Siberia – a significant infrastructure investment. Although such an arrangement could have benefited both parties, they were unable to reach a deal.[16]

However, once Russia joined the WTO, China expressed renewed interest in the idea,[17] as WTO membership was "perceived as proof of reliability...which is important for Gazprom" (Russia's state-run natural gas company) (Rosenfeld 2012, 22).[18] Moreover, though the WTO imposed few new demands on Russia's energy policies, it "constrain[ed] the bargaining space with regard to natural gas pricing policy" (Grigoriadis 2014, 11). Indeed, policy officials linked Russia's WTO accession to the pipeline proposal; for instance, both issues were discussed jointly in a 2006 meeting between Chinese premier Wen Jiabao and Russian government officials.[19] Regarding Russia's WTO membership, the deputy director of the research center on Russia under the

---

[15] See "China, Vietnam Seek Ways to Improve Bilateral Relations," *China Radio International*, October 5, 2011.
[16] See "Russia's Competition for Natural Gas Deals with China," *Stratfor*, September 12, 2013.
[17] Ibid.
[18] Other geopolitical concerns factored in as well. See Everett Rosenfeld, "Why the Russia-China Gas Deal Matters," *CNBC*, May 22, 2014.
[19] See "Sino-Russian Oil Pipeline Pending," *China Daily*, October 3, 2004.

Chinese Academy of Social Sciences stated, "These efforts are expected to greatly improve the bilateral trade environment... and pave the way for Sino-Russian economic cooperation on large projects... [as] WTO accession is likely to help Russia build an international rules-based trading system. It will enhance openness, transparency and predictability."[20] Furthermore, in addition to natural gas cooperation, overall economic relations have improved appreciably since Russia's accession.[21]

4.3 STATISTICAL TESTS OF THE WTO AND THE REDUCTION OF HOLD-UP PROBLEMS

The preceding examples illustrate instances in which states failed to undertake relationship-specific investments, resulting in low trade and investment, when they feared that powerful states with dissimilar interests would otherwise extort concessions from them. However, the WTO boosted economic exchange by permitting these states to credibly commit to not holding up their partners. I now statistically assess whether WTO membership alleviates political hold-up problems by examining several observable implications of my theory that were derived from the model developed in Chapter 2. I demonstrate that WTO membership increases trade in particular between asymmetric partners, which would otherwise suffer most from political hold-up problems. I then test the mechanism responsible for this increase in trade, showing that it occurs primarily in contract-intensive goods and that WTO members increase their fixed capital investments.

Hypotheses

Recall that the model presented in Chapter 2 predicted that WTO membership most increases trade and investment for pairs of states with dissimilar capabilities and dissimilar political preferences. The model showed that because asymmetric states are most often targeted for coercion, joint WTO membership should increase trade and investment for these states in particular.[22] To test this proposition, I follow the previous chapter's discussion and analysis by operationalizing dissimilarities in capabilities and preferences using the measures of differences in power, alliances, and regime types discussed in that chapter. Thus, I examine the following hypotheses:

---

[20] Ibid. Many reports note that Russia's WTO entry helped to diminish corruption and increase transparency, benefitting investment. Furthermore, Russia itself viewed WTO membership as a means to bolster its "international credibility" (Grigoriadis 2014, 11).
[21] See "Why Russia and China Have Cultivated Such Close Relations," *The Economist*, February 15, 2014.
[22] Because restrictions on both imports and exports are possible, the data should show less *overall* trade and investment between asymmetric pairs of states.

Hypothesis 4. *Joint WTO membership increases trade more for pairs of states with dissimilar capabilities than for pairs with similar capabilities.*

Hypothesis 5. *Joint WTO membership increases trade more for nonallied pairs of states than for allied pairs.*

Hypothesis 6. *Joint WTO membership increases trade more for pairs of states with dissimilar regime types than for pairs with similar regime types.*

Model

I test whether WTO membership increases trade between country-pairs most vulnerable to hold-up problems using data covering 185 countries from 1948 to 2009. Each observation is composed of a "directed dyad," a country-pair that includes an importer and an exporter. All country-pairs appear twice in the data set, once recording country A's imports from country B and a second time specifying B's imports from A.[23] Because many countries formed or disappeared during the period under observation, the data set comprises 846,188 directed dyads. I employ a standard gravity model of trade, which has been the workhorse for studying the determinants of dyadic trade flows for fifty years because of its strong theoretical underpinnings and robust results. In these models, distance and size enter multiplicatively, as detailed extensively in Head and Mayer (2013). This specification represents a reasonable starting point and allows for comparability with previous work in this area (Dutt and Traca 2010; Eicher and Henn 2011; Goldstein, Rivers, and Tomz 2007; Gowa and Kim 2005; Liu 2009; Rose 2004; Tomz, Goldstein, and Rivers 2007).

In the baseline specification I use year and directed dyad fixed effects, as fixed effects are robust to many types of misspecification and endogeneity concerns. In particular, the year fixed effects ensure that I account for all factors that influence trade and are common to all states in a given year such as the end of the Cold War or the 2001 U.S. terrorist attacks. Directed dyad fixed effects account for any time-invariant factors that are specific to a particular country-pair, such as the distance between two states or their colonial history. Furthermore, in all specifications, I use robust standard errors clustered at the directed dyad level to deal with the fact that the same dyads are observed over multiple years.

The outcome variable, *Log Imports*, is the log of imports of the first country in a pair from the second (in constant 1995 U.S. dollars) and comes from the IMF's "Direction of Trade Statistics." This variable is specified as

---

[23] As highlighted in Chapter 2, countries may use trade for coercion by restricting either imports or exports. Because the WTO limits both types of activities, an appropriate statistical test must use directed dyads rather than undirected dyads.

log(*imports* + 1).[24] The key independent variables include the three indicators of political dissimilarity as measured in the chapter 3. First, *Large Power Difference* is an indicator of whether the difference in power between two countries is greater than the median difference in power in the sample.[25] Second, *Non-Allied* is an indicator of the lack of joint involvement in a political-military alliance, and third, *Dissimilar Regime Types* is an indicator of whether one country in a pair is a democracy while the other is not.[26] Furthermore, the hypotheses indicate that the effects of these variables on trade flows depend on whether states are WTO members. Thus, I interact each key independent variable with *Both in WTO*, an indicator of joint WTO membership.[27]

In this parsimonious model I also include covariates that are commonly found in gravity models. First, *One in WTO* is an indicator of whether only one state in a pair is a WTO member. Because WTO members may hold up nonmember partners, only *Both in WTO* is interacted with the key independent variables. Next, countries may trade more with partners that grant them special trading privileges, which is captured using several indicators: *Currency Union* indicates joint membership in a currency union, *RTA* indicates pairs that are parties to a regional trade agreement, GSP_i indicates whether an importing country extends GSP preferences to its partner, and GSP_j indicates whether an exporter does so. Because colonizers often accord special trade privileges to their colonies, I also include an indicator of whether the importer is a *Current Colonizer* of its partner and another indicator of whether the importer is a *Current Colony* of its partner.[28] Finally, for each country, I control for log(*GDP*) and log(*GDPPC*), measured in logged constant 1995 U.S. dollars.[29]

---

[24] The results are robust to many alternative specifications, as explained below. Trade data come from Liu (2009) and are updated using Barbieri, Keshk, and Pollins (2008).
[25] Recall that the Correlates of War's CINC scores are used to measure power.
[26] Almost all states are now WTO members. For a list of WTO members and their accession dates, see the WTO's website.
[27] In my baseline specifications, I focus on formal WTO membership. Tomz, Goldstein, and Rivers (2007) note the existence of informal members, which are entitled to the majority of the rights and responsibilities granted to WTO members. However, informal members include former colonies, which did not have independent foreign policies and therefore do not fit the theory; de facto members, which could not access the DSB and thus likely found it difficult to enforce agreements; and provincial members, which only obtained rights from members that agreed to grant them as specified in Article 35. *Both in WTO* therefore indicates joint formal membership, but the results are robust to the inclusion of informal members.
[28] I do not include an indicator of colonial history due to the inclusion of directed dyad fixed effects.
[29] Some gravity specifications feature the logged product of GDPs in a country-pair and the logged product of GDP per capitas in a country-pair. These models typically specify the dependent variable as the average of imports and exports for a country-pair and therefore cannot distinguish between the importer's and exporter's GDPs and GDP per capitas. Recent scholarship typically recommends against this practice (Baldwin and Taglioni 2006), but I note that the results are robust to this specification.

Results

As shown in Table 4.1, and presented graphically in Figure 4.1, strong evidence exists that joint WTO membership increases trade most for politically dissimilar country-pairs, as these represent the main targets of coercive diplomacy in the absence of the WTO. Joint WTO membership increases trade 384 percent more for country-pairs with dissimilar capabilities relative to those with similar capabilities (column 1).[30] It also boosts trade 157 percent more for nonallies relative to allies (column 2) and 83 percent more for pairs with dissimilar regime types relative to pairs with similar regime types (column 3). Among pairs in which one or both states are not WTO members, having dissimilar capabilities reduces trade by 39 percent, whereas being nonallied depresses trade by 34 percent. Although the effect of having dissimilar regime types is marginally significant, it becomes negative and significant in many of the robustness checks detailed subsequently. Additionally, the results demonstrate that WTO members trade more on average, as do larger, wealthier countries and states that are part of a preferential trade program. The model explains more than two-thirds of the variation in trade flows, as expected from a gravity model.

These findings are particularly surprising because standard trade theory predicts the opposite results. Standard trade models show that the more states trade initially, the more trade increases after they join the WTO. In fact, the benchmark model in this area, Bagwell and Staiger (1999), shows that when states trade more prior to their WTO entry, there is more scope for tariff manipulation. Therefore, it predicts that the tariff cuts implemented after joining the WTO are larger when pre-WTO trade is larger. Thus, according to that theory, if democracies and allies trade more with each other outside of the WTO, joining the WTO has the potential to increase trade most for these pairs. This possibility may therefore work against my findings so that my estimates underreport the true effect of alleviating hold-up problems. However, concerns may remain regarding whether the results are driven by the mechanism shown in the formal model. It is to this question that I now turn by examining additional observable implications of the model.

4.4 TESTING THE CAUSAL MECHANISM

The formal model predicted that the WTO's ability to enforce long-term contracts drives the hypotheses examined previously, as this enables members to commit to not extorting concessions from their partners. Because the WTO allows states to commit to not engaging in coercive diplomacy by improving

---

[30] This is calculated by first exponentiating the coefficient on *Lg Power Diff X Both in WTO* plus that on *Both in WTO* and subtracting 1. I then exponentiate the coefficient on *Both in WTO*. Finally, I subtract the second value from the first. The effects for nonallies and for states with dissimilar regime types are calculated similarly.

TABLE 4.1. *Effect of WTO and Dissimilarity on Logged Imports*

	1	2	3
Lg Power Diff × Both in WTO	0.903***		
	(0.066)		
Large Power Diff	−0.578***	−0.214***	−0.213***
	(0.068)	(0.061)	(0.062)
Non-Allied × Both in WTO		0.471***	
		(0.091)	
Non-Allied	−0.230**	−0.494***	−0.225**
	(0.073)	(0.090)	(0.073)
Dissimilar Reg × Both in WTO			0.210***
			(0.052)
Dissimilar Regime Types	0.196***	0.187***	0.092*
	(0.032)	(0.032)	(0.040)
Both in WTO	0.961***	0.960***	1.268***
	(0.077)	(0.104)	(0.078)
One in WTO	0.732***	0.700***	0.699***
	(0.061)	(0.061)	(0.061)
$\log(GDP)_i$	1.867***	1.811***	1.815***
	(0.100)	(0.100)	(0.100)
$\log(GDP)_j$	1.989***	1.933***	1.937***
	(0.104)	(0.104)	(0.104)
$\log(GDPPC)_i$	−0.608***	−0.537***	−0.538***
	(0.096)	(0.097)	(0.097)
$\log(GDPPC)_j$	−0.747***	−0.674***	−0.674***
	(0.099)	(0.099)	(0.099)
Current Colony	0.593	0.433	0.454
	(0.597)	(0.586)	(0.589)
Current Colonizer	−0.310	−0.482	−0.454
	(0.834)	(0.819)	(0.823)
RTA	0.381***	0.425***	0.399***
	(0.068)	(0.068)	(0.068)
GSP_i	0.387***	0.381***	0.387***
	(0.084)	(0.084)	(0.084)
GSP_j	0.425***	0.420***	0.426***
	(0.084)	(0.084)	(0.084)
Currency Union	0.751***	0.705***	0.733***
	(0.155)	(0.154)	(0.154)
Constant	−46.599***	−45.780***	−46.088***
	(1.571)	(1.581)	(1.579)
R^2	0.705	0.705	0.705
N	1020182	1020182	1020182

Notes: Estimates from OLS regression. The unit of observation is the directed dyad-year and the dependent variable is the natural log of (*imports* +1). The data cover 1948–2009. Robust standard errors, clustered by directed dyad, appear in parentheses. All models include year and directed dyad fixed effects, which are not shown. * $p < 0.05$, ** $p < 0.01$, *** $p < 0.001$.

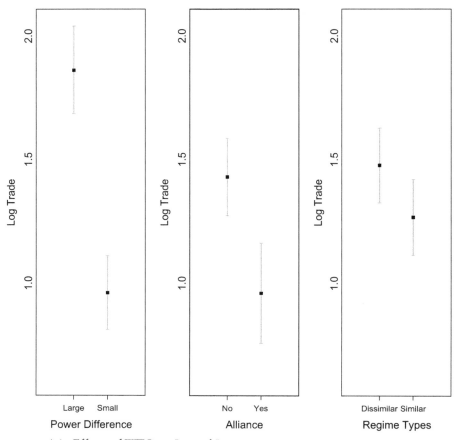

FIGURE 4.1. Effects of WTO on Logged Imports.

contract enforcement, it boosts investment and trade between members. As a result, membership increases cooperation in the production of goods that require such contracts in particular. The model thus implies the following:

Hypothesis 7. *Joint WTO membership increases investment most in contract-intensive goods.*

Furthermore, the model predicted that because WTO members face fewer concerns that their investments will make them vulnerable to coercive diplomacy, they increase their investments in fixed capital, such as infrastructure, roads, and factories, to produce goods for trade, which suggests the following:

Hypothesis 8. *WTO membership increases relationship-specific investments.*

Contract Intensity

I first examine the WTO's effect on trade in contract-intensive goods. The model is estimated using country-year and directed dyad-industry fixed effects from 1989 to 2000, with robust standard errors clustered at the directed dyad level.[31] The outcome variable, *Log Imports*, denotes the natural log of the value of imports from one country to another in a particular industry.[32] The key variable of interest is a measure of *Contract Intensity* using data from Rauch (1999), which is interacted with joint WTO membership. Contact intensity is coded as the proportion of a good's intermediate inputs that are not sold on an organized exchange, because goods sold on such an exchange have many potential buyers and sellers and thus do not tend to require relationship-specific investments (Rauch 1999). Organized exchanges do not allow a good's producers to discriminate with respect to price; instead, buyers face one price. For instance, "toys" are not sold on an organized exchange, as they can be broken down into a variety of types and brands, whereas unwrought lead is sold on an organized exchange because it has a thick and well-defined market. Note that because this measure is time-invariant over the sample period, only the interaction term appears in the regression owing to the inclusion of year fixed effects.[33] As before, I control for $\log(GDP)$, $\log(GDPPC)$, *RTA*, GSP_i, GSP_j, *Alliance*, and *Currency Union*.[34]

---

[31] I use a time-invariant indicator of contract intensity that is measured using 1997 data. I restrict the analysis to this time period because contract intensity may have differed more severely further back in time, particularly during the Cold War. The results are robust to alternative time periods, however. States that joined the WTO during this period include Albania, Angola, Bahrain, Benin, Bolivia, Brunei Darussalam, Bulgaria, Chad, Congo, Costa Rica, Croatia, Czech Republic, Djibouti, Dominica, DRC, Ecuador, El Salvador, Estonia, Fiji, the Gambia, Georgia, Grenada, Guatemala, Guinea, Guinea Bissau, Haiti, Honduras, Jordan, the Kyrgyz Republic, Latvia, Liechtenstein, Macao, Mali, Mongolia, Mozambique, Namibia, Niger, Oman, Panama, Papua New Guinea, Paraguay, Qatar, Rwanda, Saint Kitts and Nevis, Saint Lucia, Solomon Islands, Slovak Republic, Slovenia, Solomon Islands, Swaziland, Tunisia, the UAE, and Venezuela. The micro states were dropped from the analysis due to missing data in the key independent variables.

[32] For industry-level dyadic trade data, I use updated data from Feenstra (1996).

[33] The industry-level trade data are classified according to the four-digit Standard International Trade Classification (SITC) Revision 2 system, while the contract intensity data are classified according to the Bureau of Economic Analysis's (BEA) Input-Output (I-O) system. To match the data, I first converted the four-digit SITC codes into the ten-digit Harmonized System (HS) codes, using the concordance provided by Feenstra (1996). I then converted the ten-digit HS codes into I-O codes using the concordance available from the BEA. The SITC codes do not match perfectly with the I-O codes, however, because the SITC codes are at a higher level of aggregation. To deal with SITC industries that map into multiple I-O industries, I followed Nunn (2007) and chose the I-O industry for which the greatest number of HS industries link the two. If an equal number of links arose, which occurred rarely, I made the choice manually. Thus, each SITC code is mapped onto only one I-O industry.

[34] *One in WTO* does not appear in the model because it is collinear with the fixed effects. Note that the only change in currency union membership during the sample period was the transition to the European Monetary Union.

TABLE 4.2. *Effect of WTO and Contract Intensity on Logged Imports*

Contract Intensity × Both in WTO	0.327***
	(0.063)
Both in WTO	−0.175***
	(0.040)
RTA	0.169***
	(0.051)
GSP_i	0.083*
	(0.034)
GSP_j	0.060*
	(0.030)
Currency Union	0.066
	(0.215)
Alliance	0.069
	(0.043)
R^2	.7462
N	2896707

Notes: Estimates from OLS regression. The unit of observation is the directed dyad-industry-year and the dependent variable is the natural log of (*imports* +1). The data cover 1989–2000. Robust standard errors, clustered by directed dyad, appear in parentheses. The model includes importer-year, exporter-year, and directed dyad-industry fixed effects, which are not shown. Note that the measure of contract intensity is time-invariant and therefore does not appear in the analysis. * $p < 0.05$, ** $p < 0.01$, *** $p < 0.001$.

Table 4.2 provides strong evidence that WTO members trade more contract-intensive goods. The results indicate that joint WTO membership increases trade in goods with the highest level of contract intensity by about 19 percent, and decreases trade in goods with the lowest level of contract intensity by about 16 percent. The WTO's negative effect on non-contract-intensive goods likely indicates that the WTO causes economic actors to substitute away from trade in these goods toward contract-intensive ones. Prior to WTO membership, non-contract-intensive goods often provide the highest returns, but WTO membership opens up new avenues for trade in contract-intensive goods. The alleviation of hold-up problems thus allows states to engage in the type of trade that most depends on the strong enforcement of agreements.

Fixed Capital Investment

I verify that WTO membership increases fixed capital investment using data on 167 countries from 1960–2010.[35] I include year and country fixed effects and robust standard errors clustered at the country level. The outcome variable

---
[35] Owing to missing data, I am left with 4,327 observations.

TABLE 4.3. *Effect of WTO on Fixed Capital Investment*

WTO Member	0.194*
	(0.086)
log(GDPPC)	0.436**
	(0.164)
log(GDP)	−0.191*
	(0.077)
Constant	23.958***
	(0.532)
R^2	0.975
N	4327

Notes: Estimates from OLS regression. The unit of observation is the country-year and the dependent variable is logged fixed capital investment. The data cover 1960–2010. Robust standard errors, clustered by country, appear in parentheses. The model includes year and country fixed effects, which are not shown.
* $p < 0.05$, ** $p < 0.01$, *** $p < 0.001$.

is *Log Fixed Capital Investment*, which is measured in logged constant U.S. dollars and includes "outlays on additions to the fixed assets of the economy plus net changes in the level of inventories" (World Bank 2011). These comprise "land improvements (fences, ditches, drains, and so on); plant, machinery, and equipment purchases; and the construction of roads, railways, and the like, including schools, offices, hospitals, private residential dwellings, and commercial and industrial buildings" (World Bank 2011). Unlike ongoing operating expenses, fixed capital investments are sunk costs in physical infrastructure – precisely the investments that hold-up problems most affect. The variable of interest, *WTO Member*, is an indicator of whether a country is a WTO member. Because investment levels may depend on a country's size and wealth, I again control for log(GDP) and log(GDPPC). The results presented in Table 4.3 show that, as expected, WTO membership increases fixed capital investment by about 21 percent, indicating that WTO members are more apt to make highly irreversible investments because the WTO protects investments' profitability.

Threats to Inference and Robustness Checks

These results are robust to many alternative specification and coding decisions. First, a potential concern is that WTO membership may be endogenous, as countries may enter the WTO when they would have increased trade even if they had not joined the institution. However, to explain my findings, countries would have had to enter the WTO when they would otherwise have increased trade *with politically dissimilar countries in particular*, which is a more difficult claim to argue. Furthermore, many consider the inclusion of country-pair fixed effects to be the most advisable approach to dealing with this concern in the absence of a credible instrumental variable (Baier and Bergstrand 2007; Head and Mayer 2013, 31). Nonetheless, I perform two additional robustness checks designed to ameliorate this potential issue. I begin by exploiting the fact that the GATT ceased to exist in 1995 and was replaced by the WTO. The WTO's strong dispute settlement body constitutes a major difference between the WTO and the GATT, as described previously, and implies that fewer political hold-up problems should occur between WTO members than occurred between GATT members. Therefore, the WTO's establishment should increase trade most for those members most vulnerable to hold-up problems. To test this, I restrict the sample to pairs of states that were GATT members prior to 1990, circumventing possible selection bias. I then estimate the institution's impact on trade during the 1990-2000 period, finding confirmation for the theory. Then, as an additional method to deal with endogeneity, I also use the theory to identify which variables are likely important for determining WTO membership and employ a selection model, substituting the indicator of joint WTO membership with the estimated probability of joint membership.

A second potential concern is that although the log-linear gravity model provides easily interpretable estimates of average effects, it may not treat the observations containing zero trade flows adequately, particularly because the results may depend on the units of measurement. The appropriate method to deal with this issue hinges on the process that generates observations of zero trade. I adopt Eaton and Kortum's (2001) approach, which stipulates that, if ideal trade from exporter i to destination market n, X_{ni}, falls below a minimum amount of trade, no trade is observed. For example, zero trade flows may arise due to rounding or reporting thresholds or due to unobserved costs associated with trading. The dependent variable is constructed by replacing the observations of zero trade with the minimum X_{ni} for a given n, $\underline{X}_{ni}$, before taking logs.[36] The model is then estimated using interval regression. Head and Mayer (2013), who refer to the model as the "EK Tobit," argue that this model is desirable because it satisfies the following criteria: (1) no exclusion restrictions are required, (2) it has a strong structural interpretation, and (3) in Monte Carlo simulations, it is preferable to the alternatives under the assumption of log-normal errors.[37]

---

[36] Owing to the data's panel structure, I replace zero trade flows with $\underline{X}_{nit}$, where t indicates the year.

[37] Head and Mayer (2013) show that the EK Tobit dominates other approaches due to its sound structural interpretation and easier implementation. I thus follow the specification advocated by Head and Mayer (2013), which includes country and year fixed effects (rather than the directed dyad and year fixed effects used in the baseline model). However, the results are also robust to

A third possible critique is that while the baseline model represents a reasonable starting point for the analysis, many scholars have pointed to the importance of capturing the "multilateral-resistance" terms, or country-specific barriers to international trade, as described by Anderson and van Wincoop (2003). Because these terms likely vary over time, I reestimate the model including both time-varying country fixed effects and directed dyad fixed effects.[38]

A fourth potential issue is measurement; thus, I also verify that the results are not sensitive to the particular measures of the key independent variables. I first redefine *Large Power Difference* as an indicator of the one-third of dyads with the largest power differences and then as a continuous, ordinal ranking of power difference.[39] I next use alternative measures of power differences, alliances, and regime dissimilarities: power differences are measured using differences in total military personnel (Geller 1993; Reed et al. 2008), alliances are measured using Bueno de Mesquita's (1975) coding of shared security interests,[40] and different regime types are measured using differences in Polity scores.[41] I also provide an additional check that measures political similarity using UN voting behavior similarity.[42]

Additionally, there might be a concern that the findings depend on the specific covariate profile or sample. To alleviate this concern, I first add several additional control variables. I ensure that the results are not driven by countries' resource endowments by controlling for *Capital Stock per Worker* (Heston and Aten 2006). I also separate *One in WTO* into *Importer in WTO* and *Exporter in WTO*. I then show that the effects are not due to especially influential dyads

---

the inclusion of directed dyad random effects. (Note that a sufficient statistic permitting me to condition the fixed effects out of the likelihood does not exist.) Because dyadic fixed effects are not included, I add additional covariates found in standard gravity models: the log(*Distance*) between country *i* and country *j*, an indicator of a shared *Border* between *i* and *j*, an indicator of whether *i* and *j* speak the *Same Language*, an indicator of whether *i* and *j* share the *Same Religion*, an indicator of whether *i* was ever a *Colony* of *j*, an indicator of whether *i* was ever a *Colonizer* of *j*, an indicator of whether *i* and *j* ever shared a *Common Colonizer*, the number of *Islands* in a pair, and the number of *Landlocked* countries in a pair. These data come from Liu (2009).

[38] To implement the regression with high-dimensional fixed effects, I use a statistical procedure developed by Guimaraes, Portugal, and de Portugal (2010).
[39] I choose an ordinal measure because *Large Power Difference* is highly skewed.
[40] Bueno de Mesquita (1975) measures the similarity of alliance profiles for country-pairs.
[41] Polity scores are computed from measures of executive recruitment, constraints on executive authority, and political competition and range from −10 to 10 (Marshall et al. 2004). To ease comparison with other results, I normalize the scores on a scale from 0 to 1, from least different to most different.
[42] The data come from Strezhnev and Voeten (2012), who provide two measures of *Similarity*. The first measure is scored from −1 to 1, from least to most similar. See Strezhnev and Voeten (2012) for details. The second measure ranges from 0 to 1 and is calculated as the total votes on which both states agree, divided by the total joint votes. Because many states had not joined the UN during the early years of the sample, the model is estimated over the post-1990 time period.

by dropping observations for which the residuals are greater than 5 times the standard deviation and observations for which the residuals are greater than 3 times the standard deviation. Because the WTO may not have affected trade immediately, I also analyze the model using data sampled at five-year intervals.

Finally, I show that the results are not sensitive to the particular method chosen to deal with the presence of zero trade flows. There are many issues to consider with each potential alternative, so I omit the discussion of these models and their results because of space constraints, but see Carnegie (2014) for details.[43]

In sum, the theory, examples, and empirical tests examined in this chapter attest to the critical role the WTO plays in solving political hold-up problems. By limiting states' abilities to use trade agreements to target asymmetric states for political concessions, the WTO boosts trade and investment for these dissimilar states in particular.

---

[43] To account for the possibility that allies and similar regimes engaged in greater levels of trade initially, I interact the treatment variables with import levels in the year prior to the start of the analysis. Conditional on the interaction with prior trade levels, the WTO continues to boost trade for dissimilar pairs of states in particular. Furthermore, I display the robustness of dropping great powers from the analysis, and I control for similar interests using UN scores and alliance portfolio similarity.

5

Coercive Diplomacy in Comparative Perspective

> THE USE OF INTIMIDATION OF ONE KIND OR ANOTHER IN ORDER TO GET OTHERS
> TO COMPLY WITH ONE'S WISHES IS AN EVERYDAY OCCURRENCE IN HUMAN AFFAIRS.
> *Alexander George*[1]

The argument developed in this study starts from the premise that political hold-up problems represent a central feature of international relations. The theoretical model presented in Chapter 2 developed predictions regarding the conditions under which these hold-up problems pervade interstate interactions, generating testable implications to help account for variation in outcomes across WTO members. The statistical results of the previous chapters, both the baseline results and the tests of the mechanism at work, comport with these hypotheses. Yet doubts may remain about whether the particular mechanisms that my theory identifies drive the findings. It is therefore important to take a closer look at the case-study evidence to try to tease out the causal processes. Moreover, a case study analysis can help to support and enhance the theoretical approach taken in Chapter 2.

Because the theory suggests that the WTO's impact depends on the degree of similarity between pairs of states, in terms of both capabilities and political interests, it is logical to select states based on variation in these key independent variables. In particular, I consider three countries at a time: a state, which I refer to as a "primary" state for clarity, and two of its trading partners. Because I am interested in the impact of joint WTO membership, I require both trading partners to be WTO members at the time of the primary state's WTO accession. Out of this pool I then select one partner state that possesses capabilities and political interests that are highly dissimilar to those of the primary state, along with a second partner that is very similar to the primary

---

[1] See George (1994, 2).

state along these dimensions. I also ensure that primary states and their partners represent diverse regions and that primary states' WTO accession dates differ.

The case studies analyzed in this chapter thus pull together the prior chapters' discussion and findings to illustrate how these dynamics manifest themselves in specific examples. In each case I show that political hold-up problems were ubiquitous prior to the primary state's WTO accession, particularly with its dissimilar partner. These problems resulted in underinvestment and low bilateral trade, which WTO membership then remedied. In fact, in several cases, either the coercer specifically sought WTO membership to tie its hands, or the target wanted WTO membership to protect itself. Although these examples do not definitively prove the theory's claims, they illustrate how the argument operates in particular cases and demonstrate dynamics consistent with my predictions in a variety of circumstances. Furthermore, they suggest that the mechanisms I identify play an important role in interstate relations. Taken together with previous chapters, these results help to create a large body of evidence in support of my claims.

The group of examples comprises five mini-cases. First, I consider relations between Saudi Arabia, India, and Pakistan. Saudi Arabia historically maintained close political and economic relations with Pakistan, sharing religious and cultural similarities, and had similar capabilities. By contrast, Saudi Arabia and India experienced large political tensions, particularly due to Saudi Arabia's strong ties to Pakistan, and possessed dissimilar capabilities. Trade and investment remained low between Saudi Arabia and India, whereas it was high between Saudi Arabia and Pakistan. After Saudi Arabia's 2005 WTO entry, however, these trends reversed, with Saudi Arabia and India swiftly becoming more economically and politically connected.

I then turn to relations between Nepal, India, and Bangladesh. Whereas India and Nepal experienced considerable economic and political frictions prior to Nepal's 2004 WTO entry, leading to underinvestment and reduced trade, Nepal and Bangladesh enjoyed consistently friendly relations. India and Nepal also suffered from highly asymmetric capabilities, whereas Nepal and Bangladesh were similar along this dimension. Nepal sought WTO membership in part to improve its trade relations with India, as India would then be bound by WTO laws and could no longer renege on agreements to extract political concessions from Nepal. Once Nepal entered the WTO, it increased trade with India, but not with Bangladesh.

I next examine Japan's relations with the United States and India. I show that in contrast to its largely irritant-free trade and political relations with India, a relatively weak country, just prior to its GATT accession, Japan was frequently the target of trade-based coercion from the United States, a much more powerful country. After World War II, the United States pulled Japan into the GATT in part to convince Japan of the United States's reliability as a trading partner. Japan's GATT membership greatly increased bilateral trade between the two states, while trade languished between Japan and India.

Turning to the GATT's effects on relations between Mexico, the United States, and Cuba, I demonstrate that prior to Mexico's 1986 GATT accession, Mexico and Cuba frequently worked together to attempt to overcome what they perceived as U.S. dominance in the region. Constantly worried about U.S. attempts to curb its sovereignty due to both dissimilar interests and capabilities, Mexico limited trade and investment with the United States and fostered political ties with small, developing countries, such as Cuba. After its GATT entry, however, trade and investment between Mexico and the United States exploded, while remaining low between Mexico and Cuba.

Finally, I consider the impact of Taiwan's WTO membership on its relations with the United States and China. Prior to its accession, Taiwan and the United States maintained strong ties, both economically and politically. Although the United States was more capable than Taiwan, their similar interests prevented political hold-up problems from forming. By contrast, China and Taiwan's relations suffered from both asymmetric size and interests, particularly regarding their dispute over whether Taiwan should be considered an independent state or a part of China. China consistently used trade as a weapon in this battle, leading Taiwan to underinvest in economic activity with China. Once Taiwan joined the WTO in 2002, however, trade and investment surged between China and Taiwan, while it remained relatively stable between Taiwan and the United States.

5.1 SAUDI ARABIA, INDIA, AND PAKISTAN

Saudi Arabia and Pakistan have a history of exceptionally close relations due to their political similarities. During the 1970s, Pakistan actively encouraged political Islam, which linked Pakistan with Saudi Arabia, because the populations of both states are predominantly made up of Sunni Muslims. Saudi Arabia supported political Islam in Pakistan by contributing extensive funds for Islamic school construction (Noman 1990, 154–55), and many Pakistani Muslims migrated to Saudi Arabia because they viewed Saudi Arabia favorably as Islam's birthplace (Ahmad 1982). During this time, "the holy alliance with the Gulf states – especially Saudi Arabia ... [was] fully consummated" (Pasha 1992, 116).

Saudi Arabia and Pakistan's religious and cultural links led to defense and foreign policy cooperation as well, often at India's expense. For instance, official visits between Saudi Arabia and India were virtually nonexistent historically, whereas Pakistan and Saudi Arabia have a long history of visits, beginning with their first visit in 1966, during which they signed a variety of defense and economic agreements (Ahmad 1982). Saudi Arabia took Pakistan's side when India and Pakistan went to war over Kashmir in 1971 (Heptulla 1991, 158–59) and continued to do so in subsequent conflicts (Ward 1992, 82–86, 115–20). Saudi Arabia also declined to recognize Bangladesh until Pakistan permitted it to do so, and, aside from the United Arab Emirates, Saudi Arabia was the sole state to congratulate Pakistan on testing its first nuclear weapon in 1998 (Ahmad 1982). Furthermore, Saudi Arabia frequently used its friendship with Pakistan to threaten India. For instance, in 1980, the Saudi crown prince, referring to India, stated, "Any interference in the internal affairs of Pakistan would be considered interference in or injury to the kingdom of Saudi Arabia" (Ahmad 1982, 60). Pakistan also declared that its relationship with Saudi Arabia "serves notice on India... that although Pakistan may not be a match for [India] militarily, it has a powerfully ally with economic and political clout. The cost of an attack thus becomes higher."[2]

Saudi Arabia and Pakistan's many common positions on issues in the UN also attest to their similarity. For instance, Saudi Arabia insisted on a UN statement that condemned India for its aggressive stance toward Pakistan in the 1971 war and fully supported Pakistan's point of view in the UN regarding postwar issues (Ahmad 1982). In 1982, Saudi Arabia and Pakistan worked together in the UN to call for Soviet withdrawal from Afghanistan, and in 1999, the two states confirmed that they would vote together in resolutions over policies regarding Iraq (Ahmad 1982).

In addition to having mutual interests, the countries were similarly powerful. As in previous chapters, I measure how much power a state possesses using a variable constructed from the Correlates of War's CINC score (Singer 1988), which is described further in Chapter 3. According to this widely used indicator of power (Geller 1993; Reed et al. 2008), at the time Saudi Arabia joined the WTO in 2005, it had a CINC score of 0.0100, and Pakistan had a nearly identical score of 0.0136.

Owing to their symmetric power and interests, trade and investment between Saudi Arabia and Pakistan remained high, and Saudi Arabia assisted Pakistan economically even when other states refused to trade with Pakistan because of political tensions. Through the 1980s Saudi Arabia served as Pakistan's main export partner, and in turn Pakistan bought the majority of its oil from Saudi Arabia. The two states participated in many joint investment ventures, and Saudi Arabia allocated 60 percent of its FDI to Pakistan (Ahmad 1982). Furthermore, when the international community sanctioned Pakistan in 1988 because of its nuclear program, Saudi Arabia provided $3.5 billion of oil and deferred payment to assist Pakistan (Woodrow 2002). It also supplied resources to Pakistan at discounted rates and may have helped finance Pakistan's nuclear program (Woodrow 2002).

By contrast, India and Saudi Arabia suffered from large dissimilarities. While Saudi Arabia's CINC score was 0.0100 when it entered the WTO, India's was a much larger 0.0712. Compounding this size difference was the two states' dissimilar interests, which were exacerbated by Saudi Arabia's close relations with Pakistan. While Saudi Arabia took the United States's side during the Cold War, India forged close relations with the Soviet Union and remained

---

[2] See Khell, Shirin Tahir, and William O. Staudenmaeir, "The Pakistan-Saudi Arms Link," *The Illustrated Weekly of India*, September 1982, 11.

nonaligned. Unlike Saudi Arabia, India recognized Israel in 1950 and provided considerable support for the secular regimes of Egypt, Syria, and Iraq. Saudi Arabia also expressed concerns regarding India's behavior toward Muslims. Additionally, the two states remained divided in their responses to a variety of issues, such as the dispute over Kashmir, Bangladesh's independence, the Soviet Union's invasion of Afghanistan, and Iraq's invasion of Kuwait (Pradhan 2013).

In connection with their divergent views and capabilities, Saudi Arabia and India traded little prior to Saudi Arabia's WTO entry. As Saudi Arabia's ambassador to India highlighted,[3] inefficiently low trade persisted because of the many lingering tensions, leading to export bans and price regulations.[4] Furthermore, Indian companies did not feel welcome in Saudi Arabia because of Saudi Arabia's alignment with Pakistan.[5] Saudi Arabia expected its WTO accession to help to resolve such issues, as the desire to boost its credibility and accountability represented a major impetus for joining the institution (Hertog 2010, 240–41). The Confederation of Indian Industry's senior advisor outlined the problem in 2003, stating that such trade issues could not be resolved "as it [was] not a member of World Trade Organization," and adding that these disputes likely had a large impact on investment.[6]

The theory predicts that Saudi Arabia's 2005 WTO entry should have increased trade more with India than with Pakistan and as anticipated, trade between Saudi Arabia and India soared after its accession. While total bilateral trade with India remained fairly constant between 1998 and 2005, after Saudi Arabia's WTO membership, this trade increased from $3.442 billion in 2005 to $15.946 billion in 2006. The Saudi Arabian ambassador to India stated that trade irritants would no longer hinder cooperation between the two states because, "now all kinds of disputes are discussed within the framework of the WTO rules and regulations."[7] By contrast, trade between Saudi Arabia and Pakistan remained comparatively steady after its WTO accession, only increasing from $3.324 billion in 2005 to $3.781 billion in 2006.[8] Exports from Pakistan actually fell during this period, from $353 to $330 million.[9] By 2011, trade between India and Saudi Arabia reached $25 billion while trade between Pakistan and Saudi Arabia did not even hit $5 billion.[10]

---

[3] See "Riyadh: Anti-dumping Row Not to Strain Saudi-India Ties, Says Envoy," *Daijiworld*, July 20, 2011.
[4] See K.S. Ramkumar, "Indian Meat Import Ban Lifted," *Arab News*, January 27, 2004.
[5] See Zafar al-Islam Khan, "India's Middle East Energy Strategy," *Aljazeera*, May 12, 2013.
[6] See "India Inc Upset over Saudi Bid to Replace Expats," *The Financial Express*, April 19, 2003.
[7] See "Riyadh: Anti-dumping Row Not to Strain Saudi-India Ties, Says Envoy," *Daijiworld*, July 20, 2011.
[8] See "Pakistan-Saudi Arabia Bilateral Economic and Commercial Relations," Pakistan Consulate, Jeddah, February 2, 2006.
[9] Ibid.
[10] See Nick Ottens, "Despite Loan, Economic Changes Test Pakistani-Saudi Alliance," *Atlantic Sentinel*, May 26, 2013.

5.2 NEPAL, INDIA, AND BANGLADESH

Prior to Nepal's WTO entry, its relationship with India had been "marred by trade disputes and strained by mutual anxiety."[11] Although the two states shared many cultural similarities, India possessed far greater capabilities than Nepal, with a CINC score of 0.0700 versus Nepal's 0.0014 at the time of Nepal's WTO entry. India's disproportionate power led to significant involvement in Nepal's domestic politics, as it often used trade relations for political leverage, which infuriated Nepal. For example, after Nepal's 1951 political uprising, India brokered a power-sharing deal and sought to shape the new regime in many ways. When Nepal's government then collapsed, the king appointed India's preferred candidate as prime minister, creating a backlash in Nepal (Upadhya 2012, 177). In general, Nepal believed that India represented a large threat to the government's stability owing to India's negative view of Nepal's authoritarian regime. Government officials often stated their desire to dampen Indian influence over Nepal, and many worried that India was trying to turn Nepal into a "satellite colony" (Upadhya 2012, 72). India's efforts to overthrow Nepal's oligarchy and its stationing of Indian troops on Nepal's border with China resulted in Nepal's perception that India "micromanaged" Nepal's domestic and foreign affairs (Upadhya 2012, 147). Other tensions emerged as well, such as a territory dispute over the Kalapani region (Upadhya 2012, 154) and Nepal's belief that India encouraged dissent in Nepal and instigated border raids.[12]

These political spats frequently interrupted trade between the two states. A series of treaties signed in 1950, 1960, 1971, and 1978 regulated trade and transit between Nepal and India, but India frequently either violated or threatened to violate these commitments when it became dissatisfied with Nepal. Nepal charged that India had breached the 1950 Peace and Friendship Treaty, which also governed economics and commerce, to take advantage of Nepal (Subedi 2006, 24–38). Furthermore, India imposed an informal blockade in 1962 after a disagreement over whether India would send troops into Nepal in response to disruptions by Tibetan rebels (Upadhya 2012). In 1970 India again blockaded Nepal due to political disputes such as smuggling and Nepal's efforts to expand ties with China.[13] Then, in 1973, India disapproved of Nepal's proposal to become a "zone of peace" and stated that Nepal's economic benefits from India depended on "reciprocity," which Nepal interpreted as a threat to withhold trade benefits unless Nepal abandoned the idea (Subedi 2006, 39–52).

The largest disruption occurred in 1989, when India refused to renew its trade treaty with Nepal unless Nepal agreed to implement a special security

---

[11] See Bernard Weinraub, "India-Nepal Relations Running Hot and Cold," *New York Times*, August 20, 1973, 12.
[12] See Bernard Weinraub, "India-Nepal Relations Running Hot and Cold," *New York Times*, August 20, 1973, 12.
[13] See "Dispute Eroding India-Nepal Ties," *New York Times*, January 10, 1971, 11.

relationship between the two states (Upadhya 2012, 115–18). The dispute began in 1988, when India alleged that Nepal had not followed the political conditions set out in the 1950 peace treaty, as Nepal had signed a secret intelligence-sharing agreement with China and had purchased Chinese weapons consisting of light arms, ammunition, boots, uniforms, and sixteen antiaircraft guns.[14] A former prime minister of India threatened that, if Nepal did not acquiesce to India's demands, it would have "very adverse immediate and long-term effects, e.g. the advantages of economic, trade and transit and financial aid would evaporate" (Subedi 2006, 7). India then declined to renew the trade treaty, along with several other treaties, essentially blockading Nepal for longer than a year. In 1990 Nepal signed a joint communiqué that provided concessions in the areas of sovereignty, independence, and military cooperation in return for the resumption of trade (Subedi 2006, 10–13). Furthermore, India continued to use trade as a weapon; for example, during negotiations over a 1996 trade treaty's renewal, India imposed a large array of new protectionist measures on Nepal's exports, which many observers believe resulted from political frictions.[15]

The political disagreements and asymmetric capabilities resulted in lower trade and investment levels than the states would have enjoyed absent these irritants. Nepal's negative view toward India contributed to a decline in investment and exports over time (Jha 2011), and many studies cite India's inconsistent and discriminatory trade treatment with Nepal as a key factor limiting Nepal's economic growth (Khanal and Shrestha 2008). For instance, fisheries represented a particularly opportune area for joint investment with Nepal, yet the states did not invest due to fears of extortion (Upreti 2003, 265–66). Similar underinvestment occurred in hydroelectric power (Subedi 2006, 120–26). Negative views about India's propensity to use treaties to extract concessions from Nepal were so entrenched that when India and Nepal desired a mutually beneficial treaty governing investment in hydropower, the two states labeled it an "agreement" rather than a "treaty" to avoid scrutiny by Nepal's parliament. After Nepal's supreme court overruled this maneuver, the bargain fell apart as a result of the Nepalese parliament's suspicious attitude toward treaties with India (Subedi 2006, 153–60). It was estimated that eighty-three thousand megawatts of hydroelectric power could have been generated if the two states had been able to cooperate (Subedi 2006, 22). More generally, the two states signed many trade and investment treaties but failed to implement them because of Nepal's fears that India would take advantage of it. Nepal frequently opted simply to let treaty provisions fall into disuse rather than to sign new ones (Subedi 2006, 120–52).

The repeated conflicts over trade with India provided Nepal with a large incentive to join the GATT, which Nepal believed would give it a stronger

---

[14] See S.D. Muni, "Chinese Arms Pour into Nepal," *Times of India*, September 1, 1988.
[15] See Dhruba Adhikary, "India Puts Trade Squeeze on Nepal," *Asia Times*, March 7, 2002.

ability to enforce treaties with India. During India's 1989 economic blockade against Nepal, many observers pointed out that India was able to cut off trade because Nepal was not a GATT member and therefore could not enforce its MFN tariff treatment (Garver 1991). This dispute instigated Nepal's application to join the GATT, as it sought to force India to abide by its agreements (Bank 2002; United Nations 2003) and also recognized that membership could prevent India from continuing to use transit facilities as a political lever against Nepal (Subedi 2006, 57).

By contrast, relations between Bangladesh and Nepal remained friendly for most of Bangladesh's history thanks to the strong similarities between the two states. Bangladesh's CINC score at the time of Nepal's WTO entry of 0.0136 was much closer to Nepal's score of 0.0014 than was India's. Furthermore, the two countries had interacted for thousands of years, and Nepal was among the first states to recognize Bangladesh after it declared independence in 1972. After an anti-India government took power in Bangladesh in a 1975 military coup, Bangladesh and Nepal found common ground in their suspicions toward India. For instance, Bangladesh sought Nepal's support in its discussions with India over Ganges River water usage (Savada 1991). The two nations signed trade, aviation, technical, and transit agreements in 1976 and enjoyed increased economic exchange. They also issued a joint statement pledging cooperative relations in power generation and water use (Savada 1991). Nepal and Bangladesh cooperated extensively in other areas as well, as both joined several regional organizations, conducted joint peacekeeping exercises through the UN, and worked together on issues pertinent to developing countries.[16]

When Nepal joined the WTO in 2004, the theory suggests that trade ties should have increased between Nepal and India to a greater extent than those between Nepal and Bangladesh. As predicted, both Nepal and India stressed their desires to boost trade and investment immediately following Nepal's accession. Though suspicious attitudes toward India certainly remained, the WTO helped to temper them, as exemplified by Nepal's foreign secretary's statement that Nepal was finally prepared to accept investment from India,[17] and Nepal's move to foster investment by signing a bilateral investment promotion and protection agreement (Subedi 2013). Interviews with experts on Nepal's trade policy suggest that Nepal gained confidence that India would respect its rights under international law following its WTO entry. Consequently, both imports and exports increased between the two states each year after Nepal's accession, albeit gradually due to persistent domestic instability in Nepal. In 2003 Nepal's exports amounted to 31.2 billion rupees, whereas by 2006 Nepal exported goods worth 41.7 billion rupees. In 2010 exports

---

[16] See Barrister Harun Ur Rashid, "40th Bangladesh-Nepal Relations: Close Bond of Friendship," *The Daily Star*, June 13, 2012.

[17] See "Nepal, India Stress Cooperation," *BBC Monitoring International Reports*, February 24, 2004.

reached 42.9 billion rupees. Furthermore, the proportion of total trade that Nepal conducted with India rose as well, in part because Nepal had less to fear from India (Oh and Prasai 2012). In 2000, total trade with India constituted 41 percent of Nepal's total trade (Government of Nepal 2013a), whereas by 2005, it reached 65.8 percent.[18]

By contrast, Nepal's trade with Bangladesh actually decreased after its WTO entry. Its imports dropped from 0.671 billion Rs in 2003 to 0.268 billion Rs in 2006 and did not reach pre-WTO levels until 2009 (Government of Nepal 2013b), and Nepal's exports to Bangladesh fell from 0.421 billion Rs in 2003 to 0.234 billion Rs in 2005, finally reaching pre-WTO levels in 2006 (Government of Nepal 2013b).

5.3 JAPAN, THE UNITED STATES, AND INDIA

Beginning with the United States's forced opening of Japan's economy to trade in 1854 and the signing of the so-called unequal treaties, which gave the United States nonreciprocal trade privileges (Auslin 2006, 24), the United States often used trade as a coercive tool. For example, in 1932, the United States threatened to boycott Japanese goods,[19] and in 1935, Congress passed the Neutrality Acts, which limited or prohibited trade with belligerents such as Japan. After Japan invaded Manchuria, Congress repeatedly urged U.S. president Roosevelt to implement the acts, which represented a persistent threat to Japan (Powaski 1991, 106–10). Then, in 1939, the United States abrogated its trade treaty with Japan to try to influence Japan's policies in East Asia[20] and in 1940, the U.S. State Department told the Japanese ambassador that "future trade relations between the two countries would depend on the Japanese attitude to American rights in China."[21] That same year, the United States sought to halt its oil, iron, and steel exports to Japan under the Export Control Act. Then, in the leadup to World War II, the United States gradually cut exports of necessary goods to Japan, first of aircraft and several other goods, then of forty more assorted items, next of scrap iron and steel, and finally of oil. In 1941 the United States imposed a full trade embargo on Japan and froze Japanese assets, leading, in part, to Japan's attack on Pearl Harbor (Maechling 2000).

Japan reacted by striving throughout this period to become less dependent on the West for trade and capital, particularly by taking territory to provide itself with additional resources. In part to break its reliance on the West, Japan annexed the Kurile Islands from Russia in 1875, took control of Korea in the 1894 Sino-Japanese War, and took Taiwan in 1895. By 1912, Japan had

---

[18] See "Nepal Increasingly Dependent on India Trade," *Kathmandu Post*, December 22, 2005.
[19] See "Government Warns of Loss in Boycott," *New York Times*, February 29, 1932, 13.
[20] See Hugh Byas, "Treaty Action Stuns Japan; Reprisals Hinted in Tokyo; U.S. Secrecy Irks London," *New York Times*, July 28, 1939, 1.
[21] See "Japan's Hope of New U.S. Trade Treaty," *Glasgow Herald*, January 26, 1940.

closed Korea and South Manchuria off to trade with other states so that it could monopolize their resources (Graham 2004). It also cut its imports below its actual needs to reduce opportunities for coercion.[22]

These historical trade tensions continued to linger in relations between the United States and Japan after World War II, particularly as the United States continued to use trade for coercion. For instance, in 1953, it offered to increase military procurement, provide agricultural commodities, and supply a cotton credit if Japan would improve its troop strength (Schaller 1997, 68), and in 1950, the United States offered to open its markets in return for access to military bases (Schaller 1997, 47–61). The influential policy advisor George Kennan recommended economic controls "to have power over what Japan imports," which would provide "veto power over what she does" (Schaller 1997, 20). As a consequence, "the ruling Japanese conservatives and the opposition socialists were at odds over the fundamental question of whether Japan should expand its trade with the West at all" (Forsberg 1998, 188). Whereas the conservatives advocated trade and overall cooperation with the United States (Yoshida, Ken-Ichi, and Nara 2007, 242–43), the Socialists pushed for neutrality in the Cold War and trade with other states in Asia, particularly since the Left Socialists described U.S. capitalism as "exploitative and aggressive" (Forsberg 1998, 189). The Socialists' 1948 victory heightened the danger that Japan would shun trade with the United States and choose neutrality in the Cold War (Davis and Wilf 2011).[23]

In contrast, prior to Japan's GATT entry, Japan and India enjoyed similar outlooks, with no need to coerce each other as a result. For instance, after World War II, Indian justice Radhabinod Pal issued a dissenting judgment at the International Military Tribunal for the Far East on Japan's behalf (Rajamohan et al. 2008, 6), and the two nations exchanged ambassadors. Indian prime minister Nehru even sent two elephants to Japan to boost its morale after its defeat in the war, which made a very positive impression on Japan.[24] In 1951, India did not participate in the San Francisco Peace Conference because it viewed the treaty as unfair to Japan, as it impinged on Japan's sovereignty. India stated that it could not participate because "the terms of the treaty should concede to Japan a position of honor, equality, and contentment among the

---

[22] See Brendan M. Jones, "Tariff Cuts to Aid Japan Face Fight," *New York Times*, December 12, 1954, 2.

[23] While Japan and the United States signed a security agreement in 1951, Japan was coerced in to doing so as a condition of the peace treaty because the United States insisted on maintaining significant forces in Japan. By contrast, Japan got little from the agreement and "regarded the security treaty as an infringement on Japanese sovereignty" (Tiedemann 2013, 371). For the purposes of this case, therefore, Japan and the United States are considered to have significant political differences despite the formal agreement. Note also that the agreement was not revised until 1960, after Japan's WTO accession.

[24] See Mandira Nayar, "India, Japan and World Peace," *The Hindu*, February 15, 2007.

community of free nations."[25] Instead, India and Japan concluded a bilateral peace treaty, one of the first bilateral treaties signed after the war (Rajamohan et al. 2008, 6). India then suggested halting reparations and did not push Japan for its share. In 1952, India became greatly angered when Russia vetoed Japan's UN membership and promoted Japan's inclusion.[26] In return, Japan supported India with technical expertise and diplomatic exchanges (Rajamohan et al. 2008, 6–7).

India was also much closer in capabilities to Japan than was the United States, as India's CINC score at the time of Japan's WTO entry was 0.0452, Japan's was 0.0300, and the United States's was 0.2664. As a result of these similar capabilities and political ties, the two nations actively sought to expand commercial relations following World War II,[27] opening up new flight routes[28] and beginning joint investment projects.[29] India emphasized increased trade with Japan, signing a trade treaty in 1952 that included MFN status.[30]

Meanwhile, tensions between Japan and the United States led U.S. president Eisenhower and U.S. secretary of state Dulles to work toward securing Japan's GATT entry to give Japan the confidence to increase trade with the United States and thereby keep it "on the side of the free world."[31] The "growing strain" between Japan and the United States led the United States to support Japan's membership, as it worried that Japan would otherwise fail to trust the United States as a trading partner (LaFeber 1997, 311). For instance, the *New York Times* reported, "The feeling is growing among world trade leaders that if [Japan] is not permitted to break out toward the non-Communist world it will break into or be swept into the Communist world system."[32] GATT entry would help to alleviate this problem, as it would "strengthen [Japan's] economic ties with the free world and [would] also reduce the danger that Japan [would] become dependent on Communist China."[33] This was a particularly salient danger due to the Communists' victory in China's civil war (Davis and Wilf 2011).

Furthermore, the United States believed that the GATT would boost its trade with Japan by allowing the United States to commit to not using trade for coercion. The United States tried to show that it offered "the trade you can

---

[25] See "Texts of Notes Exchanged by India and U.S. on Peace Treaty for Japan," *New York Times*, August 27, 1951, 3.
[26] See "Red Ban on China Displeases India," *New York Times*, September 24, 1952, 3.
[27] See "Japan Trade Mission Seeks Ties with India," *New York Times*, September 23, 1953, 2.
[28] See "India and Japan Sign Air Pact," *New York Times*, November 27, 1955, 233.
[29] See "India Turns to Japan for Aid on New Plant," *New York Times*, April 22, 1952, 8.
[30] See "India, Japan Keep Trade Tie," *New York Times*, October 7, 1956, 3.
[31] See Brendan M. Jones, "Tariff Cuts to Aid Japan Face Fight," *New York Times*, December 12, 1954, 2.
[32] See Michael L. Hoffman, "Japanese Trade Debated by GATT," *New York Times*, November 7, 1955, 45.
[33] See "Tariff Tie Called Boon to Japanese," *New York Times*, June 10, 1955, 6.

count on" (Schaller 1997, 174). U.S. officials frequently emphasized that China, by contrast, would "use trade as a political weapon" (174) by "promising preferential trade access or threatening to withdraw favors already granted" (22) and would "choke off trade with a gun at Japan's breast and say now you either come our way or starve" (105). Treasury secretary Humphrey warned that trade with China would provide "the Chinese Communists with a terrible club to hold over Japan" (81), as nothing would stop it from "abruptly cutting off supplies to force a serious economic crisis for political purposes" (22). Even while Japan advocated the separation of trade and politics, China sought to use trade with Japan as a lever to obtain diplomatic recognition (Sayuri 1995). Conservatives in Japan, too, sought U.S. assistance with its GATT admission for similar reasons (Schaller 1997), striving to complete the GATT accession process (Yoshida, Ken-Ichi, and Nara 2007, 99–100, 295).

After Japan's 1955 GATT accession, it moved economically closer to the United States, as expected. Though this occurred for many reasons, including Cold War concerns and domestic politics, GATT-induced trade ties played an important role. Trade grew rapidly between the two states after Japan's GATT entry, as total trade between the two countries increased from $972 million in 1954 to $1,656 million in 1956 and then rose to $2,596 million in 1960 (Forsberg 2000, 230). Japan's imports from the United States doubled in the first five years after its accession, and, "helped by tariff reductions from entry into the GATT, exports more than doubled" (Schaller 1997, 109). Furthermore, Japan's exports to the United States were largely in capital-intensive goods, such as transistor radios (Schaller 1997, 109), indicating that hold-up problems were likely resolved.

Although the United States and Japan still encountered trade frictions in their relationship, these tensions were minimized by their ability to settle disputes within the GATT framework (Davis 2012, 109, 188). Subsequent trade irritants were negotiated in the shadow of the GATT, such that merely identifying potential GATT violations often led to their resolution. For instance, South Carolina and Alabama passed laws in 1956 requiring their stores to hang notices stating, "Japanese textiles sold here." Japan asserted that these signs violated GATT rules, so the states removed them (Schaller 1997, 109).[34]

By contrast, trade with India remained relatively low and stable after Japan's accession. In the first five years following Japan's GATT accession, India's imports from Japan actually declined slightly, while exports increased by only about 18 percent in real terms (Liu 2009).[35]

---

[34] Although Japan had gone along with the United States's desire to violate GATT rules in some cases, such as the semiconductor agreement and voluntary export restraint, it has also been active in bringing cases against the United States in the WTO (Davis 2012).

[35] It should be noted that India went along with many other GATT members by invoking GATT Article 35 against Japan, which allows for nonapplication of the agreement, though India ceased to apply it by 1958.

5.4 MEXICO, THE UNITED STATES, AND CUBA

From the time of Mexico's independence, Mexico and the United States faced considerable dissimilarities in capabilities and political views, as exemplified by Mexico's active promotion of developing countries' initiatives to which the United States often objected. For example, Mexico proposed the Charter of Economic Rights and Duties of States at the UN in 1972, which would help to facilitate benefits for developing countries,[36] and, in 1975, assisted Venezuela in creating the Latin American and Caribbean Economic System (SELA), which enabled its twenty-six Latin American and Caribbean members to form common positions on economic matters. Importantly, SELA provided an alternative to the OAS, which the United States dominated (Domínguez and De Castro 2009, 56). Mexico also actively participated in the Group of 77 at the UN to try to achieve greater benefits for developing nations, leading the group from 1974 to 1975. Additionally, Mexico was instrumental in forming a Third World voting bloc in the UN, which frequently conflicted with U.S. interests (Purcell 1997).

Furthermore, throughout the 1980s, Mexico assisted many revolutionary groups that the United States opposed. For instance, Mexico supported the Sandinistas in Nicaragua, providing oil and other supplies (Leiken 2001), while the United States worked against them by funding and training anti-Sandinista guerrillas, known as the Contras. Mexico similarly diverged from U.S. policy by backing rebels in El Salvador (Leiken 2001). More generally, Mexico frequently resisted U.S. involvement in the region, maintaining a firm stance of nonintervention in other states' domestic affairs (Leiken 2001).

In line with its political views, Mexico also explicitly geared its economic policies toward avoiding dependence on the United States, as Mexico consistently exhibited unwillingness to trade with the United States due to political tensions and concerns over sovereignty (Salvucci 1991). Mexico treated the United States "with a degree of indifference and suspicion as extraordinary as it was to be regretted."[37] It used import substitution in part as a strategy to rely less heavily on this trade and applied a variety of restrictions on foreign capital as well (Purcell 1997). Mexico's hesitation to invest in trade with the United States continued through the 1980s owing to these political hold-up problems. For instance, in 1976, the United States and Mexico discussed constructing a natural gas pipeline, which had the potential to improve both countries' welfare through gains from trade. However, Mexico expressed concerns that once they built the pipeline, the United States could violate the agreement's terms to extract political concessions (Grayson 1981, 186–90). The United States and Mexico therefore failed to reach an agreement at the time. In another example,

---

[36] See "Charter of Economic Rights and Duties of States," General Assembly Resolution 3281 (XXIX). New York, December 12, 1974.

[37] Van Buren to Chargé d'Affaires in Mexico, Washington, DC, October 16, 1829, in *Message from the President*, 44.

when Mexico first contemplated entering the GATT in 1979, many Mexicans alleged that the United States had threatened to raise tariffs on Mexico if it did not join (Contreras 2008, 88). Indeed, upon Mexico's rejection of GATT membership, the United States increased its countervailing duties on Mexico's imports (Davis and Wilf 2011).

By contrast, Cuba and Mexico were similar politically and in terms of their capabilities. Whereas Mexico and the United States had very dissimilar CINC scores at the time of Mexico's WTO entry, 0.0115 and 0.1321 respectively, Cuba's score of 0.0033 indicated that the two states were much more alike. Cuba and Mexico also have a long history of close relations, initially based on their common struggles against Spain and later on their joint resistance against the United States, as Mexico assisted Cuba in its fight for independence. Mexico's assistance in planning Cuba's rebellion against Spain and its decision to host Cuban rebels and exiles led Cuban president Fulgencio Batista to write to the Mexican ambassador in 1953, "We will never forget that... [Mexico] was asylum and home... for Cuban patriots in the past century" (White 2007, 47). Furthermore, Mexico's revolutionary history led it to view the Cuban revolution with sympathy, resulting in strong public support for Cuba, which Mexico considered its "sister republic" (Pellicer de Brody 1972). The tight bonds between Mexico and Cuba allowed Mexico to use Cuba to balance against the United States and to justify its own nationalist policies.

Mexico demonstrated its strong similarities with Cuba frequently in the international arena. For instance, Mexico opposed both Cuba's expulsion from the OAS in 1962 and the U.S. blockade of the country in 1964. Furthermore, even after all other Latin American countries had cut relations with Cuba by 1964, under pressure from the United States, Mexico refused to do so (White 2007, 99). Mexico's recognition of Cuba led Fidel Castro to present Mexico's president with an award in 1980, stating, "Mexico alone maintained the worthy and courageous position of not breaking relations with Cuba... which we Cubans will never forget" (White 2007, 103). Because Mexico considered Cuba a critical partner, it actively worked to bring Cuba back into the international system. Between 1970 and 1976, Mexico stepped up efforts to reinstate Cuba in the OAS, which the United States strongly opposed. Then, between 1976 and 1982, relations improved still further as the two states participated in joint education and industry projects, held many cultural celebrations, and conducted multiple state visits (White 2007, 4).

Mexico and Cuba's strong affinity and symmetric capabilities led to significant economic exchange. Trade between Mexico and Cuba began to grow during the early 1970s, when the two states signed several trade treaties, and then rose more rapidly after 1976, as Mexico provided oil and loans to Cuba (Tsoutouras and Sagebien 1998, 173). Trade remained strong in the early 1980s, and Mexico became Cuba's second largest trade and investment partner.[38]

[38] UN Trade Commission data.

However, due in part due to Mexico's 1982 bankruptcy, Mexico decided to join the GATT in 1986. By making trade relations "binding and predictable," the GATT was expected to create a strong trade partnership between Mexico and the United States (Nafey 2007, 167), and in fact, there is widespread agreement that Mexico's GATT accession greatly boosted economic ties between the two (Leiken 2001). GATT membership proved essential for liberalizing Mexico's economy, locking in crucial economic reforms (International Monetary Fund 1993). Prior to Mexico's GATT entry, trade between the United States and Mexico had been relatively stable, hovering around $20 million since 1980. Between 1986 and 1993, however, trade tripled, increasing steadily each year (Gilderhus 2008). The United States became Mexico's largest trading partner, and Mexico became the third largest U.S. trading partner and the United State's second largest export destination (U.S. Census Bureau 2013). Indeed, after Carlos Salinas de Gortari was elected president in 1988, he stressed the importance of improving trade ties with the United States because Mexico wanted "to be part of the First World, not the Third."[39] Salinas felt that the economic integration would "turn Mexico's proximity to the world's largest economy into a permanent advantage by modifying... the uncertainties that dominated trade" (De Gortari, Hearn, and Rosas 2002, 42).

But while Mexico's GATT accession stimulated closer economic relations with the United States, it had the opposite impact on Mexico's relations with Cuba. After Mexico's GATT entry, trade growth slowed (Sagebien and Tsourtouras 1999). Cuba's exports to Mexico made up a negligible fraction of Mexico's market throughout the 1990s and beyond, and Mexico's exports to Cuba remained flat until 1993. Although a brief increase in exports to Cuba occurred from 1993 to 1995, they then fell back down to pre-1993 levels (Gilderhus 2008).

5.5 TAIWAN, THE UNITED STATES, AND CHINA

Before Taiwan's 2002 WTO entry, the United States and Taiwan shared many political similarities, as the United States treated Taiwan "as though it were designated a major non-NATO ally" (Kan 2013, 27). Throughout the 1990s, the United States displayed increasingly strong support for Taiwan: it violated an agreement with China to reduce arms sales to Taiwan by providing Taiwan with 150 F-16 planes in 1992; it improved its protocol for the treatment of Taiwan's diplomats in 1994; it provided a visa for Taiwan's president to visit the United States and give a speech at Cornell in 1995; and it demonstrated its resolve to defend Taiwan after China sent missiles into the Taiwan strait in 1996 (Ross 2000). Since signing the 1979 Taiwan Relations Act, the United States

---

[39] Carlos Salinas de Gortari, Second State of Nation Address, November 1, 1990. Secretary de Relaciónes Exteriores, *20 Años de Political Exterior a Travel de los Informes Presidencies, 1970–1990*, 130–31.

had remained committed to "maintain the capacity of the United States to resist any resort to force or other forms of coercion that would jeopardize the security, or the social or economic system, of the people on Taiwan" and to provide Taiwan with arms for defense.[40] U.S. president George W. Bush made the especially strong statement in 2001 that the United States would "do whatever it took to help Taiwan defend itself" (Kan 2013, 8).

The friendly relationship between the United States and Taiwan was evident in U.S. congressional activity around the time of Taiwan's WTO accession. Senator Jon Kyle referred to Taiwan as "a close, long-standing ally...that respect[s] the rule of law" and emphasized the importance of signaling "America's determination to meet our commitments and our resolve to support Taiwan."[41] Representative Doug Bereuter also highlighted the United States's "unshakable, long-term commitment to America's critically important relations with Taiwan."[42] Similarly, the U.S. congressional tribute to Taiwan's president Chen Shui-Bian, who held the presidency when Taiwan joined the WTO, also reflected the political similarity between the United States and Taiwan. Representative Tom Lantos stated, "President Chen has been an instrumental component as Taiwan moves along the path of democratization and wide economic reform. Moreover, President Chen deserves recognition for repeatedly demonstrating his commitment to human rights and rule of law.... President Chen has shown a continued commitment to the long-standing economic and cultural relationship that exists between the United States and Taiwan."[43] Representative Scott McInnis echoed the sentiment, stating, "The relationship between our countries stands as a great example of the cooperation and understanding that can be reached between two nations that share the goals of fostering democracy and human rights, protecting the world against terrorism and expanding the global economy through trade.... Under this President's guidance, Taiwan's vibrant democracy has continued to thrive, human rights have been safe-guarded, and freedom of the press has never been stronger."[44]

Although the two states were dissimilar in size, with CINC scores of 0.1435 for the United States and 0.0010 for Taiwan at the time of its WTO entry, investment and trade between the United States and Taiwan remained high due to their robust political ties. When Taiwan acceded to the WTO, Taiwan stood as the United States's eighth largest trade partner, and the United States was Taiwan's largest trade partner. Furthermore, the United States served as Taiwan's main investment destination (Kan and Morrison 2013, 30–31).

[40] See "Taiwan Policy Act of 2013," H.R.419, January 25, 2013.
[41] See "U.S.-China Relations Act of 2000. Kyle Amendment No. 4133," H.R. 4444, September 11, 2000, 5.
[42] See "American Institute in Taiwan Facilities Enhancement Act," *Congressional Record*, Vol. 146, No. 36, March 28, 2000, H1436.
[43] See "A Tribute to President Chen Shui-Bian," *Congressional Record*, Vol. 149, No. 10, May 22, 2003, 13175.
[44] Ibid.

By contrast, China and Taiwan held highly dissimilar political views and had dissimilar capabilities, as China's CINC score was 0.1674 at the time of Taiwan's WTO entry. Prior to its accession, Taiwan – China relations had become very strained as a result of political disputes, particularly regarding the issue of Taiwan's sovereignty. Their cultural disparities and dissimilar regime types exaggerated these tensions; in a 1999 white paper regarding its policy toward China, Taiwan stated, "The current totalitarianism of the Beijing government causes the cultural differences of both sides to be greater" (Democratic Progressive Party 1999). Owing to China and Taiwan's difficult history, they had little interaction after the cross-strait wars of the 1950s, remaining in a state of war until 1979. After a brief thawing of relations, Taiwan's democratic reforms in the 1980s and early 1990s motivated it to adopt a stance emphasizing its sovereignty, with which China vehemently disagreed. This dispute led Taiwan and China to engage in competition for international recognition, offering bribes such as increased foreign aid to partner states in return (Dumbaugh 2008). China became so agitated by Taiwan's pro-independence stance that top Chinese officials warned in 1992 and 1993 that China might take "drastic" and "resolute" measures to prevent its independence (Kan 2013, 20).

Relations deteriorated into an escalating crisis after Taiwan president Lee's highly political speech at Cornell University during Lee's first official visit to the United States in 1995 (Christensen 2011, 235). In response, China cut off all ongoing discussions with Taiwan. President Lee continued to push for independence, claiming that Taiwan and China should negotiate as equal states. In the run-up to Taiwan's elections, China conducted six large military exercises and then fired missiles into the Taiwan Strait in 1995 and again in 1996, which many interpreted as a tactic to scare Taiwanese voters into selecting a more pro-China government (Ross 2000). The United States responded by threatening China with a major demonstration of military power, the largest military maneuver in Asia since the Korean War, to emphasize its support for Taiwan (Ross 2000). Taiwan then continued to favor pro-independence candidates by electing Chen Shui-bian in the 2000 election. Chen agitated China by referring to China and Taiwan as "one country on each side" of the strait, pushing for a new constitution that would establish Taiwan's sovereignty, and favoring a referendum on the threats made by China during Taiwan's election (Kan 2013).

These political concerns resulted in low trade and investment; Taiwan banned Chinese investment in the 1980s, and cross-strait trade remained negligible due to worries that increased trade would provide China with political leverage (Lin 1999), with which it could hold Taiwan hostage (Cho 2005). The United States recognized this possibility as well, stating that it would "consider any effort to determine the future of Taiwan by other than peaceful means, including by boycotts or embargoes, a threat to the peace and security of the Western Pacific area" (Godwin, Wilhelm, and Sutter 1996, 140, 216). China, too, emphasized its intention to "use business to pressure the politicians" and to "use the people to pressure the officials" (Tong 2007, 2). China issued warnings to investors in Taiwan that it could prohibit them from doing business with China if they supported Taiwan's sovereignty[45] and reportedly conducted an investigation into investor support for independence.[46]

In response, Taiwan maintained a variety of restrictions on investment throughout the 1990s, such as mandates on licensing for investments greater than $5 million; bans on investment projects greater $50 million; and prohibitions on investment in China's high-technology industries, energy sector, infrastructure, and service sector. Taiwan further strove to develop the capacity to closely monitor investment and trade with the mainland and regulated the types of goods that could be traded to try to minimize its vulnerability to coercion. In particular, early investments tended not to exceed $1 million and mainly occurred in non-relationship-specific sectors such as footwear, foodstuffs, textiles, and toys (Tanner 2007, 113). Moreover, Taiwan regulated whether China's companies could list shares on Taiwan's stock market and tried to depress the listing of Taiwan's companies on China's stock market. It also limited Chinese financing sources for its companies (Tanner 2007, 39–50).

These restrictions on investment occurred explicitly due to political hold-up problems. For instance, the Cheng Shin Rubber International Company sought to invest $20 million in a tire factory in 1991, but Taiwan banned the investment at the time as a result of fears that China would use it to blackmail Taiwan (Tanner 2007, 43). A white paper from Taiwan stated that the restrictions reflected concerns about antagonistic Chinese behavior because of "cultural conflicts" (Democratic Progressive Party 1999). However, the paper expressed the hope that both nations would join the WTO so that investment prohibitions could be relaxed, as Taiwan believed that one of WTO membership's key benefits would be enhanced economic integration with China (Cho 2005). Many scholars pointed out that WTO accession would prevent China from using economic pressure to try to extract political concessions from Taiwan, as "such attempts could land Beijing in a WTO mediation hearing" (Gilley and Pao 2001). Since Taiwan had cut off official communication prior to Taiwan's WTO entry, many saw the WTO's consultative mechanism as a key venue for enforcement, and it indeed proved effective in enhancing compliance with WTO regulations once Taiwan joined the institution (Cho 2005).

The theory indicates that after Taiwan's 2002 WTO accession, trade should have increased in particular with powerful partners that held dissimilar political views, like China, which in fact occurred. Considerable evidence shows that the WTO allowed China and Taiwan to depoliticize their trade relations (Charnovitz 2006), resulting in strong trade growth (Wu 2012, 15–24). After

---

[45] See James Kynge, "China in Warning to Taiwan Businesses," *Financial Times*, April 10, 2000, 10.
[46] See "Pro-Independence Taiwanese Firms to Face Squeeze in China," *Taipei Times*, April 20, 2000.

Taiwan's WTO entry, trade and investment between the United States and Taiwan increased only slightly, as U.S. exports to Taiwan rose by 1.5 percent and U.S. imports from Taiwan grew by 3.5 percent during 2002 (Hsieh 2008). By contrast, exports from Taiwan to China grew by 35.4 percent and imports from China grew by 30.7 percent from 2002 to 2003. Trade continued to climb dramatically over time, from $27.8 billion in 2001 to $76.4 billion in 2005. Specifically, Taiwan's exports to China rose from $21.9 billion to $56.3 billion, and its imports from China increased from $5.9 billion to $20.1 billion during this period. Daily direct flights and the potential for opening representative offices also accompanied WTO accession to facilitate further trade.[47]

In effect, China became Taiwan's biggest trading partner, while the United States sunk to Taiwan's eleventh largest partner (Kan and Morrison 2012). According to one study, Taiwan's economy received an extra $3 billion because of the WTO-induced elimination of trade restrictions with China (Ianchovichina and Martin 2004). Furthermore, Taiwan's investments in trade with China not only rose but also changed in composition from those requiring few fixed capital investments, such as toys and clothes, to industries requiring large relationship-specific investments, such as high-tech industries (Tanner 2007, 44), indicating the resolution of political hold-up problems.

Discussion and Summary

This chapter presented a variety of illustrative examples to demonstrate that across states and over time, political hold-up problems have been a central feature of international relations. In countless instances, pairs of countries seek cooperation by, for example, liberalizing their trading relations, but fail to do so because one or both countries could exploit this cooperation at a later time. Furthermore, the greatest risk occurs when countries differ significantly in their political power or interests.

However, WTO membership does not occur at random. Could it be the case that states join the WTO once they become more similar to their asymmetric trading partners? Further examination of the cases presented in this chapter shows that this is not likely. For example, Nepal's push toward WTO accession occurred at the height of its tensions with India and reflected its desire to restrain India rather than any sort of improvement in their relations. Similarly, Taiwan's WTO entry did not signal a better relationship with China. Instead, most scholars believed at the time that political relations between Taiwan and China would remain difficult (Mastel 2001). Turning to Saudi Arabia's WTO entry, scholars attribute the specific timing of its accession primarily to domestic factors rather than to its relationship with India (Hertog 2010, 232–37). Furthermore, Mexico's GATT entry was largely due to its new economic strategy of free trade following its economic downturn rather

---

[47] See Harry Kazianis, "Has the United States 'Lost' Taiwan?," *The Diplomat*, June 22, 2013.

than changing political relations with the United States (Davis and Wilf 2011). Finally, although Japan's GATT entry did reflect Cold War politics, it did not *result* from changing relations with the United States as much as *foster* these improved relations. As detailed previously, the United States's primary motivation for supporting Japan's GATT membership was to ensure that Japan would trade with the United States and its allies going forward. Furthermore, in each case, new entrants expected their WTO membership to reduce the potential for coercion in their trade relations with their dissimilar partners. The states themselves thus seem to believe that the WTO can alleviate political hold-up problems.

This chapter therefore demonstrated many cases that are consistent with the theory that the WTO helps to restrain states from using trade for coercion by increasing the costs of doing so. Having established this, I next test an additional implication of the model: WTO members do not simply give up on exercising coercive diplomacy – they substitute other mechanisms to wield influence. In the following chapter, I explore this prediction by examining members' selection of coercive tools.

6

Agreements and the Displacement of Coercion

TACTICS MEAN DOING WHAT YOU CAN WITH WHAT YOU HAVE.

Saul Alinsky[1]

To this point, I have shown that international institutions help states to solve political hold-up problems, which occur when one state fails to undertake an otherwise productive investment due to the increased ability it would give another state to extract political concessions. While ameliorating these issues facilitates cooperation within the domains of the institutions, member states also experience limitations in their abilities to exercise coercive diplomacy within these policy areas. Because states often offer (or retract) foreign policy concessions to influence other states, such as lowering trade protection, increasing foreign aid, or granting security concessions, the policy rigidity induced by these institutions constitutes lost political leverage over other members.

However, the model developed in Chapter 2 predicted that rather than abandoning their attempts to engage in coercive diplomacy, members of international institutions replace policies made more costly by institutional membership with more flexible policy options. In fact, cost represents a key factor shown to govern foreign policy substitution; leaders choose between economic, military, and diplomatic levers of influence as a function of the costs of the policies available to them.[2] But while scholars have proposed numerous

---

[1] See Alinsky (1971, 126).
[2] See Clark, Nordstrom, and Reed (2008) and Most and Starr (1989, 36–39, 75–79). The motivations for choosing certain foreign policies over others have been explored in many areas, including enduring rivalries (Bennett and Nordstrom 2000), alliances and aid (Diehl 1994; Milner and Tingley 2012; Morgan 2000; Palmer and Morgan 2010), interventions (Regan 2000), sanctions (Clark and Reed 2005; Lektzian and Sprecher 2007), and repression (Moore 1998).

factors which shape the burdens imposed by certain policies, the role that international institutions play remains undertheorized. This chapter demonstrates that by limiting members' options in specific policy realms, institutions lead these states to coerce their partners using tools the institutions do not regulate. International institutions thus create ripple effects across policy arenas, bolstering cooperation in some areas, while politicizing others.

Specifically, I show that because the WTO constrains its members' abilities to condition their trade policies upon their political relationships with their trading partners, members instead manipulate policies that remain unregulated by the WTO to pursue their political objectives. In what follows, I first detail the alternative instruments of coercion that WTO members rely on. Next, I illustrate WTO-induced policy substitution by providing specific examples from the EU's experience with coercive diplomacy. I then test these claims systematically, demonstrating that once states join the WTO, their trade flows become less correlated with political tensions, while other levers of influence become more responsive to these political issues.

6.1 INSTRUMENTS OF COERCION

To exercise coercive diplomacy, states may select a variety of tools as alternatives to WTO-regulated trade policies.[3] First, states often turn to bilateral foreign aid provisions to pressure their partners. When recipients comply with donors' demands, the donors allocate additional aid, but when recipients ignore their requests, donors withhold assistance (Crawford 2001; Dunning 2004; Morrissey 2004). Donors often apply these measures formally by inserting clauses in aid agreements which mandate that recipients make concessions to receive aid, or informally by simply withholding or extending aid in response to political factors. For example, the EU's Lomé IV and Cotonou Conventions and the United States's Millennium Challenge Account place conditions on receiving aid, such as showing respect for human rights and exhibiting good governance.

Second, states frequently rely on preferential trade programs to pressure their partners, such as those discussed in Chapter 3. These programs specify goods on which recipients receive lower tariffs if they meet specific criteria. While eligibility requirements vary by program and donor, they typically include political and economic factors, and if countries do not meet these qualifications, tariff preferences may be withdrawn at any time. For instance, states often revoke eligibility for the most common preference program, GSP, if a recipient

---

[3] Although I focus on alternative foreign policy instruments, governments may also substitute using alternative economic tools because the WTO also restricts tariff manipulation for economic purposes. For instance, states may substitute nontariff barriers (Rickard and Kono 2013) or exchange rate policies (Copelovitch and Pevehouse 2013). See also Broz and Werfel (2011).

violates human rights, nationalizes property, or experiences high economic growth (UNCTAD 1998).

Third, numerous financial restrictions exist that states may employ as leverage. For example, recipient countries often greatly desire foreign direct investment (FDI) to bolster their economies. Although private economic actors determine FDI flows in many countries, governments can use FDI for political leverage by threatening to place restrictions on its flow. For instance, a 2008 U.S. Congressional Research Service report describes the "good governance requirements, human rights conditions, approved-project restrictions, and environmental quality regulations that characterize U.S. and European government investments" (Dumbaugh 2008). Similarly, China often requires host countries to adopt a "one-China" policy and to use Chinese companies, suppliers, and banks to receive FDI.

Loans constitute another financial tool that states employ for coercion. For example, the U.S. Export-Import (Ex-Im) Bank loans money to other countries at low interest rates to allow them to buy U.S. products. However, the Ex-Im Bank requires human rights and political clearances by the U.S. State Department before it will agree to lend (GAO 1994). Furthermore, in deciding whether to accept an application for Ex-Im Bank programs, the bank may consider the extent to which a state has been helpful in combating terrorism, among other criteria (Jackson 2003). The bank can therefore threaten not to lend unless recipients comply with its demands.

The treatment of foreign assets represents an additional financial tool commonly used for political leverage, as countries may render their partners' assets inaccessible or unprofitable to gain political influence. For instance, states frequently freeze key government officials' assets until they comply with their demands. I provide examples of this in Chapter 7.

Diplomatic levers can also allow states to coerce their partners. These tactics represent relatively low-cost signals of disapproval of other states' policies and thus are commonly used. States may punish each other by recalling ambassadors, boycotting conferences and events, tarnishing a partner's reputation, or refusing to allow participation in international forums. For instance, U.S., German, and British heads of state did not attend the 2014 Olympics held in Sochi, Russia, to protest Russia's poor human rights record.

States also can make entry into international agreements contingent on the fulfillment of specific criteria such as economic or political reforms. Accession agreements that provide a pathway to EU membership in exchange for numerous concessions constitute a well-known example of this practice (Kelley 2004; Levitz and Pop-Eleches 2010; Schimmelfennig 2005; Schneider 2009; Vachudova 2005). Similarly, existing NATO members generally demand stringent reforms prior to offering membership to other states.

Additionally, many states use military instruments when practicing coercive diplomacy, including military invasions, force, military basing policies, and security guarantees. Perhaps the most commonly implemented military punishment is an arms embargo, which limits the flow of weapons to specific countries or groups. The possible avenues for military coercion are too extensive to discuss here, but see Stevenson (2012) for an overview.

Other levers exist as well and include policies in diverse areas such as currencies, visas, the environment, technology, immigration, and intelligence. Although the specific tactics available vary by state, most states have at least some of these tools at their disposal. Typically, the more powerful the state, the wider the array of instruments it can wield.

In sum, once states join the WTO, they may select from a variety of tools for influence that do not fall under the WTO's purview. But how do states choose between their various policy options? States clearly do not employ every tool they have to address every problem that arises. Instead, scholars have shown that states adopt policies based on their associated costs and benefits, which depend on many factors, including partner countries' welfare, national security concerns, costs to specific domestic groups, potential retaliation by other states, and lobbyists' and constituents' interests. While the precise considerations involved in choosing a particular set of policies differ by state, I argue that the WTO increases the costs associated with manipulating WTO-regulated trade policies and thus causes the substitution of alternative tactics.

6.2 THE EU AND WTO-INDUCED POLICY SUBSTITUTION

To illustrate how the theory operates in practice, I consider the EU's experience with coercive diplomacy. As a powerful force in international relations that frequently seeks concessions from partner states, the EU represents an instructive example. I analyze more in-depth cases in Chapter 7; however, the following vignettes are meant to illustrate the theory's applicability to a variety of prominent policy choices.

I examine recent EU decisions to sanction partner states, both WTO members and nonmembers, to show the WTO's impact on these considerations. I demonstrate that although the EU does not generally apply trade sanctions to WTO members and explicitly cites WTO membership as the reason for its restraint, it implements trade penalties against non-WTO members without hesitation. The EU does so because the WTO prohibits unilateral discrimination, except under the exceptions detailed in Chapter 4. The national security exception (Article XXI) is perhaps most salient, as it allows states to take any action to protect their "essential security interests." As explained previously, although this exception seems extremely permissive, in reality countries only invoke it in exceptionally rare circumstances because of fears of undermining the entire trading system, incentives to follow international norms, and concerns about retaliation (Alford 2011). Although the WTO does not prevent states from enacting any and all trade sanctions, WTO membership does curtail their use, which leads the EU to substitute alternative coercive strategies.

Zimbabwe

Election monitors found Zimbabwe's 2002 elections to be neither free nor fair, as they were "marred by a high level of politically motivated violence and intimidation." Subsequently, numerous reports of human rights violations surfaced, which included torture, politically motivated arrests, and severe lack of freedom of assembly and association. The EU therefore decided to sanction Zimbabwe by freezing its assets, restricting visas for key officials, and cutting off foreign aid to the Zimbabwean government. Zimbabwe was also suspended from the commonwealth "until the government complies with the Harare Declaration and takes concrete steps to restore rule of law, restores respect for human rights and holds perpetrators of human rights violations accountable."[4]

However, the EU did not administer sweeping trade sanctions due to Zimbabwe's WTO membership. Instead, a large Zimbabwean newspaper reported the WTO director for information and external relations's statement that states were limited in their abilities to apply trade sanctions because "as a member of the WTO, Zimbabwe is able to enjoy the rights of all members. What this means in practice is that WTO members cannot discriminate against Zimbabwe's trade in goods and services.... Zimbabwe has access to the dispute settlement system which means it can defend its rights through our binding system of dispute resolution."[5] Thus, to punish Zimbabwe for human rights violations, the EU relied on tactics other than trade manipulation.

Burma

Burma, a GATT member since 1948, had been led by its military from 1962 to 1988, when pro-democracy protests broke out across the country. After the military massacred thousands of protesters, a new military regime took control and agreed to hold an election in 1990. The National League for Democracy won the election, but the military refused to relinquish power. The EU therefore imposed sanctions by cutting off nonhumanitarian aid, implementing an arms embargo, and removing military personnel from embassies. In 1996, the EU also enacted travel bans and asset freezes for key figures of the regime, suspended Burma's GSP status, and cut off contact with it (Giumelli 2013).

Burma then joined ASEAN in 1997, but more protests occurred, followed by another military crackdown. In response, the EU refused to allow Burma to accede to the ASEAN-EU Economic Cooperation Agreement that would

---

[4] See David Danzig, "Zimbabwe Suspended Indefinitely from Commonwealth," *Human Rights First*, December 8, 2003.
[5] See Kudzai Chimhangwa, "Stop Whining about Sanctions, Zim Told," *The Standard*, November 29, 2010. Although, as stated earlier, this statement is only true while sanctions remain outside of the UN's purview.

provide it with EU development aid. EU president Jacques Poos stated, "The EU will agree to extend assistance to Burma under the ASEAN framework only if five conditions are met – release political prisoners, restore democratic dialog, stop arresting political dissidents, fix a date for democratic elections, and allow freedom of democracy and movement" (Pedersen 2008, 36). In an attempt to tighten the screws further, asset freezes were implemented in 2000.

However, although the EU imposed numerous measures designed to coerce Burma to institute democratic reforms and improve its human rights policies, it did not enact large-scale trade sanctions during this time. The EU explained, "Since Burma is a member of the WTO, the possibility of imposing sanctions in the field of trade in goods and services is subject to the rules of those agreements falling under the WTO to which Burma is a party.... Future EU policy in the field of restrictive measures will have to take into account the international commitments of the EU, in particular WTO agreements" (Pedersen 2008, 39).

In 2007, the EU further strengthened its sanctions regime by restricting imports on textiles, gems, timber, and precious metals (Hose and Genser 2007). However, discussions about these measures centered on whether such bans would violate WTO laws, as the EU wanted to avoid doing so. Indeed, many policy makers argued that these measures were compatible with the WTO's Article XX, which permits restrictive measures "necessary to protect public morals" (Hose and Genser 2007).

Furthermore, the EU and Japan also brought a WTO case against the United States, charging that the United States's sanctions violated WTO laws. In particular, the U.S. state of Massachusetts had sanctioned Burma, passing a law in 1996 that restricted government procurement of Burma's goods, which violated the WTO Government Procurement Agreement. The Massachusetts law was repealed after the U.S. Supreme Court struck it down, which occurred before the WTO could rule on the case (Barker 2000), but this illustrates the general principle that the WTO limits the its members' abilities to use trade policies to sanction states unilaterally.

Note that this example represents a particularly tough case for the theory, because Burma's human rights violations stood as a major international concern for a prolonged period of time. However, as this illustration highlights, WTO membership can restrain states from using trade for coercive purposes even when strong incentives to do so exist. Although the EU wanted to implement large-scale trade sanctions, it instead relied mainly on foreign aid cuts, visa restrictions, asset freezes, arms embargoes, and other tactics for coercion due to its desire to abide by the WTO's rules.

Iran

In contrast to the previous two examples, the EU faced different considerations when deciding what types of sanctions to apply to Iran, which was not a WTO member. In 2006, the international community demanded that Iran stop its uranium enrichment and reprocessing activities, but Iran would not suspend this program. The International Atomic Energy Agency (IAEA) Board of Governors further found that Iran was not in compliance with the safeguards agreement, but Iran refused to cooperate with the IAEA or to report to the UN Security Council. High-level negotiations with Iran were attempted, which failed in part because Iran was not willing to meet the international community's demands (Giumelli 2013).

In response, the UN Security Council approved sanctions on Iran, which included asset freezes on specific individuals, nuclear material and technology bans, arms embargoes, travel bans, financial restrictions, and monitoring mandates. The EU implemented these measures and imposed further penalties that went well beyond those agreed to in the UN, including additional financial restrictions and an oil and gas embargo, followed by an economic embargo (Clyde and Co 2013). The EU stated that it supported these policies because "trade with Iran is subject to the EU general import regime, since Iran is not a member of the WTO" (European Commission 2014). Additionally, many experts called for EU sanctions by pointing out that the EU's treatment of Iran was not restrained by WTO rules, and as a consequence, "the world community can be equally uninhibited toward Iran" (Feldman 2006).

Turkey

The WTO affects bilateral relations between individual EU members and third parties, as well. Consider the WTO's effect on a dispute between France and Turkey, both of which are WTO members, though only France is an EU member. In 2011 the French National Assembly introduced legislation that would criminalize the denial of what France refers to as the Armenian genocide, during which more than a million Armenians were killed from 1915 to 1918. However, Turkey denies responsibility for their deaths, arguing that they were the result of Armenian Christians and Muslims fighting against each other during World War I (Lewy 2005, 90–99). In response to the bill, Turkey's prime minister Erdogan announced, "We are stopping all kinds of political consultations with France. We are canceling bilateral military activities and joint exercises from now on. We are canceling the permission granted annually for all military overflights, landings and take-offs. We are starting a permission process for every military flight individually. From today on, we are rejecting the permission requests of military ships to visit ports. We will not attend or hold the bilateral Turkey-France joint economic and trade partnership committee meeting that was planned for January 2012 under the co-chairmanship of the economy ministers of the two countries."[6] He also threatened that, if

---

[6] See "French National Assembly Passes Armenian Genocide Bill," *CNN*, December 22, 2011.

the bill passed, Turkey would consider applying additional penalties to France and would do so "with determination without any hesitation."[7]

However, although Turkey implemented a variety of retaliatory measures, it refrained from enacting WTO-inconsistent policies. When asked whether Turkey would boycott French goods, Turkey's ambassador to France replied, "Turkey has obligations. The Turkish state can't do this given the WTO and Customs Union rules."[8] Turkey thus relied on alternative tactics that did not violate WTO laws.

6.3 STATISTICAL TESTS OF THE WTO AND POLICY SUBSTITUTION

The preceding section supplied anecdotal evidence that WTO membership can cause states to alter their tactics of coercion, but it could be argued that these represent isolated instances. I now provide empirical support for the theory's claim, demonstrating that it holds systematically over time and across many countries.

Hypothesis and Measures

Recall that the model presented in Chapter 2 predicted that joint WTO membership would lead states to substitute other policy tools in place of trade policies for coercive diplomacy due to the WTO's ability to enforce states' trade commitments. Furthermore, while the examples highlight extreme cases in which formal sanctions were implemented to coerce the EU's partners, states routinely implement smaller punishments and rewards, such as raising or lowering tariffs either overall or on specific products, extending or revoking moderate amounts of aid, and freezing the assets of certain officials. Members often do this discretely, such that the general public may not even be aware of it. Accordingly, I anticipate the following:

Hypothesis 9. *WTO members decrease the use of trade policy for coercion and increase the use of other policy tools to extract foreign policy concessions from other members.*

To operationalize this hypothesis, I focus on a particular policy area and on two alternative policy tools. Although states seek a variety of policy concessions from partner states, such as democratization, intelligence cooperation, technology sharing, access to military bases, votes in the UN, support for foreign policy positions, and others, a particularly salient and long-standing objective of many powerful states has been to promote respect for human rights. For example, the UN Universal Declaration of Human Rights promises

---
[7] Ibid.
[8] See "Turkey to Abide by WTO Norms in French Boycott," *Today's Zaman*, December 23, 2011.

Agreements and the Displacement of Coercion

to protect all people's "equal and inalienable rights." Similarly, the EU's founding 1957 Treaty of Rome states that its goal is "developing and consolidating democracy and the rule of law, and...respecting human rights and fundamental freedoms" (Article 177).[9] OECD members have also long expressed concern with their partners' human rights records. This group's stated mission is to "promote policies that will improve the economic and social well-being of people around the world." They declare, "The common thread of our work is a shared commitment to market economies backed by democratic institutions and focused on the wellbeing of all citizens" (OECD 2011). Accordingly, these states frequently condition their policies upon recipients' respect for human rights (Dobbins 2008, 81–82, 153–55). A reflection of the significant role that respect for rights plays in their foreign policy decisions is their explicit linkage between the foreign policy instruments discussed previously and human rights promotion (Crawford 2001; Conrad and Moore 2010; Dobbins 2008; Hafner-Burton 2005, 2009; Sikkink 2011; Simmons 2009). Indeed, states belong to the OECD primarily because of their liberal orientation and alignment (Davis 2014).

Thus, to test this hypothesis systematically, I focus on OECD states' coercive methods in the area of human rights. As a result of the salience of human rights in interstate relations, the international community's role in advancing rights and freedoms has attracted a good deal of attention, and scholars have demonstrated that international commitments have secured significant improvements in many states' human rights records.[10] International institutions, in particular, can promote rights (Hafner-Burton 2012, 2013) by offering material benefits in exchange, helping states overcome domestic barriers to political liberalization, and fostering liberal norms (Checkel 2005; Pevehouse 2002). However, the effect of international institutions on the particular policy tools states use to foster human rights remains opaque.

I argue that WTO membership curtails OECD countries' abilities to promote rights using trade policies by increasing the cost associated with trade policy discrimination. Accordingly, I anticipate that OECD countries condition their imports upon non-WTO members' human rights records to a greater extent than they condition their imports upon those of WTO members. Yet I do not expect OECD countries to abandon their efforts to encourage respect for human rights among WTO members; rather, I expect them to use other tools instead. If the hypothesis holds, I thus expect OECD countries to condition policy instruments that the WTO does not regulate upon WTO members' human rights records to a greater extent than they condition these instruments upon those of non-WTO members.[11]

---

[9] See Simmons (2009) for an overview.
[10] See Hafner-Burton (2012) for an overview.
[11] I do not argue that outside of the WTO, states care about human rights more than they care about trade. To be sure, states would typically like to commit ex ante not to use trade to

I test these claims using data from three foreign policy areas: international trade, bilateral foreign aid, and GSP programs. I select foreign aid and GSP policies because, for a long period of time and across many donors, respect for human rights has been an important criterion in both of these programs' administration. Many scholars have shown that virtually all OECD members have altered their foreign aid flows to some degree to encourage respect for human rights (Crawford 2001; Uvin 1993; Uvin and Biagiotti 1996), and Chapter 3 detailed the frequency with which states employ GSP to promote rights. Thus, although states differ in terms of their access to potential tools of coercion and issue areas they target, the instruments and policy domains selected here remain relevant for this large sample of states.

Statistical Model

To test whether OECD countries implement policy conditionality in their trading relationships with non-WTO members to a greater extent than with WTO members, I estimate a model of bilateral trade flows. As in previous chapters, I adopt the traditional work-horse model in the trade literature, the log-linear gravity model. The model includes year and country-pair fixed effects and robust standard errors, clustered at the directed dyad level. The sample consists of country-pairs composed of OECD importers and their trade partners that are also eligible for foreign aid, which includes 30 OECD states and 165 recipient states observed from 1981 to 2009.[12] I focus on trade partners that receive foreign aid for two reasons. First, because I am interested in foreign policy substitution, concentrating the analysis on aid recipients ensures that the importers can substitute using other policies. Second, using the same sample for both this analysis and the next allows for comparability and consistency.[13]

The outcome variable is the log of bilateral imports (in constant 1995 U.S. dollars). I select OECD imports as the dependent variable rather than OECD exports, because when an OECD member uses its trade policies to punish a trading partner for human rights violations, it usually reduces imports of goods from that partner by increasing trade protection. In other words, OECD states typically condition imports, rather than exports, upon a partner's respect for human rights.

---

elicit human rights concessions. However, states commonly cannot resist using trade ex post to punish or reward their partners.

[12] The year 1981 represents the first year that my key independent variable is measured. None of the OECD members joined the OECD during the sample period, circumventing issues of selection bias. OECD members include Australia, Austria, Belgium, Canada, the Czech Republic, Denmark, Finland, France, Germany, Greece, Hungary, Iceland, Ireland, Italy, Japan, Korea, Luxembourg, Mexico, the Netherlands, New Zealand, Norway, Poland, Portugal, the Slovak Republic, Spain, Sweden, Switzerland, Turkey, the United Kingdom, and the United States.

[13] The results hold when the full sample is used and also when the set of donors is restricted to Development Assistance Committee members.

A key variable of interest is respect for *Human Rights*, which is measured using data from the Cingranelli – Richards (CIRI) Human Rights Project (Cingranelli and Pasquarello 1985) and is scored on a 14-point scale ranging from least to most respect for rights. The CIRI index is compiled using annual reports from Amnesty International and the U.S. State Department, which record specific human rights violations. Because the CIRI index is measured using actual violations instead of expert opinions, it may be more credible than alternative measures.[14] To ease interpretation, I rescale *Human Rights* such that it ranges from 0, indicating no respect for rights, to 1, indicating full respect for rights. Furthermore, the theory implies that the effect of *Human Rights* on trade flows differs for WTO members versus non-WTO members. To account for the hypothesized conditional effect of rights, I interact *Human Rights* with *Both in WTO*, an indicator of joint WTO membership.

While the fixed effects account for any time-invariant country-pair characteristics as well as factors that are common across country-pairs in a given year, I must still include relevant variables that vary both over time and by country-pair. I therefore follow the extensive empirical work on gravity models (Head and Mayer 2013) and add the following: an indicator of whether states are members of an *RTA*, an indicator of whether an importing country extends *GSP* tariff preferences to its partner,[15] and measures of both the importer's and exporter's log(*GDP*) and log(*GDPPC*) measured in logged constant 1995 U.S. dollars.[16] I also include *Alliance*, which is an indicator of a strategic military alliance. Note that the colony measures and the customs union control variable used in the analysis presented in Chapter 4 are now collinear with the fixed effects because of the shorter time period under analysis.

Table 6.1 presents results that comport with the hypothesis. The coefficient on *Human Rights* is positive and statistically significant ($p = 0.001$) and indicates that among non-WTO trading partners, OECD countries import 339 percent more from regimes that fully respect rights relative to those that do not respect rights. Furthermore, the estimated effect of respect for human rights on OECD imports is much smaller for WTO members and is not statistically significant ($p = 0.317$), indicating that the effect is not significantly different from zero. This result is consistent with the hypothesis that OECD states condition their imports on respect for rights when exporters are not WTO members. When exporters are members, the effect disappears, which accords with the

---

[14] This variable is constructed using the following indicators: *Foreign Movement, Domestic Movement, Freedom of Speech, Freedom of Assembly and Association, Workers' Rights, Electoral Self-Determination*, and *Freedom of Religion*.
[15] None of the exporters in the analysis extend GSP to OECD importers.
[16] Many gravity models include an indicator of whether only one state in a pair is a WTO member. However, because virtually all OECD members were also WTO members during the sample period, this variable is collinear with the fixed effects. Additionally, because WTO laws do not bind WTO members' trade relations with nonmember partners, only *Both in WTO* is interacted with the key independent variable. The source of these data was described in previous chapters.

TABLE 6.1. *Effect of WTO and Human Rights on Logged Imports*

Human Rights × WTO	−1.648***
	(0.292)
Human Rights	1.480***
	(0.303)
Both in WTO	1.198***
	(0.210)
$\log(GDP_i)$	5.589***
	(1.070)
$\log(GDP_j)$	0.160*
	(0.361)
$\log(GDPPC_i)$	−6.720***
	(1.166)
$\log(GDPPC_j)$	0.978
	(0.347)
RTA	0.175
	(0.101)
GSP	0.314
	(0.187)
Alliance	−0.902***
	(0.115)
Constant	−39.897***
	(12.260)
R^2	0.756
N	55,863

Notes: Estimates from OLS regression. The unit of observation is the directed dyad-year and the dependent variable is the natural log of (*imports* +1). The data cover the years 1981–2009. Robust standard errors, clustered by directed dyad, appear in parentheses. Year and directed dyad fixed effects are not shown. * $p < 0.05$, ** $p < 0.01$, *** $p < 0.001$.

claim that the WTO restrains states from using their trade policies for coercion.

In addition to these results, I verify the robustness of my findings to many alternative empirical specifications. Because this is an observational study, it is important to be careful when making causal claims based on the results. However, demonstrating the strong robustness of the results should boost confidence in the findings. To do so, I add additional control variables and fixed effects, drop outliers, and use alternative measures of the key independent variables.[17]

---

[17] Because only 7 percent of the observations contain zero trade flows, models that account for a high percentage of zeros in the dependent variable are inadvisable here.

One possible concern with the preceding results is that the model does not account for time-varying factors specific to the importing country. For example, importers' strategic goals, political environments, policy priorities, and other characteristics may change over time. To deal with this possibility, I include time-varying importer fixed effects (in addition to the year and directed dyad fixed effects). I cannot add time-varying exporter fixed effects because I would no longer be able to estimate the impact of the key independent variables on trade. However, only time-varying factors specific to the exporting country are not captured by this model, minimizing potential bias.

Furthermore, it is possible that the model does not include other time-varying factors that could affect whether states use trade policy to punish or reward their partners for human rights violations. Thus, I also add several other control variables: log(*Foreign Aid*) is the natural log of the foreign aid given by the importer to the exporter and *Alliance* is an indicator of a strategic military alliance.[18]

Another potential concern is that the results could depend on the specific measure of human rights used. I thus employ a measure of civil liberties and a measure of political rights as alternative measures of this variable (Freedom House 2006). Civil liberties are defined as policies that "allow for the freedoms of expression and belief, associational and organizational rights, rule of law, and personal autonomy without interference from the state," while political rights "enable people to participate freely in the political process." These variables are again rescaled such that they range from 0, indicating no government respect for rights, to 1, indicating full respect for rights. Because these data are available for a longer time span than the data used in the baseline analysis, the model is now estimated over the period 1972-2009.[19] I find that the results are robust to each of these specifications.

WTO Membership and Coercion Using Aid and GSP

Whereas the previous results support the first aspect of the hypothesis – that WTO members use means other than trade for coercion – the second part of the hypothesis remains to be tested. Thus, I now investigate whether OECD countries condition nontrade policy instruments upon WTO members' human rights records to a greater extent than they do upon those of non-WTO members. To do so, I examine two specific policy levers: foreign aid allocation and GSP investigations. Foreign aid and GSP programs serve as ideal settings in which to assess the strength of the hypothesis because respect for human

---

[18] Alliance data come from Leeds et al. (2002), and aid data are from OECD (2011).
[19] Additionally, because colonizers tend to accord special trade privileges to their colonies, I include an indicator of whether the importer is a *Current Colonizer* of its partner. This indicator was collinear with the fixed effects in previous specifications but can now be included due to the larger time frame.

rights is commonly included in OECD states' criteria for governing both policy domains.

Foreign Aid

I first examine whether OECD members increase their use of foreign aid conditionality once their partners become WTO members. I test this hypothesis using data on OECD donor states' aid flows from 1981 to 2009. To estimate the model, I again include year and country-pair fixed effects in all specifications. The dependent variable is the logged net official development assistance (ODA) disbursements from OECD donor countries, measured in constant U.S. dollars.[20] The key independent variables are *Human Rights*, measured by Cingranelli and Pasquarello (1985), and that variable's interaction with *Both in WTO*, both of which were defined previously.

The inclusion of the fixed effects ensures that I need only control for key factors that vary over time and across country-pairs. The foreign aid literature specifies recipient need, recipient merit, and donor interests as important determinants of aid flows; thus, measures of these elements should be found in any such model (Hoeffler and Outram 2011). I account for recipient merit using respect for *Human Rights* (which is one of the key variables of interest) along with *Growth*, measured as growth in GDP per capita, and *Democracy*, measured using a binary indicator from Cheibub, Gandhi, and Vreeland (2010). For recipient need, I include log(*GDPPC*), measured in logged constant 1995 U.S. dollars, the *Infant Mortality* rate (per 1,000 live births), and log(*Population*). Because donor motivations for aid giving generally hinge on the donor's strategic environment, I include an indicator of a military *Alliance* between the donor and recipient, as alliances have been shown to drive aid flows (Hoeffler and Outram 2011; Leeds et al. 2002), along with *Power*, which I have argued influences both trade and aid. Additionally, donor interests may depend on the donor's trade relations with the recipient, so I include log(*Imports*) from the recipient. Many other common indicators of donor interest, such as the donor's colonial history with the recipient, global economic shocks, and geography, are controlled for by virtue of the fixed effects. Additional control variables can be found in the robustness checks.

The results of the analysis, presented in Table 6.2 and shown graphically in Figure 6.1, show strong support for the hypothesis. Among non-WTO members, the relationship between human rights and foreign aid is weak and insignificant. However, WTO members that show complete respect for human rights receive a large and statistically significant increase in aid relative to WTO members that do not respect rights, obtaining 243 percent ($p = 0.0001$) more aid than the most repressive states receive. These results are consistent with the claim that donors use foreign aid as a tool to promote human rights among

---

[20] The OECD defines ODA as nonmilitary grants and net loan disbursements which contain at least 25 percent in the form of a grant. The data come from OECD (2011).

TABLE 6.2. *Effect of WTO and Human Rights on Logged Foreign Aid*

Human Rights × *WTO*	0.742*
	(0.360)
Human Rights	0.491
	(0.305)
Both in WTO	−0.427
	(0.254)
log(*GDPPC*)	−0.419***
	(0.105)
Growth	0.022***
	(0.003)
Democracy	−0.153
	(0.112)
Infant Mortality	−0.021***
	(0.005)
Power	−7.920
	(14.755)
log(*Imports*)	0.011
	(0.007)
log(*Population*)	1.615**
	(0.588)
Alliance	−0.569**
	(0.216)
Constant	32.166***
	(5.821)
R^2	0.604
N	48883

Notes: Estimates from OLS regression. The unit of observation is the directed dyad-year and the dependent variable is the natural log of (*aid* +1). The data cover the years 1981–2009. Robust standard errors, clustered by directed dyad, appear in parentheses. Year and directed dyad fixed effects are not shown.
* $p < 0.05$, ** $p < 0.01$, *** $p < 0.001$.

WTO members, as there exists a strong correlation between aid and human rights for these states. However, for non-WTO members, the effect disappears. Taken with the previous results, this likely indicates that states tend to rely on trade for influence over these states instead. Figure 6.1 displays these results graphically, plotting the marginal effect of human rights on logged aid for WTO members versus nonmembers, along with the associated 95 percent confidence intervals.

I perform the same robustness checks as above, considering a variety of alternative model specification and coding decisions. First, I account for any time-varying factors affecting donor strategies or aid priorities. For example, donors' aid preferences, domestic political environments, ideologies, or other

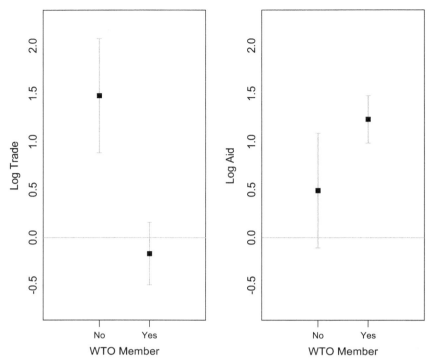

FIGURE 6.1. Effects of WTO and Human Rights on Logged Imports and Logged Aid. OLS regression estimates of the effect of full respect for human rights relative to no respect for human rights on logged imports and logged aid, conditional on WTO membership. Estimates presented with 95 percent confidence intervals.

variables that influence aid-giving may change over time in ways that are difficult to measure. I thus include time-varying donor fixed effects in addition to the country-pair and year fixed effects. Next, I respecify the outcome variable. Because the effect may take time to appear, I average the outcome variable over three periods, as is common in the foreign aid literature (Alesina and Dollar 2000). I then add additional control variables, including an indicator of *GSP* status, an indicator of an *RTA*, a measure of *FDI* inflows, and a measure of *Government Spending*. Finally, I use the alternative measures of human rights described earlier from Freedom House (2006). The results remain robust to each of these specifications.

Unilateral Preference Programs

Unilateral preference programs constitute a second area in which I expect states to use conditionality more frequently once their partners become WTO members. In particular, I focus on the U.S. GSP program, which places strong emphasis on human rights as an explicit criterion for eligibility, rendering it an instructive test of the theory. Under the program, if interested parties believe a GSP recipient has violated rights, they may file a petition requesting an investigation into that state's eligibility. The AFL-CIO files the vast majority of petitions in protest of recipients' poor human rights records.[21] The Office of the U.S. Trade Representative then chooses whether to investigate each claim and, if it does so, whether to suspend the recipient's GSP eligibility. I described this process more thoroughly in Chapter 3, where I also demonstrated that states frequently commence GSP investigations to pressure recipients to improve their human rights records.

The theory implies that these investigations should occur more frequently once states join the WTO. To test this, I collected data on all instances of U.S. GSP investigations due to violations of workers' rights, which I obtained directly from the Office of the U.S. Trade Representative. The data set begins in 1985, the year that the United States added workers' rights as a criterion for GSP eligibility, and ends in 2012, the most recent year for which data are available. Using these data, I first present some descriptive statistics: I compute the number of years that each GSP recipient was under investigation and compare the number of investigations that occurred in the five years prior to the recipient's WTO accession to the number of investigations that took place in the five years after that recipient joined the WTO. Thus, the sample contains GSP recipients that both joined the WTO between 1985 and 2012 and were under investigation within a ten year window of WTO entry; this includes sixteen countries. As shown in Table 6.2, in the five years prior to WTO accession, investigations occurred in only three country-years, whereas in the five years after joining, investigations took place in sixteen country-years.

While the large difference in the number of investigations conducted before versus after WTO entry is striking, I now investigate whether such a relationship between WTO membership and human rights investigations holds more systematically, using a sample containing all GSP-eligible states. The dependent variable is an indicator of the presence of a GSP investigation on the basis of workers' rights. The data set contains a total of 190 country-years during which investigations occurred. I conduct the analysis using a logit model, a statistical model that is often considered more appropriate when the outcome variable is binary, and include year and county fixed effects in all specifications. I thus estimate the effect among countries that were investigated at least once.

The variable of interest is an indicator of whether the recipient is a *WTO Member*. I also control for several other factors that could influence whether workers' rights investigations occur. First, such a decision should depend on the recipient's respect for *Workers' Rights*, which is measured by Cingranelli and Pasquarello (1985) on a scale from 1, indicating no respect for rights, to 3, indicating full respect. Second, a recipient may be investigated more frequently if it is less able to meet eligibility criteria for other reasons. The GSP guidelines

---

[21] Calculated using data collected from the Office of the U.S. Trade Representative.

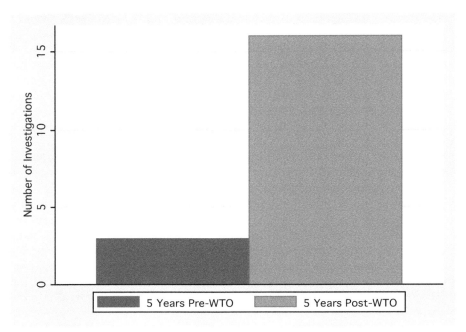

FIGURE 6.2. Years Under GSP Investigation Before and After WTO Entry.

explicitly state that eligibility depends on economic development; therefore, I add measures of log(*GDP*) and log(*GDPPC*). The guidelines also highlight the importance of trade openness, so I control for a recipient's total *Imports* and *Exports* as a percentage of GDP.[22] I also include *Terms of Trade*, the ratio of the price of exportable goods to that of importable goods, because this is an observable indicator often used to evaluate GSP eligibility.[23] Note that although an indicator of an alliance might be expected to affect investigations, there is no variation in this variable over the sample period, and so it drops out.

Table 6.3 demonstrates that the hypothesis is borne out by the data as WTO membership increases the likelihood of investigation strongly and significantly. The coefficient on *WTO Member*, 1.363, indicates that the odds of an investigation grow by 3.908 for WTO members relative to non-WTO members. Reassuringly, improvements in workers' rights significantly decrease the likelihood of an investigation based on violations of those rights. This result suggests that, as predicted, WTO membership leads to more GSP investigations because

---

[22] Imports and exports are common measures of openness. For instance, imports, exports, and GDP are used to calculate Deardorff's "openness index."
[23] All economic data come from World Bank (2011).

TABLE 6.3. *Effect of WTO on GSP Human Rights Investigations*

WTO Member	1.363*
	(0.642)
log(GDP)	5.323
	(2.865)
log(GDPPC)	−4.841
	(2.663)
Exports (% GDP)	0.064*
	(0.032)
Imports (% GDP)	−0.076**
	(0.031)
Terms of Trade	−0.004
	(0.006)
Workers' Rights	−0.962***
	(0.274)
Log likelihood	−167.032
Chi square	65.450
N	609

Notes: Estimates from logistic regression. The unit of observation is the directed dyad-year and the dependent variable is an indicator of the presence of a GSP investigation. The data cover the years 1985–2009. Year and directed dyad fixed effects are not shown. * $p < 0.05$, ** $p < 0.01$, *** $p < 0.001$.

states move away from using trade policies regulated by the WTO for coercive diplomacy and rely more heavily on GSP eligibility instead.

I also demonstrate the results' robustness to the addition of other variables that may affect whether an investigation occurs. I include measures that reflect the United States's economic relationship with the recipient, including log(*U.S. Aid*), *Total Aid*, and log(*U.S. Imports*). Finally, I include a measure of *Property Rights Enforcement*, which is sometimes considered when determining GSP eligibility, along with *Economic Growth*.[24] The results remain statistically and substantively significant, providing confidence in the robustness of the findings.

One potential worry is that these results could be explained by some other mechanism. For instance, perhaps states join the WTO once they improve human rights, which impacts trade and aid. Or maybe joining the WTO reduces other members' desires to exercise coercive diplomacy if the new entrant implemented significant reforms during the accession process. However, I find it unlikely that these processes drive the results for several reasons. First, while

[24] Property rights data are from Gwartney, Lawson, and Norton (2008).

some studies show that more democratic states which exhibit similar UN voting behavior to existing WTO members are more likely to enter the WTO (Davis and Wilf 2011), the results are robust to the inclusion of these variables. Second, the results are robust to the use of lagged human rights – the level of respect for rights preceding WTO entry – as the key independent variable. However, this is not completely satisfactory because lagged respect for human rights is highly correlated with current respect for human rights. More generally, selection bias may be an issue with each set of results in this chapter because states do not enter the WTO at random. This important issue is taken up and discussed extensively in the concluding chapter.

I now turn to other types of evidence to help assess my claims. In particular, historical and case study evidence can complement the statistical results presented here. In the following chapter, I thus adopt a qualitative approach to enrich and extend the analysis and to test an additional implication of the formal model. Specifically, I examine the United States's response to five prominent WTO accessions, showing that rather than reduce the United States's need to exercise coercion, WTO entry created strong incentives to identify alternative tools to use as leverage. Because the United States anticipated its persistent and strong desire to influence these states, it sought new means to do so. Furthermore, I show that in each of the five cases, the United States's ability to maintain comparable leverage over these states declined.

7

Reduced Effectiveness of Coercion
Evidence from the United States

The theoretical account provided in this study posits that political hold-up problems represent a central feature of interstate relations. Although international institutions can help to solve them, spurring investment, they displace coercive behavior into other policy areas. The statistical evidence shown in the previous chapters comports with the hypotheses developed in the formal model. Nonetheless, questions may remain regarding the underlying mechanism at work. In this chapter, I thus turn to a qualitative assessment of the process driving states' observed behavior and test an additional observable implication of the model.

In particular, in addition to the argument presented thus far, the theoretical account developed in Chapter 2 also clarifies the impact of international institutions on their members' *abilities* to exercise coercive diplomacy. This question is particularly important as states hold memberships in numerous international institutions, and yet they still seek to exert influence over other members. However, the theoretical framework showed that these institutions reduce their members' capacities for coercion. The model specifically predicted that whereas non-WTO members may rely on both trade and other tools to influence their partners, WTO members face higher costs from using trade for coercion against other WTO members. Because members rely less on a key source of leverage, these members should forfeit some coercive power.

This chapter integrates this additional insight with the findings from previous chapters to demonstrate how the model's many predictions all work together to explain the interplay between international institutions and coercive diplomacy. I focus in particular on coercion in the domain of human rights, showing that WTO membership diminishes states' capacities to influence their partners' human rights records. However, my purpose is not to develop a full theory of human rights treatment; rather, the limited objective is to demonstrate that accepting trade constraints limits leverage over human rights, with potential negative implications for human rights outcomes. Analyzing the causal relationship between WTO membership and human rights outcomes more generally is beyond the scope of my analysis.

7.1 WTO ENTRY AND U.S. INFLUENCE

To operationalize the model's prediction, this chapter examines the coercive strategies of a particular country: the United States. Closely following the United States's interactions with multiple partners allows me to demonstrate that its actions represent a pattern of behavior rather than a few isolated incidents. Furthermore, as the most powerful state in the international system, the United States possesses a wide range of tools, which illustrates the diversity of policies that serve as substitutes for trade. I thus explore all cases in which the United States strongly resisted providing WTO benefits to particular trade partners. I expect to find that when the United States's partners entered the WTO, the United States possessed less leverage over those states, or:

Hypothesis 10. *The United States experiences a diminished ability to exercise coercive diplomacy over WTO members, relative to non-WTO members.*

I begin the analysis at the WTO's creation in 1995, as I exclude GATT membership cases due to space constraints. I investigate the effects of each prominent WTO accession by a dissimilar partner since the WTO's creation, which includes Russia, China, Vietnam, Cambodia, and Romania. I show that, prior to these nations' WTO accessions, political hold-up problems persisted in the trade domain, but that once these states joined the WTO, the United States became less apt to use its WTO-regulated trade policies to extract reforms. The United States instead switched to other tools, such as asset freezes, foreign aid cuts, unilateral preference programs, and NATO membership conditionality. However, because the WTO reduced the United States's ability to apply a particularly powerful tool of coercive diplomacy – trade policy – these alternate levers typically achieved less success in realizing U.S. policy goals.

The cases also show that the United States relied heavily on trade policy manipulation to gain influence over non-WTO members. Specifically, when the U.S. Congress disapproved of policies enacted by nonmembers, it regularly offered MFN status renewal in exchange for policy concessions and threatened to revoke this status if the recipient would not meet Congress's demands. As explained previously, MFN treatment entitles countries to nondiscriminatory trade policies such that a country cannot alter tariffs for a partner with MFN status without altering its tariffs for all partners with MFN status. Although all WTO members must grant each other this treatment, extending it to non-WTO members remains unrestricted, and, indeed, the United States has taken full advantage of this option.

In particular, 1972 marked the passage of a bill that included the "Jackson-Vanik amendment," which blocked MFN status for countries that curbed emigration. The amendment required that the president grant yearly MFN waivers to countries disallowing emigration and that Congress renew MFN agreements every three years. The United States consistently applied the amendment to try to encourage political reforms, particularly in the human rights domain (Lilley and Willkie 1994, 8, 80–97). For example, the United States revoked MFN status from Poland after it became more repressive but then restored it in 1987, when Poland implemented liberalizing reforms (Pregelj 2005). Similarly, the United States rescinded it from Afghanistan in response to the kidnapping and killing of a U.S. ambassador in 1979 (Gladstone 2001, 40) and from Serbia and Montenegro due to "war-like activities" in 1992 (Pregelj 2005). The United States also used the threat of removing it to try to extract policy concessions from Albania, Georgia, Laos, and Ukraine and denied MFN status to Cuba and North Korea because of political frictions (Pregelj 2005).

However, when these countries joined the WTO, the United States lost its ability to revoke this status, because the WTO requires its members to grant each other permanent MFN treatment, also known as permanent normal trade relations (PNTR).[1] The United States often explicitly recognized that this would be a particular benefit of its partner's WTO accession and, similarly, the potential entrant often sought membership to restrain the United States. Thus, when the United States gave its dissimilar partners PNTR (along with WTO membership), it switched to alternative levers of influence to pursue its policy goals, though it generally became less able to obtain concessions from its partners. I now examine specific, detailed cases in which this occurred.

7.2 RUSSIA: THE MAGNITSKY ACT AND HUMAN RIGHTS

Prior to Russia's WTO entry, the United States had long used its trade policies for coercion on states with highly dissimilar policy preferences. The Export Control Act of 1949 represented perhaps the most prominent effort to do so. This act allowed the United States to curb exports to the Soviet Union, and it was then formalized with the establishment of the Coordinating Committee for Multilateral Export Controls (COCOM). COCOM created lists detailing prohibited exports, limited exports, and exports under surveillance and was often used in attempts to extract political concessions from the Soviet Union (Dobson 1988). For instance, the United States warned that it would implement even stricter sanctions and strengthen COCOM if the Soviet Union invaded Poland (Dobson 2005).

---

[1] An exception to this rule occurs if a particular member invokes GATT Article XXXV, as discussed later.

Similar examples abound. After the USSR's invasion of Afghanistan in 1979, the United States placed an embargo on wheat, corn, and soybeans to the Soviet Union, canceling $17 million worth of contracts. It also suspended high technology and other export licensing, reduced fishing privileges in U.S. waters, and enacted additional penalties. The United States hoped the embargo would pressure the USSR to withdraw its military from Afghanistan (Heritage Foundation 1981), and many analysts suggested that such an embargo could be used to obtain other concessions too. For instance, the U.S. secretary of agriculture stated, "Food is now a great weapon for keeping peace" (Heritage Foundation 1981). Later that year, after the United States attributed rights violations in Poland to the USSR's activities, the United States strengthened the sanctions, which included the suspension of all export licenses and new restrictions on energy technology.

The impact of these sanctions on the USSR depended on the relationship specificity of the goods in question. For instance, though the USSR found alternative sources of grain from Argentina, Australia, Canada, and domestic producers, this switch was not cost-free. Furthermore, unlike grain, technology and machinery represented areas in which the USSR could not secure alternative supplies (Smith 1984, 25). Instead, it was forced to purchase lower quality goods from Eastern Europe and through illegal means. According to the U.S. Department of Defense, doing so was much more costly, making this a relatively effective trade weapon (U.S. Government 1985).

Subsequently, the United States continued to make many trade threats and concessions to push for improvements in other areas such as the Soviet Union's human rights record (Columbus 2003, 67–68), particularly once U.S. president Reagan took office. Indeed, "trade pressure became a central plank of America's trade policy towards Moscow when Reagan was elected to the Presidency. The political Cold War was thus supplemented by an economic Cold War" (Ishaq 1999, 67). For instance, Reagan tried to link trade between the two nations to concessions in the Strategic Arms Limitation Talks (SALT) treaties (Knorr and Trager 1977, 68). Furthermore, both Reagan and Nixon explicitly tied trade to human rights, promising to expand trade in exchange for concessions in this area. For instance, Nixon wrote in *Foreign Affairs*, "for the United States to increase trade... at a time when they [the USSR] are engaging in political activities that are opposed to our interests would be stupid and dangerous" (Nixon 1985, 6). In particular, emigration, treatment of dissidents, and freedom to dissent represented the United States's main objectives, especially due to the hundreds of thousands of Jews who wanted to emigrate but were not allowed to do so (Buwalda 1997, 197–97).

The United States also connected emigration and human rights to the yearly renewals of normal trade relations status under the Jackson-Vanik amendment. While the United States had signed a 1991 bilateral trade agreement with Russia, which came into force in 1992 and provided Russia with normal trade relations status, the United States used its renewal to threaten Russia each year with the reapplication of the tariff levels imposed under the Smoot – Hawley act. These tariff levels were enacted during the Depression and reached up to 50 percent ad valorem, which would cut off Russia's imports from the U.S. market if implemented (Aslund and Hufbauer 2011, 2). Russia's desire to join the WTO stemmed in part from its wish to end these annual reviews, which represented a "key irritant in Russian-U.S. relations."[2]

This persistent reliance on trade as a weapon led to underinvestment in trade between the two states, as the Soviet Union had "never made itself dependent in these matters on the benevolence of Western partners" (Knorr and Trager 1977, 106). For instance, in the years following the U.S. grain embargo, the Soviet Union dramatically decreased its livestock sector because it relied extensively on U.S. grain (American Farm Bureau Federation 2012) – a mildly costly adjustment. Even after the United States lifted the embargo in late 1981 and Reagan pledged not to use grain as a political tool again, the USSR did not purchase its grain from the United States due to its belief that the United States was an unreliable source. In fact, the United States's share of grain exports did not rise to their pre-embargo levels until 1988 (Ishaq 1999, 72). The United States anticipated this behavior, as it worried that the embargo might lead the USSR to trade and invest less with the United States as a result (Heritage Foundation 1981).

More generally, "the President made clear his desire to deny the USSR advanced Western technology and punish it economically through the use of American trade and economic coercion.... [Thus,] the USSR never amounted to more than 1% of overall American foreign trade with the exception of 1979.... America accounted for less than 2% [of the USSR's imports] (in 1980) and never rose above 2% again during the 1980s" (Ishaq 1999, 69). Indeed, it was widely acknowledged that trade between the United States and Russia remained low due to continuing political frictions (Cain 1995). For example, former U.S. secretary of state Madeline Albright stated that bilateral trade fell "significantly short of its potential" but that she anticipated that granting Russia PNTR status along with its WTO entry would help to rectify the situation.[3] Ishaq (1999, 69) succinctly sums up the state of affairs between the two countries: "As two superpowers confronting each other on a global scale their mutual mistrust spilled over into the economic sphere. In the early days of the Cold War economic ties were almost unthinkable."

However, manipulating trade policies for coercive diplomacy was somewhat effective in eliciting certain concessions from the Soviet Union due to the Soviet Union's desire for increased trade with the United States, particularly once Gorbachev took office. Though the Soviet Union was relatively

---

[2] See Valeria Korchagina and Stephen Boykewich, "WTO Agreement Expected in Weeks," *Moscow Times*, June 26, 2006.
[3] See Madeline Albright, "A New Agenda for U.S.-Russia Cooperation," *International Herald Tribune*, December 30, 2012.

powerful and therefore was not very vulnerable to coercive tactics, it did make marginal improvements as a result, as "the dire state of the economy made Moscow conscious that competition and confrontation with Washington was not profitable" (Ishaq 1999, 62). Although many factors likely led to these concessions, it is widely thought that the United States's economic pressure represented an important catalyst. Ishaq (1999, 174) argues, "It would be incorrect to conclude that the use of economic pressure by America had no influence whatsoever on Soviet political thinking. There is no doubt that U.S. trade pressure had some bearing on the conduct of Soviet behavior, with Gorbachev in particular sensitive to the damage to East-West relations and to the Soviet Union's reputation done by international criticism of its actions in the domestic and international arenas." Furthermore, "Gorbachev's realization of the need for change in Soviet policy on human rights and in its involvement in areas of regional instability was driven by domestic concerns, and was certainly influenced by the adverse effect of U.S. trade pressure on the USSR which was depriving Moscow of much-needed Western technology and credits" (Ishaq 1999, 177).

For instance, when U.S. president George H. W. Bush took office in 1988, Gorbachev made a speech at the UN in which he promised to cut back on arms unilaterally, reduce involvement abroad, allow emigration, stop persecution for religious or political reasons, and accept decisions on human rights agreements by the World Court. In addition to making promises, several laws were altered as well. In 1987, freedom of demonstration was allowed, debates on previously outlawed subjects were permitted, the submission of scripts for censorship by the media was no longer required, psychiatric abuse was made punishable, many political prisoners were authorized to leave psychiatric institutions, and criminal law was amended to reduce the applicability of the death penalty.[4] The USSR took concrete actions, including allowing 8,000 Jews to emigrate prior to a 1987 summit with the United States, the most permitted to do so since 1982, and then let 19,292 more emigrate in 1988 (Buwalda 1997, 154–60). Reagan declared that these measures represented a "sizable improvement," and the U.S. State Department concluded that they were "more than cosmetic and less than fundamental."[5]

As a result, during debates in the U.S. Congress over a bill that would extend PNTR to Russia – which would pave the way for its WTO accession – members worried that doing so would diminish the United States's leverage over the country. For example, Congressman Devin Nunes argued against granting PNTR to Russia, stating, "The 1974 Jackson-Vanik amendment [MFN conditionality] effectively pressured the Soviet Union over its appalling human rights

---

[4] See "Gorbachev's Speech to the U.N.," *CNN*, 43rd U.N. General Assembly Session, December 7, 1988.
[5] See U.S. Department of State, "Human Rights Policy and Practice," *Country Reports on Human Rights Practices for 1987*, 1987, 47.

record."⁶ Similarly, Congressman Peter DeFazio warned, "We are giving up the tools we have to try and push Russia.... We have more power today with the capability of depriving them of a normal trade relations status with the United States. If we want to use our clout, we should vote this bill down."⁷ Congressman Bill Pascrell also opposed the bill, stating, "I'd like to use trade as leverage."⁸

As these members of Congress anticipated, the United States lost its ability to exercise coercive diplomacy using WTO-regulated trade once Russia entered the WTO in 2012, and trade between the United States and Russia thus began to grow. In the year following Russia's WTO entry, U.S. exports to Russia increased 29 percent, and rose by another 10.5 percent in the first quarter of the following year, which a U.S. report attributed to Russia's WTO entry.⁹ While exports from Russia to the United States remained relatively stable, this was in large part due to U.S. technological innovation. The primary product the U.S. imports from Russia is oil, and with the United States's improvements in fracking technology, these imports plummeted (Energy Information Administration 2014). Taking this into account, it appears that Russia's WTO membership facilitated trade between the two states, albeit not dramatically.¹⁰

Furthermore, because Congress worried that Russia's WTO entry would remove its ability to influence Russia, it attached additional human rights provisions to the bill granting Russia's PNTR status. These provisions were derived from the Magnitsky Act, which was named after a lawyer who had been imprisoned in Moscow due to his investigation of tax fraud by Russian officials. The provisions prohibited the officials blamed for the incident as well as any other individuals involved in human rights violations from entering the United States and from using the U.S. banking system.

Members of Congress readily acknowledged that the bill's purpose was to create other forms of pressure because Congress could no longer rely on using the United States's trade policies. Congressman Howard Berman stated, "Just as Jackson-Vanik [MFN conditionality] became a tool to deal with one aspect of a horrible set of policies by the Soviet Union during the Cold War, we now, using the Magnitsky legislation, deal with some very serious human rights issues remaining in Russia, but not in the context of restricting trade."¹¹ Senator Cardin added, "Today we close a chapter in the U.S. history on the advancing of human rights with the repeal basically of Jackson-Vanik [MFN

---

⁶ See "Russia and Moldove Jackson-Vanir Repeal and Sergei Magnitsky Rule of Law Accountability Act of 2012," *Congressional Record*, Vol. 158, No. 147, November 16, 2012, H6410.
⁷ Ibid., H6414.
⁸ Ibid.
⁹ See Doug Palmer, "U.S. Puts Russia on Notice in First Report on WTO Compliance," Reuters, June 19, 2013.
¹⁰ See ibid.
¹¹ See "Russia and Moldove Jackson-Vanir Repeal and Sergei Magnitsky Rule of Law Accountability Act of 2012," *Congressional Record*, Vol. 158, No. 147, November 16, 2012, H6409.

conditionality]. It served its purpose. Today, we open a new chapter in U.S. leadership for human rights with the Sergei Magnitsky Rule of Law Accountability Act."[12] Similarly, Congressman Robert Brady stated that because PNTR would eliminate a source of leverage over Russia, "this legislation also creates important new tools to continue to pressure Russia to make progress on the important issue of human rights."[13] As the surrounding congressional testimony makes clear, the U.S. Congress approved PNTR for Russia only after it had instituted visa bans and asset freezes to gain leverage over the country's human rights policies.

These alternative measures, however, do not appear to have persuaded Russia to make concessions. For instance, rather than "conduct a proper investigation and hold those responsible for [Magnitsky's] death accountable," as the U.S. State Department specifically requested, Russia responded to the Magnitsky bill by prohibiting U.S. citizens from adopting Russian children, restricting U.S. funding for NGOs in Russia, and banning eighteen U.S. citizens from entering Russia.[14] In addition, because the Magnitsky bill allowed the United States to use asset restrictions for leverage, many Russian officials withdrew their assets from the United States.[15]

More generally, while the WTO's impact on trends in human rights and democracy in Russia are difficult to assess, because Russia entered the WTO very recently (in 2012), it is possible to compare its human rights scores in the two years prior to its entry to the two years following its entry. Though CIRI has only released its data through 2011 at this time of this writing, Freedom House has published its scores through 2014. Examining Freedom House scores, which range from 0 to 16 from least to most respect for rights, movement only occurred in two of the seven categories over this four-year period. Specifically, Russia's associational and organizational rights fell from an average score of 4.5 in the two years prior to entry to 4 in the two years post, and personal autonomy and individual rights fell from an average of 7 in the two years prior to 6.5 in the two years post. Thus, if anything, Russia's respect for human rights has declined since its accession.

7.3 CHINA: THE CHINA COMMISSION AND RIGHTS VIOLATIONS

Prior to China's 2001 WTO entry, the United States relied heavily on trade policy manipulation to place political pressure on China. For instance, the

---

[12] See "Russia and Moldova Jackson-Vanir Repeal and Sergei Magnitsky Rule of Law Accountability Act of 2012," *Congressional Record*, Vol. 158, No. 155, December 5, 2012, S7437.
[13] See "Russia and Moldove Jackson-Vanir Repeal and Sergei Magnitsky Rule of Law Accountability Act of 2012," *Congressional Record*, Vol. 158, No. 147, November 16, 2012, H6410.
[14] See Jim Heintz, "Russia Responds to U.S. Magnitsky Act by Placing 18 Americans on Blacklist," Associated Press, April 13, 2013.
[15] See Philip Aldrick, "Sergei Magnitsky Death: US Politicians Move to Ban Russians from Entering America," *The Telegraph*, September 29, 2010.

Trading with the Enemy of Act of 1917 outlawed U.S. exports to Communist countries, including China, and the Export Control Act of 1949 essentially had the same effect. These bans were formalized in 1952, when the United States set up the China Commission (CHINCOM) to oversee the restrictions, particularly due to China's involvement in the Korean War (Grzybowski 1973). In 1979 the United States and China signed a bilateral trade agreement that granted China short-term MFN status and was renewed yearly by the United States.

After the Tiananmen Square incident, the United States imposed numerous sanctions including Ex-Im Bank financing restrictions; Overseas Private Investment Corporation (OPIC) and Trade and Development Program project suspensions; aid cuts; and military, nuclear, and satellite export bans. Furthermore, this incident triggered a yearly debate in the U.S. Congress regarding whether to suspend China's MFN status. During each renewal period, Congress repeatedly threatened China with tariff increases unless China addressed the United States's concerns regarding human rights, weapons proliferation, and trade (Lilley and Willkie 1994, 24). The potential impact of these higher U.S. tariffs on the Chinese economy was severe, because the United States represented China's most important export market, and no other market was large enough to absorb such a high volume of Chinese goods. In 1993 the World Bank estimated that if MFN were rescinded, China would lose $7 to $15 billion annually in exports to the United States, and the U.S. – China Business Council estimated that its import tariffs would increase ninefold on average.[16]

Although the initial sanctions did not elicit much of a response from China, as highlighted by President Bush's statement that "there hasn't been much give" in its human rights policies,[17] the MFN renewal debates did elicit small improvements, particularly in the areas of extrajudicial killings and the jailing of political prisoners. Indeed, although many other sanctions were quickly lifted, the MFN threats persisted, leading China to make concessions in advance of the votes each year. For instance, in early May 1990, China released 211 prisoners who were arrested in the Tiananmen Square protests. Reports stated, "Diplomats and Chinese intellectuals say the move seems aimed at improving China's image abroad and, in particular, derailing U.S. lawmakers' efforts to take away China's most-favored-nation trade status."[18] Then, in June 1990, China permitted emigration by Fang Lizhi (a prominent dissident) and his wife to the United Kingdom, which represented a major issue during the controversy over whether to grant MFN to China that month.[19]

---

[16] See "Case Studies in Sanctions and Terrorism," Peterson Institute for International Economics, Case 89–2.
[17] See Robert Pear, "Bush Distressed as Policy Fails to Move China," *New York Times*, March 11, 1990.
[18] See "Case Studies in Sanctions and Terrorism," Peterson Institute for International Economics, Case 89–2.
[19] See "China Allows 2 Dissidents to End Yearlong Refuge," *Deseret News*, June 25, 1990.

President Clinton also explicitly linked MFN renewal to human rights improvements in 1993, stating that China must allow emigration, permit investigations into goods made with prison labor, provide the Red Cross with access to prisons, release political prisoners, permit open media broadcasting, and agree to dialogue on Tibet (Lilley and Willkie 1994, 13–14, 29). In response, to "give Clinton just enough of a political fig leaf to reject calls to punish China with stiff trade tariffs," China released political prisoners from Tibet, initiated talks to permit the Red Cross to visit prisons, and stated it would allow the United States to inspect five prisons that were suspected of producing goods for export.[20] China then let U.S. technicians visit to talk about China's "Voice of America" broadcast jamming. Each of these concessions was attributed to the upcoming MFN vote.[21]

This back and forth continued through the early 1990s, and between 1990 and 1993, China made many policy concessions in exchange for low U.S. tariffs: it released 881 Tiananmen prisoners, lifted martial law, provided information on high-profile political prisoners, agreed not to export products made with prison labor, allowed the Red Cross to visit prisoners, sent two human rights delegations to the United States, and gave passports to many families of political exiles (Lilley and Willkie 1994, 86). Though these represented real reforms, many reports concluded that they "amount[ed] to incremental rather than fundamental change[s] in China's hard-line policies on human rights."[22] China admitted as much, as officials stated to a U.S. envoy that they would make human rights concessions to the United States but would not implement large political changes.[23]

However, this extensive use of trade for coercion dampened economic exchange between the United States and China. Bilateral investment declined in the 1990s (Walmsley, Hertel, and Ianchovichina 2006), suggesting that prior to China's WTO membership, hold-up problems persisted between the two states. Furthermore, WTO accession was recognized as a means of increasing investment and trade. For instance, Senator Paul Wellstone argued, "I think the evidence is pretty clear. [Permanent MFN status] will result in ... more investment."[24]

Thus, the United States commenced a debate over whether to provide China with PNTR in 2000, the last major hurdle to its WTO entry. Both China and the United States recognized that once China entered the WTO, any leverage

---

[20] See Clay Chandler and Daniel Southerland, "China Moving Slowly on Rights Issues; Steps May Yet Meet Minimum Demands Set for U.S. Trade," *Washington Post*, January 20, 1994.
[21] Ibid.
[22] Ibid.
[23] See "Case Studies in Sanctions and Terrorism," Peterson Institute for International Economics, Case 89-2.
[24] See "To Authorize Extension of Non-Discriminatory Treatment to the People's Republic of China," *Congressional Record*, Vol. 151, Part 13, September 19, 2000, 18340.

over the country through trade would be dramatically curtailed. In fact, China's desire to end the annual MFN renewals represented one of its incentives to join the WTO (Prime 2002). Many U.S. government officials acknowledged the reduced coercive ability that would accompany China's WTO entry as well. For instance, Congressman Chris Smith urged Congress to "deny China's PNTR today – require them to move in the direction of reform and the protection of human rights."[25]

For its part, China sought to convince the United States that relinquishing its ability to use trade for leverage was unimportant because the United States would not need to exercise coercive diplomacy against it. In the run-up to the U.S. Congress's debate over China's WTO entry, China launched a $7 million public relations campaign in the United States that received funding from corporations that sought China's WTO entry.[26] The *New York Times* called it "a touring cultural extravaganza intended to introduce Americans to China,"[27] which featured performances, exhibitions, lectures, and question-and-answer sessions with top Chinese officials. China's president stated that the tour was intended to "allow the American people to hear first-hand its peaceful intentions, and help foster good relations with the United States," and the Chinese ambassador to the United States underscored its intention to promote "mutual understanding and friendship." The touring group proclaimed that China strongly respected human rights and that China and the West had much in common.[28] Thus, to persuade the United States to relinquish its capacity to use its trade policies opportunistically, China tried to highlight that the United States would not need the trade tool.

The U.S. Congress agreed to provide PNTR to China in 2000, leading to China's 2001 WTO entry, which caused investment and capital stocks to grow rapidly (Walmsley, Hertel, and Ianchovichina 2006). Both imports and exports roughly doubled from 2000 to 2004, as U.S. exports rose from $16.185 billion to $34.428 billion, and its imports increased from $100.018 billion to $196.662 billion (U.S. Census Bureau 2013). U.S. reports note the WTO's significance for trade between the two states, stating, "China's WTO membership offers an important tool for managing the increasingly complex U.S.-China trade relationship. A common WTO rulebook and an impartial body in Geneva have helped the two sides resolve differences and the United States has not hesitated to pursue its rights with China through WTO dispute settlement" (House Hearing 2011). The China Commission also stated, "In defense of the

---

[25] See "To Authorize Extension of Non-Discriminatory Treatment to the People's Republic of China," *Congressional Record*, Vol. 146, Part 7, May 24, 2000, 9100.
[26] See Elisabeth Rosenthal, "China's U.S. Road Show, Aimed at Making Friends," *New York Times*, August 23, 2000.
[27] Ibid.
[28] Ibid.

WTO and the agreement that was reached, it has in fact worked in terms of the dispute settlement process when the cases have been brought to the WTO. China has been willing to engage in that process. The Chinese have adhered to the results when the results have gone against them" (House Hearing 2011). As a result, "trade and investment also expanded dramatically between China and its many trading partners, including the United States. Indeed, this expansion in trade and investment has provided numerous and substantial opportunities for U.S. businesses, workers, farmers and service suppliers, and a wealth of affordable goods for U.S. consumers" (House Hearing 2011).

However, many members of Congress argued that because PNTR would reduce the United States's ability to pressure China using trade policy, the United States should promote its policy goals through other mechanisms. Congress therefore introduced the Levin – Bereuter proposal, which established a commission to monitor China's human rights performance. Congressman Robert Underwood explained, "Once China is a member of the WTO, the United States still can impose sanctions on China but they have to be 'WTO consistent.'... There are many other processes to affect this 'leverage' over China. For example, the U.S. could use the power of the Export-Import Bank, TDA [Trade and Development Agency] and OPIC to apply pressure on China. Finally, the Levin-Bereuter language... will annually grant this body the opportunity to investigate and criticize China's abuse in these areas."[29] Similarly, Congressman Steny Hoyer claimed that monitoring China's human rights performance would allow Congress to maintain diplomatic influence over China, arguing, "A China commission will be a more effective mechanism for maintaining pressure on China on human rights, worker rights, and rule of law issues than our brief annual [MFN] reviews."[30]

The United States introduced other tools as well. Congress put forward a bill that would link China's ability to host the 2008 Olympics to its human rights performance. Congressman Christopher Cox stated, "In the few days since Congress has approved expanding trade with the PRC through the World Trade Organization, there has already been backsliding. Conditioning any future Olympics in the PRC on compliance with Olympic principles will help increase international pressure for human rights improvements," where the "backsliding" was in reference to China's statement that the Tiananmen Square incident was "fabricated."[31] In addition, the day after U.S. president Clinton stated that the United States would take an "all out" effort to secure China's WTO entry,[32] he also announced that the United States would introduce a

---

[29] See "To Authorize Extension of Non-Discriminatory Treatment to the People's Republic of China," *Congressional Record*, Vol. 146, Part 7, May 24, 2000, 9131.
[30] Ibid., 9112.
[31] See "Lawmakers Introduce Measure on 2008 Olympics, Human Rights," *Washington File*, September 29, 2000.
[32] See "Remarks to the American Embassy Community in Ankara, Turkey," November 15, 1999.

UN resolution condemning China's human rights record, which elicited mild improvements.[33] Indeed, using other venues to criticize China's human rights abuses was a central aspect of the U.S. administration's plan to allow China to join.[34]

China's impending WTO entry thus led the United States to switch its focus from trade policy conditionality to other levers of influence. The China Commission, composed of nine senators, nine members of the House, and five senior officials appointed by the president, began to report annually to the president and Congress. Its mission is explicitly linked to China's WTO membership, as a recent report stated, "Ten years ago this week, China acceded to the World Trade Organization (WTO). Prior to that, the United States granted China permanent normal trade relations, or PNTR. This Commission was formed in that process with a mandate to monitor human rights and the development of the rule of law, or the lack of progress thereof, in China" (House Hearing 2011). In addition to the commission, other avenues for dialogue were used in place of the PNTR tool to pressure China. As the USTR highlighted in the China Commission's hearing, "the WTO framework does not deal directly with labor rights, however the U.S. Trade Representative's Office participates in several forums where these issues are dealt with. One is the labor dialogue, which also involves our Labor Department, which is an important venue for dealing with some of these issues. In addition, we participate in the human rights dialogue, which is led by the State Department, which also deals with these questions. I think there is no question that this was part of the reason why your Commission was created" (House Hearing 2011).

However, rather than improve its human rights in line with U.S. requests, China became less apt to comply with U.S. demands and generally retaliated against the United States instead. Whereas China exhibited minimal compliance with U.S. requests prior to its WTO entry, it made few, if any, concessions in response to U.S. pressure afterward. Prominent dissident Wei Jingsheng wrote in the *New York Times*, "In my time, the Communist Party kept its promise for as long as one year because human rights were directly linked with trade. Now that such international pressure does not exist, the party no longer feels the need to keep its word."[35] Numerous accounts highlight the lack of improvement in China's human rights. For instance, a recent assessment states, "As a member of the WTO ... China continues to massively violate the basic human rights of its own people," before going on to detail these violations. It also notes, "Far from becoming freer, the Chinese people are burdened with limited or no rights to basic freedoms of speech, religion, and assembly. And it's getting worse" (House Hearing 2011). Furthermore, in 2008, the U.S. State

---

[33] See "Case Studies in Sanctions and Terrorism," Peterson Institute for International Economics, Case 89–2.
[34] See "Prepare for Fireworks," *The Economist*, January 20, 2000.
[35] Wei Jingsheng, "Don't Believe China's Promises," *New York Times*, May 4, 2012.

Department released its assessment of China's human rights record in which it cited considerable evidence from the China Commission's studies. In response, China published a paper on the United States's human rights performance in which it condemned U.S. policies.[36] Indeed, critiques of China's human rights policies have never been particularly effective; for instance, China also released a retaliatory report in 1999 in response to a similarly critical human rights review (Wan 2001, 21). However, once the United States relinquished its trade tool, it had to rely on this form of pressure instead.

Human rights statistics also point toward the conclusion that the United States lost a modest amount of leverage over China after its WTO entry. While Freedom House scores are only available in the aggregate over this time period, CIRI Human Rights scores provide detailed information for all of the years under study. Looking at the average human rights performance in sixteen categories four years before WTO entry versus four years after, variation exists in the categories of disappearances and extrajudicial killings, which are measured on a scale of 0-2, and physical integrity, which includes "the right not to be tortured, extrajudicially killed, disappeared, or imprisoned for political beliefs" and is measured on a scale of 0-8. China's performance regarding disappearances regressed after entry from an average of 2 to an average of 0.75, its score regarding extrajudicial killings dropped from an average of 0.25 to 0, and its physical integrity performance fell from an average of 2.25 to 0.75.

7.4 VIETNAM: THE HUMAN RIGHTS ACT

During the period between the normalization of U.S.-Vietnam relations in the mid-1990s and Vietnam's 2007 WTO accession, the United States depended primarily upon its trade policies to pressure Vietnam to improve its human rights record. Prior to 1998, the United States held out MFN status as a potential reward if Vietnam made improvements in its human rights and emigration policies. The United States lifted the economic embargo in 1994, in part due to cooperation regarding missing prisoners of war (POW) (Usa 2009, 22). In 1996, the two states launched the Resettlement Opportunity for Vietnamese Returnees (ROVR), which offered "a final chance at a U.S. resettlement interview to eligible Vietnamese who were then still in first asylum camps in Southeast Asia, or who had recently returned to Vietnam" (U.S. Department of State 2004). In 1997 the United States and Vietnam targeted fifteen hundred potential citizens per month for the program. After a rocky start, the U.S. ambassador and secretary of state both made it clear that MFN would not be granted unless the ROVR agreement were successfully implemented. In response, Vietnam abandoned many cumbersome requirements and

---

[36] See "The Human Rights Record of United States in 2008," *China View*, February 26, 2009.

bureaucratic red tape, leading thirteen thousand citizens to be cleared for the program.[37]

Citing progress in these areas, President Clinton granted Vietnam conditional MFN trade status in 1998, which the United States renewed yearly depending upon Vietnam's human rights record.[38] Furthermore, owing to these renewals, Vietnam continued to make concessions, such as reducing similar bureaucratic requirements under the Orderly Departure Program (ODP), which allowed virtually all 480,000 applicants to emigrate by the end of 1998. This led the assistant secretary for East Asian and Pacific affairs to declare,

> The Jackson-Vanik Amendment is working just as its authors intended. The prospect of obtaining a waiver prompted Vietnam to simplify processing procedures for ROVR last October. It then served to encourage significant progress in clearing applicants for interview. With the waiver granted in March but a review process around the corner in June, Vietnam understood the need to demonstrate a further positive evolution, hence the additional procedural simplifications made in April and June. Next year Vietnam will again be required to face review; to continue enjoying the benefits that the Jackson-Vanik waiver provides, the GVN [Government of Vietnam] will be constrained to continue taking steps to advance the freedom of emigration. (Roth 1998)

He then went on to highlight Vietnam's human rights improvements. While acknowledging that Vietnam needed to do more in this area, he commended Vietnam for providing the United States with access to many POW records and discussing enhanced cooperation in locating POW remains using new technologies (Manyin 2006). Similarly, the U.S. ambassador to Vietnam stated, "The yearly renewal of the Jackson-Vanik waiver, it seems clear to me, influenced Vietnam to facilitate ODP processing."[39]

Because Congress and the U.S. president consistently threatened to revoke trade concessions over human rights concerns,[40] Vietnam made several human rights reforms, such as signing an agreement on religious freedom in which it pledged to improve conditions for religious citizens (Manyin 2006).[41] Improvements, although real, were also not comprehensive. A U.S. report prepared to provide background for Congress prior to the vote over PNTR indicated,

> [Vietnam] appears to have followed a strategy of generally relaxing most restrictions on most forms of personal and religious expression while selectively repressing individuals

---

[37] See Stanley Roth, "Waiver of Jackson-Vanik for Vietnam," State Department, Testimony before the Senate Finance Committee, July 7, 1998.

[38] See the discussion in the *Congressional Record* each year the waiver was granted. For example, in the 1998 act titled "Disapproving Extension of Waiver Authority with Respect to Vietnam," members of Congress make many arguments that the waiver should not be approved because of human rights violations.

[39] See Douglas Peterson, "Jackson-Vanik Waiver for Vietnam," *State Department, Testimony before the House Ways and Means Committee, Subcommittee on Trade*, July 18, 1998.

[40] See the numerous bills introduced in Congress to prohibit trade with states such as Vietnam, that violate human rights, including, among others, H.R. 967 in February 17, 2005.

[41] The agreement has not been released publicly.

and organizations it deems a threat to the party's monopoly on political power. Vietnamese living in the country's urban areas generally enjoy wide and expanding latitude to exercise their civil, economic, and religious liberties. In contrast, conditions are more restrictive in more rural areas.... Many observers have pointed to evidence of improvements in the general human rights situation in Vietnam in 2005 and 2006, even as conditions remain difficult for certain individuals, groups, and in certain regions. (Manyin 2006, 21)

Furthermore, a 2008 U.S. report declared, "Since late 2004 the Vietnamese government has responded positively to many U.S. human rights demands" (Manyin 2008). The U.S. National Economic Council also lists numerous improvements resulting from the linkage between trade and political concessions, citing the release of prisoners, POW concessions, and the resettlement of refugees (National Economic Council 2000).

In 2001 the United States signed a bilateral trade agreement with Vietnam that represented the last major hurdle to Vietnam's WTO accession. The agreement did not require any concessions from the United States; rather, it laid out Vietnam's WTO accession terms (Manyin 2001).[42] The U.S. Congress intensely debated the agreement's passage, as it recognized that Vietnam's near-certain WTO accession would eliminate the United States's ability to credibly threaten to terminate Vietnam's MFN status if Vietnam violated human rights. For instance, Representative Zoe Lofgren argued for continuing to tie human rights to MFN renewal rather than passing the agreement because "if we insist that Vietnam improve its human rights record as a condition to trading with America, we would gain human rights advances in Vietnam, so I think it is a tragic mistake for the United States to decline to use this tool."[43]

However, once Congress relinquished trade as a lever of influence, trade between the United States and Vietnam increased dramatically. Prior to Vietnam's WTO entry, trade between the two states had increased very gradually each year. Afterward, trade shot up dramatically, as U.S. exports to Vietnam grew from $1.1 billion in 1996 to $2.789 billion in 2008, and its imports rose from $8.566 billion to $12.901 billion over the same period (U.S. Census Bureau 2013).

To compensate for losing leverage over Vietnam in the trade realm, the U.S. Congress sought to tie Vietnam's aid allocation and GSP status to its human rights practices instead. On the same day that Congress passed the trade agreement, the House approved a companion bill, H.R. 1587, by a vote of 410–1 to prohibit nonhumanitarian increases in aid for Vietnam unless the

---

[42] Although note that, until Vietnam's official entry into the WTO, the United States still exercised considerable leverage in its trade relations with Vietnam, as exemplified by their dispute over catfish (Davis 2006).
[43] See "Disapproval of Normal Trade Relations Treatment of Products of Vietnam," *Congressional Record*, Vol. 147, No. 106, July 26, 2001, H4640.

Vietnamese government "made substantial progress toward releasing all political and religious prisoners from imprisonment, house arrest, and other forms of detention... respecting the right to freedom of religion... respecting the human rights of members of ethnic minority groups... [and was not] complicit in a severe form of trafficking in persons."[44] Congressional debate emphasized that the bill's purpose was to connect aid to respect for human rights due to the decoupling of MFN status and human rights after the trade agreement's passage. Congressman Henry Hyde stated, "This bill makes clear that progress towards freedom and democracy will continue to be a central theme of U.S. foreign policy toward Vietnam. It uses forms of leverage other than trade sanctions to promote this objective, such as conditions on non-humanitarian foreign assistance."[45]

Congress also sought to tie Vietnam's GSP status to its human rights record. Senator Barbara Boxer introduced the Vietnam Human Rights Act of 2008, which would prohibit GSP authorization for Vietnam unless it was certified as making progress in labor rights."[46] The bill proposed this new lever of influence because, it stated, "since Vietnam's accession to the WTO on January 11, 2007, the Government of Vietnam arbitrarily arrested and imprisoned numerous individuals for their peaceful advocacy of religious freedom, democracy, and human rights."[47]

However, relying on aid and GSP left the United States with reduced leverage over Vietnam. For instance, Vietnam "is sensitive to any form of aid conditionality and shows a strong resistance when donors push on policy reform" and thus limits foreign advisors' access to occasional visits (Ohno and Ohno 2005). Vietnam therefore seems to have reduced its cooperation with the United States in many areas. Human Rights Watch stated, "Vietnam's overall human rights record remains poor, and has deteriorated since Vietnam joined WTO."[48] Interestingly, non-WTO-regulated trade represents one of the few areas over which Vietnam made a few concessions, as Vietnam released several dissidents prior to talks regarding the Trans-Pacific Partnership trade agreement.[49]

The human rights data provide further evidence of the United States's reduced coercive capacity. Vietnam's average scores four years before its 2007

---

[44] See "Viet Nam Human Rights Act," *Congressional Record*, Vol. 147, Part 12, September 6, 2001, 16479.
[45] Ibid., 16486. Perhaps under pressure from the United States, other countries also moved to tie their aid allocations to Vietnam's human rights record around this time, as Japan did in 2004. See AFP, "Japan Lays Out New Aid Policy for Vietnam," *Channel NewsAsia*, November 3, 2004.
[46] See "Vietnam Human Rights Act of 2008," The Library of Congress, S.3678, October 1, 2008.
[47] Ibid.
[48] See "Vietnam: Sharp Backsliding on Religious Freedom," *Human Rights Watch*, October 18, 2009.
[49] See Luke Hunt, "Vietnam Frees Some Dissidents amid TPP Trade Talks," *The Diplomat*, April 16, 2014.

WTO entry versus four years after were the same in all categories, except for freedom of domestic movement, freedom of foreign movement, physical integrity, political prisoners, torture, women's economic rights, and women's political rights. Each of these categories ranges from 0 to 2, except for physical integrity, which ranges from 0 to 8. Whereas Vietnam improved from an average score of 0 to an average score of 1 in the area of foreign movement, it regressed from an average of 1 to 0 in domestic movement, from 4 to 3 in physical integrity, from 0.25 to 0 in political prisoners, from 4 to 0.25 in torture, from 1.75 to 1.25 in women's economic rights, and from 2.25 to 2 in women's political rights.

7.5 CAMBODIA: FOREIGN AID, VISAS, AND FREEDOM

Prior to granting Cambodia PNTR in 1996, the precursor to its WTO accession, the United States frequently conditioned its trade policies upon Cambodia's human rights performance. From 1975 to 1992, the United States maintained a trade embargo against Cambodia as punishment for its frequent civil and political rights violations. The United States lifted the embargo only after Cambodia held elections and improved its human rights record (Lum 2009).

The United States also exerted trade pressure on Cambodia by exploiting an MFN loophole in the textiles sector, allowing the United States to sign a trade agreement with Cambodia that regulated quotas on Cambodia's textiles. Specifically, as stated in the text of the agreement posted on the USTR's website, the United States signed the U.S.-Cambodia Bilateral Textile Trade Agreement in 1999, which had to be renewed in 2001 contingent on Cambodia's labor rights performance. Furthermore, at the beginning of each agreement period, which lasted twelve months, the United States would assess working conditions in the Cambodian textile and apparel sectors and, if they were found satisfactory, increase Cambodia's textile, cotton, wool, fiber, and silk export limits by 14 percent. The agreement was monitored and reports on working conditions in specific factories were made public. Furthermore, after the states renegotiated the agreement in 2002, the United States and Cambodia held formal labor consultations, and Cambodia received assistance with the labor law's implementation. As in the previous agreement, Cambodia again received quota increases for improvements in working conditions, this time of up to 18 percent (USTR 2002).

This treatment was found to be effective in encouraging labor rights in Cambodia, as the agreement's extension states, "The quota for most textile exports from Cambodia in 2002 will be fifteen percent higher than in 2001, a nine percent increase in recognition of Cambodia's progress in reforming labor conditions in textile factories over the last three years."[50] The USTR

---

[50] See "U.S.-Cambodian Textile Agreement Links Increasing Trade with Improving Workers' Rights," Office of the U.S. Trade Representative, January 7, 2002, 1.

said that the agreement represented an "excellent example of the way trade agreements... promote a greater respect for workers' rights."[51] Indeed, when Cambodia entered the agreement, it had very poor conditions in this sector, but, at the end of 2004, the World Bank survey of large buyers in the United States and EU gave the garment industry the highest ranking (Rosenthal 2006). However, this quota system expired shortly after Cambodia joined the WTO in 2004, as textile quotas were phased out by 2005 and standard WTO principles applied in this sector as well.

In its debates over whether to offer Cambodia PNTR, which Congress viewed as the last major step to its WTO entry (Lum 2009), the United States recognized that doing so would diminish trade as a tool to pressure Cambodia to improve its human rights performance. Senator John McCain stated, "Granting [PNTR] to Cambodia should not be interpreted as disinterest in the course of Cambodian democracy. The United States Senate is committed to helping democracy and human rights to flourish in Cambodia." He warned, "Our efforts will not end with this vote."[52] As expected, once the United States removed trade as a coercive tool, trade soared. Whereas bilateral trade had remained stagnant for many years prior to Cambodia's accession (U.S. Census Bureau 2013), both imports and exports increased greatly each year afterward, roughly doubling between 2003 and 2007 (U.S. Census Bureau 2013).

Owing to concerns over potential future human rights abuses, however, the United States sought other tools for leverage over Cambodia. For example, the U.S. House of Representatives unanimously passed House Resolution 345, which linked foreign aid to Cambodia's human rights record. Senator Roth explained, "Recently, Congress sent to the President H.R. 1642, a bill to extend permanent most-favored-nation tariff treatment to Cambodia.... The resolution we have passed today is meant to send a parallel message – that the United States Senate remains deeply concerned about problems in Cambodia."[53] The Congressman went on to detail the problems he was referring to, listing several human rights issues in Cambodia that included corruption, politically motivated deaths, and lack of political freedom. The resolution also urged other aid donors to condition Cambodia's foreign aid allocation upon its human rights record, stating, "The Secretary of State should encourage Cambodia's other donors... to raise concerns with the [government] over Cambodia's record on human rights."[54] Similarly, Senator Thomas argued, "The United States and other donor nations should reconsider the amount and extent of our financial aid [to Cambodia]."[55] Accordingly, each year after PNTR was granted,

---

[51] Ibid.
[52] See "Extending Most-Favored-Nation Treatment for Cambodia," No. 398, July 25, 1996, S8931.
[53] See "Relative to Cambodia Human Rights Record," *Congressional Record*, Vol. 142, No. 137, September 28, 1996, S11640.
[54] Ibid., S11639.
[55] See "Democracy in Cambodia," *Congressional Record*, Vol. 142, No. 88, June 14, 1996, S6274.

international donors met to set political conditions for providing Cambodia foreign aid (Lum 2009).

In addition to connecting aid flows to human rights, Congress created other coercive tools. For example, it developed a second tool when the Senate introduced a resolution to "impose visa restrictions on members of the Cambodian National Assembly and their families" who were found guilty of human rights offenses.[56] Similarly, the United States stepped up military ties "to maintain leverage" (Lum 2013). Thus, once Cambodia made significant strides toward joining the WTO, the U.S. Congress moved to link aid disbursements, visa applications, and military cooperation to Cambodia's human rights record but refrained from using trade policy conditionality.

As expected, once Cambodia joined the WTO, the United States lost leverage over Cambodia, as it noted abundant human rights issues following on the previous decade's improvements (Lum 2009). Furthermore, its aid's ineffectiveness was noted (Lum 2013), as Cambodia even threatened to expel the NGOs from the country rather than implement reforms.[57] While the United States recognized Cambodia's cooperation in trafficking prior to Cambodia's WTO entry, it found that Cambodia was less apt to comply afterward (Lum 2009). Perhaps most dramatically, after the U.S. Congress threatened to cut aid to Cambodia as a result of electoral irregularities, Cambodia instead delayed military aid from the United States due to the conditions the United States had imposed.[58]

Examining Cambodia's CIRI scores, a similar pattern emerges. The average score in the four years prior to its WTO entry compared with the four years after differs in the following categories: the empowerment rights index, extrajudicial killings, the physical integrity index, political prisoners, religious freedom, free speech, and women's economic rights. All categories range from 0 to 2, except for the physical integrity index, which ranges from 0 to 8, and the empowerment rights index, which ranges from 0 to 14. The empowerment rights index is constructed from the foreign movement, domestic movement, freedom of speech, freedom of assembly and association, workers' rights, electoral self-determination, and freedom of religion indicators. (The physical integrity index was defined earlier.) The data show that although religious freedom improved marginally from 1.75 to 2, each of the other categories listed declined. Empowerment rights dropped from 8.75 to 7.75, extrajudicial killings from 0.5 to 0.25, physical integrity from 4.5 to 3, political prisoners from 2 to 1, speech from 1 to 0, and women's economic rights from 1.5 to 1.25.

---

[56] See "Calling for the Government of Cambodia to Release Cheam Channy from Prison, and for Other Purposes," Senate Resolution 65, February 17, 2005.
[57] See "Cambodia NGOs Protest Gov't for Threatening to Expel Overseas NGO," *Kyodo News*, March 29, 2007.
[58] See Khuon Narim and Simon Lewis, "Cambodia Delays US Military Aid," *Cambodia Daily*, August 14, 2013.

7.6 ROMANIA: ACCESSION AGREEMENTS AND POLITICAL REFORMS

Although Romania entered the WTO in 1971, the United States had invoked its right under the GATT Article XXXV to withhold PNTR until Congress chose to grant it.[59] However, once Congress approved PNTR, it could not revoke it without violating WTO law; thus, in terms of U.S.-Romania trade relations, granting PNTR was akin to its WTO entry.

Prior to the decision to grant PNTR to Romania, the United States employed MFN status renewal as its primary tool to elicit improvements in Romania's human rights record, particularly with regard to religious freedom and the release of political prisoners (Kirk and Raceanu 1994, 6). As a result, through the 1980s, Romania agreed not to impose an emigration tax, allowed many more citizens to emigrate prior to MFN renewal deadlines, and issued a debt reduction program after Congress became irritated about Romania's increasing foreign debt (Kirk and Raceanu 1994, 9). Furthermore, once Romania made human rights improvements, Romanian president Ceausescu sent a personal envoy to the United States to convince the government that Romania respected rights and to ask for MFN status in return (Kirk and Raceanu 1994, 7). However, in 1988, Romania became increasingly repressive and, as punishment, the United States did not renew its MFN status until Romania held democratic elections and provided greater rights and freedoms to its citizens in 1993. Indeed, the U.S. assistant secretary of state Rozanne Ridgway stated that the United States had "used [its] MFN leverage to secure a distinct improvement" in Romania's human rights policies, which she went on to detail (Kirk and Raceanu 1994, 71). Similarly, Representative David Funderburk, a former ambassador to Romania, stated, "Denial of permanent MFN to Romania was, during those years, a valuable means of exerting some pressure on that regime."[60]

However, temporary MFN status hurt business interests due to underinvestment in trade between the two states. In fact, Romania feared that the United States would use its MFN policies to extract concessions and thus initially rejected MFN treatment by the United States (Kirk and Raceanu 1994, 182). These issues also came up repeatedly during the U.S. congressional debate over whether to extend PNTR to Romania in 1996. The president of Mobile Transatlantic Oceanic Corporation testified, "We have delayed making investments in Romanian enterprises that could export products to the United States or in importing Romanian products ourselves because... we need to be sure that our operations will not be subject to political winds before we can commit

---

[59] This treatment is very rare; WTO entry and PNTR are typically granted together. PNTR was withheld from WTO members only a handful of times in the past (Suzumura 1997).

[60] See "Extending Most-Favored-Nation Status to Romania," *Congressional Record*, Vol. 142, No. 104, July 16, 1996, H7594.

scarce resources to new projects. We will significantly expand our import trade with Romania if, and only if, Romania's MFN status is made unconditional."[61] Furthermore, Congressman Gregory Laughlin argued that PNTR was essential because "Romania realizes that its new-found industrial emphasis will require significant infrastructural modernization and a number of new facilities."[62] Senator Crane then read a letter from retired ambassador Alan Green Jr. that stated, "It is difficult to do business in this world and the need for permanent M.F.N. status is the guarantee of stability for all parties. This improvement of reliability will work to the benefit of the U.S.A. and Romania."[63] Similarly, Armand A. Scala, the president of Romanian Americana, argued before Congress that denying PNTR to Romania would deter "importers, exporters and investors from entering a new and very promising market."[64] Thus, impermanent MFN status depressed investment and trade due to the United State's willingness to use the agreement for coercion.

As expected, once Congress granted PNTR to Romania, political hold-up problems dissipated, and trade boomed. Prior to the United States's PNTR decision, trade with Romania remained low, actually decreasing in many years from the previous year. However, trade increased each year following the decision, as U.S. exports to Romania grew from $253 million in 1995 to $337 million in 1998 and its imports rose from $222 million to $393 million over the same period (U.S. Census Bureau 2013).

However, members of Congress also expressed concerns about relinquishing the ability to influence Romania through WTO-regulated trade policies. Congressman and former ambassador to Romania Funderburk stated, "We need to apply a little bit of pressure, get a little bit of leverage, try to get a quid pro quo somewhere before granting this. Certainly we do not need to... say OK, you have done well with your dictatorship in Romania since Ceausescu's days, and now what we want to do is give you permanent MFN and reward you for this, so you will forever be able to do whatever you want to do."[65] Congressman Smith agreed, stating, "If we now say, you have MFN, we are not going to review this anymore, I think we take away that pressure, that vigilance which that review, connected with most-favored-nation status will give us.... The annual review gives us that ability to say, Wait a minute, let's look at the record and then let's look whether or not we want to confer for

---

[61] See "Permanent Extension of Most-Favored-Nation (MFN) Trade Status to Romania," hearing before the Subcommittee on International Trade of the Committee on Finance United States Senate, June 4, 1996, H7597.
[62] See "Extending Most-Favored-Nation Status to Romania," *Congressional Record*, Vol. 142, No. 104, July 16, 1996, H7597.
[63] Ibid., H7594.
[64] Ibid., H7594.
[65] Ibid., H7592.

another year most-favored-nation status on Romania. Let us not remove that little bit of pressure which we have at this stage."[66] Similarly, Congressman Frank Pallone argued, "We must first insist that it follows the democratic paths of its European neighbors.... A vote on this critical piece of legislation now would seriously hamper any efforts by the pro-democratic forces in Romania to continue to reform the Government and improve Romania's human rights record."[67] Marshall F. Adair, the U.S. deputy assistant secretary of European and Canadian affairs, concurred, stating that MFN renewal "was a useful kind of leverage to try and move Romania onto the right path."[68]

To compensate for losing the ability to use trade to extract concessions from Romania, many members advocated capitalizing on its aspirations to enter NATO and the EU. During the debate over PNTR, deputy assistant secretary Adair argued that the United States could rely on these other forms of influence, stating, "We do have a lot of leverage with them to continue working with them, to continue encouraging democratic reform, human rights reform, and economic reform. They are desperate to become full-fledged members of the Western community of nations. They want to get into NATO, they want to get into the EU."[69] Senator Chuck Grassley concurred, arguing that Congress should use Romania's "desire to become integrated into the European community and to become a member of NATO."[70] Congressman Tom Lantos similarly advocated a focus on "Romania's quest to join NATO."[71] The PNTR issue therefore shifted the locus of power from trade policy to Romania's accession agreements.

However, the accession agreements proved to be weaker tools than the MFN renewals. Consequently, the United States held less influence over Romania once it provided PNTR. To be sure, Congress expected this; as Representative Funderburk stated, "without annual MFN, the United States will surely lose what little leverage it has in encouraging improvement in the areas of human rights, privatization, economic freedom, press and media freedom and political democratization."[72] For instance, while NATO and the EU placed pressure on Romania to reform (Levitz and Pop-Eleches 2010), Romania exhibited hesitation in cooperating with the reforms the EU demanded.[73] Furthermore, once Romania joined NATO and the EU, even fewer tools remained, leading

---

[66] Ibid., H7593.
[67] Ibid., H7596.
[68] See "Permanent Extension of Most-Favored-Nation (MFN) Trade Status to Romania," hearing before the Subcommittee on International Trade of the Committee on Finance, United States Senate, June 4, 1996, H7597.
[69] Ibid., H7592.
[70] Ibid., H7597.
[71] Ibid., H7592.
[72] Ibid., H7596.
[73] See Jovanovic (2013, 921) and Morrison (1995).

members of Congress to believe that "the reform momentum in Bucharest may have dissipated."[74]

Romania's CIRI scores corroborate this deterioration in respect for rights during the post-WTO era. The average score in the four years prior to its WTO entry compared with the four years after differs in the following categories: empowerment rights, independence of the judiciary, extrajudicial killing, physical integrity, religious freedom, freedom of speech, and women's political rights. All categories range from 0 to 2, except for the human empowerment index, which ranges from 0 to 14, and the physical integrity index, which ranges from 0 to 8. While independence of the judiciary improved from 0.25 to 1 and women's political rights improved from 1 to 2, the remaining categories declined. Human empowerment dropped from 10 to 9.5, killings from 2 to 1.5, physical integrity from 6.5 to 6, religious freedom from 0.75 to 0.5, and speech from 1.25 to 1. Overall, then, joining the WTO seems to be negatively associated with Romania's human rights performance.

Summary and Discussion

This chapter demonstrated that political hold-up problems represent a central feature of international relations. Focusing on trade with the United States, I showed that countries often seek to cooperate by liberalizing their trading relations, but fail to do so because the United States could capitalize on this cooperation at a later time, particularly when these states differ in terms of capabilities and interests. I then provided evidence for the contention that the WTO can alleviate political hold-up problems by increasing the costs associated with exploiting the relationship. However, this success comes with a price. Because the WTO makes wielding some foreign policy tools more costly – for example, trade protection and sanctions – the United States moved toward less costly policies in its efforts to influence other countries. Because it was relegated to using second-best tools, the United States experienced reduced coercive powers.

In particular, the cases presented in this chapter suggest that the United States was less able to influence WTO members' human rights policies once these states joined the WTO, as summarized in Table 7.1. Because the United States typically used coercion to pressure states in the area of physical integrity in particular, this measure, along with its constituent parts, is displayed in the table, though the other available CIRI measures were also described in the text. The table records the trajectory of states' human rights performances, comparing their average scores in the four years prior to their accessions into the WTO with their average scores in the four years following them. It demonstrates the significant drop in human rights performance after their WTO entrances. It is important to note, however, that while these scores are suggestive, these results

[74] See "Taking Stock in Romania," *Congressional Record*, Vol. 149, No. 67, May 7, 2003, E889.

TABLE 7.1. *Human Rights Before and After WTO Entry*

Indicator	China	Vietnam	Cambodia	Romania
Physical Integrity	–	–	–	–
Disappearance	–	0	0	0
Extrajudicial Killings	–	0	–	–
Political Prisoners	0	–	–	0
Torture	0	–	0	0

Notes: The table displays the trajectory of the physical integrity score along with its constituent parts, comparing the score's average in the four years prior to WTO accession with its average in the four years afterward. Note that CIRI scores are not available for Russia; thus, Russia is not reported in the table. Plus, minus, and zero denote a positive change, negative change, and no change respectively.

should not be interpreted to indicate a causal relationship between WTO membership and human rights performance. Instead, they are merely consistent with the account given in this chapter. It is of course possible that many other factors could be responsible for such a correlation.

Nonetheless, these findings suggest that MFN renewals represent more than simply symbolic politics. While states sometimes impose punishments due to domestic pressures rather than genuine desires for policy change (Whang 2011), these penalties impose real costs on the target. Thus, regardless of the coercer's underlying motivations, such punitive measures can elicit policy change when the target seeks to avoid them in the future. Irrespective of whether the government or domestic groups' desires to exert coercive diplomacy drive the coercer's actions, the net result of these pressure tactics is often (at least partial) compliance with the coercer's requests.

Moreover, these cases also showed that substitution was not the result of rent-seeking activities by domestic actors. Unlike accounts that argue that substitution occurs when industries that benefit from protection lobby for its continuation through alternative, less transparent forms, I demonstrated that states move toward tactics that would not assist such groups. For instance, if substitution were driven by trade interests, the United States would have likely imposed nontariff barriers rather than adopting naming-and-shaming tactics, foreign aid cuts, asset restrictions, and visa bans. Thus, the mechanism behind the theoretical results also seems to drive the observed behavior.

Finally, while this chapter demonstrated that coercive capacity is constrained when states are forced to use alternative levers of coercion rather than their preferred tools, these results in no way suggest that trade is the only effective instrument of influence. Other tools can certainly be persuasive in alternative domestic and international scenarios. However, the United States's reliance on trade for coercion in each case indicates that trade was selected as its preferred instrument, likely in part due to its efficacy. Because the United States was then induced to increase its use of other policy tools instead, it lost coercive capacity. In other settings, other policies may be more or less optimal. Trade is a prevalent tool, but it is not always the most effective instrument.

Having developed a theory of coercive diplomacy and tested a variety of this theory's observable implications, I now turn to a discussion of the account's significance. This powerful argument has numerous welfare, policy, and scholarly implications, which I examine in the following chapter.

8

Conclusion

Attempts to support national interests and achieve political objectives without waging war engross leaders worldwide. Yet despite its importance, coercive diplomacy has remained something of a mystery. When do states succeed in coercing their partners, and how do their targets defend themselves? What are the political and economic implications of these efforts?

This book considered these questions in detail, showing that the capacity to coerce other states can create political hold-up problems, as states reduce cooperation that would make them vulnerable to opportunistic behavior. Because coercive diplomacy represents an indispensable part of interstate interactions, hold-up problems are pervasive in international relations. However, states can use membership in international institutions to solve these problems because these bodies both allow members to credibly commit to not wielding certain tools to extort concessions from other members and protect members from having these instruments used against them. Yet, because institutions ban the use of some forms of leverage, members attempt to do so using alternative means, altering the sites of coercion in international relations and reducing the effectiveness of their efforts.

In support of the theory, I supplied evidence obtained using a multimethod approach. After developing this logic formally, I tested the implications of the model using statistical analyses, case studies, and other descriptive evidence. While none of my results on its own demonstrates irrefutable proof of the theory's claims, as a whole my findings present a compelling picture of the relationship between political hold-up problems and the practice of coercive diplomacy, particularly in the context of international institutions. In this concluding chapter, I explore the possibility that states are held up during the process of accession to international institutions, and explain what this might mean for my argument. I then close the chapter with a discussion of the theory's implications for both policy making and scholarship.

8.1 HOLD-UP AT ACCESSION

While membership in an international organization can solve political hold-up problems, states may also hold up their partners that try to join one. Often, once states comply with initial entry requirements, existing members demand additional concessions. However, because states fear that members will increase their demands once they invest in meeting the initial criteria, they hesitate to invest in the first place. Therefore, accession may not occur even when it could benefit both current and aspiring members. This possibility represents both an interesting additional domain in which my theory applies, and also presents a potential threat to inference. I first explain when these hold-up problems occur and then offer thoughts about how this might affect the conclusions of this study.

Perhaps the most well known accession agreements are those that provide pathways to EU and NATO membership. To join the EU, states first sign association agreements, in which the EU offers political, economic, and security ties to aspiring entrants in exchange for reforms. Many of these are highly relationship-specific, as potential members must integrate their political systems with those of the EU member states and make their economies EU-compatible (Kelley 2004; Levitz and Pop-Eleches 2010; Schneider 2009). Similarly, potential NATO entrants must undertake many relationship-specific investments such as establishing "democratic institutions, free market economies, civilian control of their armed forces, protection of minority rights, and the rule of law" (Gilman 1994). They must also obtain particular military equipment and capabilities which states may only use within the alliance, necessitating purchases from limited suppliers (Wallander 2000). Turkey's 2013 attempt to purchase a cheaper long-range air defense system from China highlighted such investments' irreversibility: its NATO membership required Turkey to use an aligned air defense architecture – the NATO Air Defense Ground Environment – which it could not integrate with the Chinese system, forcing Turkey to back away from the deal.[1]

Both EU and NATO expansion have been explicitly used as tools of influence and have therefore stimulated many changes. Although states have implemented these reforms unevenly, a large body of literature demonstrates that the desire for European integration has resulted in at least some political and economic liberalization (Kelley 2004; Vachudova 2005; Levitz and Pop-Eleches 2010; Schimmelfennig 2005). The U.S. Congress also recognized the changes that accession conditions brought about. For instance, Senator Christopher Bond noted, "Poland, Hungary, and the Czech Republic as well as other countries in Central and Eastern Europe that aspire to join NATO, have worked to alleviate historical grievances and build relationships with their neighbors

---

[1] See "In Turkey, Some Potential Success for the Chinese Arms Industry," *Stratfor*, October 1, 2013.

based on mutual trust, respect and cooperation."[2] Accession was also recognized as a key tool for encouraging further changes. Senator Wellstone stated, "The administration [contends] that a key reason NATO expansion is necessary is that it will promote democracy, stability and economic reform in Central Europe." He then went on to argue, "The single best way that we could exert our leverage for Poland, for Hungary, for the Czech Republic, if the goal of this is to expand markets and democracy, would be for the United States to be the leader, the leading voice in calling for expansion of the European Union."[3] Secretary Perry also claimed, "NATO enlargement is a carrot encouraging reforms."[4]

However, once states invest in cooperation with NATO or the EU, they may be held up for additional concessions. Both groups monitor potential members' progress every year, allowing the threat of rejection from the group to be reactivated periodically. The danger is that once states invest in democratic reforms or human rights improvements, these groups could decline to admit them unless they meet new requirements. Fearing this, some states have exhibited unwillingness to reform in the first place. For example, Ukraine chose to stop efforts geared toward joining NATO, as former Ukrainian president Viktor Yanukovich said that Ukraine was "a hostage to accelerated integration into NATO."[5] Similarly, Serbia refused to comply with the EU's demand that it reach an agreement with Kosovo, because it did not believe that it would be rewarded with membership.[6]

Many policy makers also acknowledge this possibility. Deputy U.S. Trade Representative Jeffrey Lang argued that when states "have met the minimum criteria" to join an institution, Congress should "get them in the system and work with them there.... [Otherwise] it says to them that, even though you have accomplished most of the things – all of the things – that we said you need to accomplish, we are not going to give it to you quite yet. That gives fuel to the argument of those who are against this kind of reform."[7] In other words, when states fear that they will not be let into an institution when they have met the stated requirements for membership, they may not implement those reforms at the outset.[8]

---

[2] See "Protocols to the North Atlantic Treaty of 1949 on Accession of Poland, Hungary, and the Czech Republic." *Congressional Record*, March 19, 1998, 4163.
[3] Ibid, 4159.
[4] See "Secretary Perry's Wehrkunde Address," *Congressional Record*, Vol. 142, No. 25, February 28, 1996, S1396.
[5] See "Ukraine, Not Planning to Speed up Accession to NATO," Interfax, Russia & CIS Business and Financial Newswire, October 14, 2010.
[6] See "Serbia's Stance on NATO and the EU," *Stratfor*, August 2, 2012.
[7] See "Permanent Extension of Most-Favored-Nation (MFN) Trade Status to Romania," hearing before the Subcommittee on International Trade of the Committee on Finance, U.S. Senate, H.R. 3161 and S. 1644, June 4, 1996, 14.
[8] This occurs with accession to many other organizations, such as the OECD, as well (Davis 2014).

Similar dynamics may play out in the context of the WTO, as membership can be held out as a carrot and exclusion as a threat to coerce concessions from aspiring members. Members may thus hold up countries that wish to enter until those countries make concessions, since the members know that they will lose trade leverage once their partners join the WTO. Such actions are entirely consistent with the theory presented in this book; however, they also introduce potential selection bias into the statistical analysis if countries are allowed to join the WTO once they improve their human rights records and become more similar to powerful members. The concern is that WTO membership is not random, and instead may be contingent on factors such as human rights and dissimilarity, which are key independent variables in the empirical analysis presented previously. Although I explored this possibility in the case studies and found no evidence to support it, it is possible that such dynamics occured in cases I did not consider.

Potential selection bias is an issue with which most studies of the WTO's effects must contend, and although a perfect solution has not been found, I took many steps to address it. First, I conducted a number of robustness checks designed to alleviate concerns about this issue, including lagging my key independent variables, analyzing the effects associated with the transition of the GATT to the WTO (which was not conditioned on human rights or dissimilarity), employing a selection model, and other tests that were described more extensively in the statistical chapters. Second, because no single test can fully prove my argument, I relied on many types of evidence to make my claims, including a formal model, multiple statistical tests, and case study evidence. Although concerns may remain with each test individually, taken as a whole, this evidence represents strong support for my argument.[9]

8.2 IMPLICATIONS FOR INTERNATIONAL RELATIONS

The framework developed in this manuscript can shed light on many persistent puzzles in international relations. Most immediately, the theory facilitates an understanding of states' strategies of coercive diplomacy. While scholars have examined the conditions that lead states to exercise coercion successfully, they have paid insufficient attention to the ways in which states choose to influence their partners and the effects of these attempts on economic and political relations. I provided an account of the tactics states adopt, the problems caused by the selection of certain tools, the remedies states turn toward to ameliorate these problems, and the impact of these solutions. My theory can thus explain a wide range of state behavior in a variety of settings.

---

[9] The WTO could also reduce dissimilarity after states join. This would represent a post-treatment effect, however, and therefore would not pose a threat to inference.

Relatedly, this theory adds to knowledge of the motivations underlying foreign policy selection. This book suggests that states choose particular policies for coercive diplomacy based on the costs and benefits associated with each. However, states' inabilities to commit to not employing certain policies as leverage creates additional costs due to political hold-up problems. These losses are present regardless of whether states actually use the policies for coercion; merely possessing the option leads their partners to reduce cooperation with them when such cooperation requires relationship-specific investments. States thus join international institutions to reshape the costs connected to wielding these policies; by increasing the penalty associated with using certain tools, states can commit to not doing so, alleviating these problems. Incorporating this insight provides a more complete picture of the calculus by which states choose policies from an array of options.

My theory also speaks to international institutions' role in the international system. Although many scholars acknowledge that these bodies can increase cooperation, their capacity to solve political hold-up problems has been underappreciated. Furthermore, because scholarship on international institutions tends to overlook hold-up problems, it has not recognized that institutions alter the tactics of coercive diplomacy, reducing its effectiveness. These institutions can therefore have unintended consequences in realms that they do not govern, which is important to appreciate when evaluating their impact on interstate relations.

These findings also inform debates over institutional creation and design. I showed that strong enforcement mechanisms allow international institutions to solve political hold-up problems. When assessing an institution's structure, it is therefore important to analyze whether the institution governs relationship-specific investments and, if so, whether it has a strong enforcement capacity. I emphasized several important components of such a capability, including transparency, impartiality, and multilateral punishments for violations. The theory suggests that when political hold-up problems are common in a particular area, states should either strengthen existing institutions' abilities to govern the policy realm or perhaps create new international institutions for this purpose.

Furthermore, this logic contributes to the literature examining issue linkage in international relations; although this body of work tends to depict bargaining over multiple areas as beneficial for cooperation, I showed that such linkages can actually hinder cooperation due to political hold-up problems. Although settling many issues jointly can help states reach agreements, political hold-up problems occur when states link multiple issues but do not resolve them simultaneously. Instead, hold-up problems occur because states fear that once they reach a deal on a particular issue, their partners will renege at a later date to extract concessions in other domains. Thus, whereas haggling over many items at once improves states' welfare by facilitating agreements, political hold-up problems can make states worse off by preventing mutually beneficial investments.

Finally, my argument speaks to the body of literature on the causes of trade protection. My results imply that the proportion of trade intervention that can be attributed to coercive diplomacy as opposed to domestic politics has diminished overtime. The finding that WTO membership has had little effect for similar states suggests that the restraint of coercive diplomacy provides a primary explanation for the WTO's effectiveness, implying that political hold-up problems were a prevalent cause of trade barriers prior to membership. Over time, the WTO's membership has increased, so that today almost all states have joined the institution. This indicates that the share of trade barriers caused by political hold-up problems is much lower than it was and, instead, that many current barriers are due to pressure from vested interests and uncompetitive industries.

My analysis thus has broad implications for diverse bodies of work. Exploring how international institutions can prevent states from holding their partners hostage permits an understanding of these bodies' broader impacts and an ability to make sense of otherwise confusing state behavior.

8.3 IMPLICATIONS FOR WELFARE

An important finding from the analysis of political hold-up problems' effects on coercive diplomacy is that states rely on international institutions to restrain themselves from using some tools for coercion. This insight has many implications for understanding which states benefit from membership in these institutions and when they reap these benefits.

For states that exercise coercive diplomacy, membership constitutes a trade-off. On one hand, WTO membership increases trade and investment between states that would experience political hold-up problems otherwise. The WTO thus provides the biggest trade boost to dissimilar pairs of states, because extortion is most prevalent between such states outside of the institution. On the other hand, the WTO negatively impacts these states when they would like to use trade for coercive purposes and cannot to do so because of their WTO commitments. Trade frequently represents an easy-to-use and relatively effective instrument, so taking this option off the table constitutes a sacrifice. This impact likely varies depending on the degree to which a particular state used trade for coercion prior to membership and the state's ability to substitute other tactics. For instance, some states have small foreign aid programs, manage limited foreign assets, and provide few loans. These states may not easily switch to other means of coercion; thus, their capacities for coercion may greatly diminish as a result of their WTO memberships.

For targets of coercion, however, membership in international institutions most immediately brings benefits. For example, the WTO both boosts economic exchange and leads targets' partners to substitute less effective levers of influence, increasing the target's foreign policy autonomy. Thus, the extent to which such a state gains from membership depends on the size of the resulting trade benefits and the degree to which it wants to exert influence over its partners. It also has additional, more subtle effects, to which I now turn.

Domestic Actors

Importantly, changes in states' strategies of coercive diplomacy affect nonstate actors as well. Whether domestic actors benefit from a particular institution depends on which policies it constrains and which instruments states chose as substitutes. For instance, when states join the WTO, trade policy becomes more difficult to use as a political weapon. A large body of literature in political science suggests that trade sanctions often indiscriminately and inefficiently impact the target's population. If coercers instead opt for more efficient, targeted penalties against WTO members, such as diplomatic sanctions, reduced government aid, or visa denials, then shifting the sites of pressure away from trade may improve conditions for these states' citizens. Conversely, coercers could select even less desirable measures instead.

Furthermore, changes in states' coercive capabilities affect nonstate actors as well. For instance, suppose a state attempts to foster respect for human rights in another country. If trade conditionality is highly effective in this endeavor relative to other policies, then WTO membership will decrease this state's capacity to improve its partner's human rights record. Repressed domestic actors will then suffer as a result. On the other hand, if the coercer wishes to persuade its partner to undertake a less noble action, the coercer's reduced ability to do so may positively impact domestic actors.

Shifting the points of pressure used for coercion may also affect industries differentially. For instance, because WTO membership causes states to rely less heavily on trade policy conditionality, some groups, such as businesses that stand to gain from increased bilateral trade, benefit from the resulting trade stability. However, if states adopt, say, foreign aid conditionality instead, businesses that tend to receive aid contracts may be harmed by the new aid requirements. International institutions therefore create domestic winners and losers by increasing predictability in some areas while causing disruptions in others. While the specific consequences depend on which tools institutions constrain and which instruments states adopt as substitutes, such shifts in domestic actors' welfare may have ramifications for many domestic issues including political stability, electoral prospects, and lobbying behavior.

Politicization of Other Areas

Furthermore, because WTO-induced substitution can politicize nontrade policy areas, these tools can become less effective in achieving their nonpolitical objectives. Consider the example of foreign aid. WTO membership leads states to substitute using aid to attain political concessions; however, this can reduce aid's ability to reach its economic goals, such as stimulating economic growth for recipients (Carothers 2011, 46–47). When aid is repurposed toward political ends, economic benefits may shrink as a consequence, as many scholars have noted trade-offs between promoting poverty alleviation versus democracy (Resnick and Van de Walle 2013, 8, 142, 200).

Indeed, when donors tie aid to political conditions, many recipients simply reject aid altogether as a result of anger and unwillingness to fulfill specific donor demands. Consider the examples of Turkey and Greece. The United States has provided foreign aid to these countries since 1940, which has long been conditioned on human rights and democracy. For instance, from 1967 to 1974 the United States cut aid to Greece because of Greece's military rule, and in 1992, the United States threatened to withhold 25 percent of Greece's aid unless Greece agreed to sanction Serbia. The United States also suspended aid to Turkey from 1974 to 1978, after it invaded Cyprus. Once aid was restored, Congress required certification of progress on the Cyprus issue before aid could be disbursed to Turkey and withheld 25 percent of aid to Turkey unless it stopped intimidating the Kurdish population. Subsequent legislation, such as the 1996 Humanitarian Aid Corridor Act, made such links to human rights permanent by requiring Turkey to withdraw troops from Cyprus, improve its human rights record, and stop blockading Armenia (Migdalovitz 1996). As a result, both Turkey and Greece often refused to accept aid in the first place.

On August 1, 1994, the United States passed legislation withholding 10 percent of its loans to Turkey until the United States certified that Turkey respected rights, and it withheld 10 percent of its aid to Greece until it certified that Greece sanctioned Serbia; however, both Turkey and Greece rejected the portion of aid that was tied to these conditions (Migdalovitz 1996). On May 29, 1996, the United States tightened the restrictions on aid under the Humanitarian Aid Corridor Act and voted to limit aid to Turkey unless Turkey recognized the Armenian genocide, after which Turkey stated it would not accept U.S. foreign aid. Then, on November 13, 1996, Turkey terminated the delivery of ten U.S. Supra Cobra helicopter gunships – a form of military aid – stating that "Turkey cannot allow its defense requirements to be held hostage" (Migdalovitz 1996).

More generally, many instances exist in which recipients rejected aid due to political hold-up problems. For instance, Iran turned down U.S. foreign aid in the wake of its 2012 earthquake, noting that "it is not uncommon for a country to reject aid from other countries" for political reasons.[10] Similarly, domestic actors in Pakistan frequently demand that the government refuse foreign aid, believing that it is a Western tool that undermines sovereignty.[11] Furthermore, many parts of Pakistan have rejected foreign aid when it comes with conditions,

---

[10] See Maya Shwayder, "Iran Rejects Foreign Aid to Help Earthquake Victims … Or Do They?," *International Business Times*, August 15, 2012.

[11] See "Pakistani Taliban: Reject Foreign Flood Aid," *CBS News*, August 10, 2010.

although, notably, they have continued to accept aid from multilateral institutions and certain bilateral partners who would not attempt to use it for coercive purposes.[12] Egypt, too, has rejected budgets that emphasize foreign aid, as they have sought to evade the conditions that come with it.[13] Bangladesh also declined aid in 2013,[14] as did India in 2005.[15] Perhaps most prominently, Eritrea decided not to accept any foreign aid in 2007 and instead would only permit joint investment projects to lessen its aid dependence and vulnerability to conditionality.[16] Kenyan human rights and aid groups urged their government to do the same, stating that aid is "used as an instrument of power. . . . and conditionalities are the most blatant expression of this fact."[17] Therefore, if the WTO increases the use of conditionality in aid or other domains, these instruments may become less effective as states resist this linkage.

Incorporating political hold-up problems into the study of coercive diplomacy thus facilitates understanding of many aspects of interstate relations and reveals important consequences of these dynamics for both states and domestic actors. This brief concluding discussion suggests the substantive value and theoretical potential of addressing political hold-up problems in studies of international relations. Further investigating the issues raised by this book's theory and empirical analysis and adapting the model to other empirical domains represent promising directions for future research.

---

[12] See Ivy Mungcal, "Pakistani State Says It Rejects Foreign Aid with Strings Attached," *Devex*, May 18, 2011.
[13] See Hannah Allam, "Egypt Rejection of U.S. Aid a Sign of Future Rifts?," *McClatchy Newspapers*, June 29, 2011.
[14] See Andrew North, "Bangladesh Defends Rejection of Foreign Aid for Collapse," *BBC News*, April 29, 2013.
[15] Somini Sengupta, "Pride and Politics: India Rejects Quake Aid," *New York Times*, October 19, 2005.
[16] See Edmund Sanders, "Eritrea Aspires to Be Self-Reliant, Rejecting Foreign Aid," *Los Angeles Times*, October 2, 2007.
[17] See Njeri Rugene, "Kenya: Reject Conditional Aid, Say Lobbies," *The Nation*, September 5, 2008.

Bibliography

Accominotti, Olivier, and Marc Flandreau. 2008. "Bilateral treaties and the most-favored-nation clause: The myth of trade liberalization in the nineteenth century." *World Politics* 60(2):147–88.

Acharya, Amitav, and Alastair Iain Johnston. 2007. *Crafting cooperation: Regional international institutions in comparative perspective.* Cambridge University Press.

Adelman, M. A. 1970. "Economics of exploration for petroleum and other minerals." *Geoexploration* 8(3–4):131–50.

Aghion, Philippe, George-Marios Angeletos, Abhijit Banerjee, and Kalina Manova. 2010. "Volatility and growth: Credit constraints and the composition of investment." *Journal of Monetary Economics* 57(3):246–65.

Ahmad, J. 1978. "Tokyo rounds of trade negotiations and the generalised system of preferences." *The Economic Journal* 88:285–95.

Ahmad, Naveed. 1982. "Pakistan-Saudi relations." *Pakistan Horizon* 35(4):51–67.

Aiello, F., P. Cardamone, and M. R. Agostino. 2010. "Evaluating the impact of nonreciprocal trade preferences using gravity models." *Applied Economics* 42(29):3745–60.

Ala'i, P. 2000. "A human rights critique of the WTO: Some preliminary observations." *George Washington International Law Review* 33:537.

Alesina, A. and D. Dollar. 2000. "Who gives foreign aid to whom and why?" *Journal of Economic Growth* 5(1):33–63.

Alford, Roger P. 2011. "The self-judging WTO security exception." *Utah Law Review* 3:697.

Alinsky, Saul D. 1971. *Rules for radicals: A pragmatic primer for realistic radicals.* Vintage.

Allee, T. L. and P. K. Huth. 2006. "Legitimizing dispute settlement: International legal rulings as domestic political cover." *American Political Science Review* 100(2): 219.

Allen, Robert Loring. 1959. "State trading and economic warfare." *Law and Contemporary Problems* 256–75.

American Farm Bureau Federation. 2012. "From Cold War enemy to key trade partner – a historical look at U.S.-Russia agricultural trade." American Farm Bureau Federation.

Anderson, J. and E. van Wincoop. 2003. "Gravity with gravitas: A solution to the border problem." *American Economic Review* 93(1):170–92.

Appleton, Arthur E. 2000. "The World Trade Organization: Implications for human rights and democracy." *Thesaurus Acroasiuml* 19:415–60.

Araral, Eduardo, Jr. 2005. "Bureaucratic incentives, path dependence, and foreign aid: An empirical institutional analysis of irrigation in the Philippines." *Policy Sciences* 38(2–3):131–57.

Art, Robert J. 2003. "Coercive diplomacy: What do we know?" In *The United States and Coercive Diplomacy*, 359–420. United States Institute of Peace.

Aslund, Anders and Gary Clyde Hufbauer. 2011. *Why it's in the US interest to establish normal trade relations with Russia*. Peterson Institute.

Auslin, Michael R. 2006. *Negotiating with imperialism: The unequal treaties and the culture of Japanese diplomacy*. Harvard University Press.

Bader, Julia, Jörn Grävingholt, and Antje Kästner. 2010. "Would autocracies promote autocracy? A political economy perspective on regime-type export in regional neighbourhoods." *Contemporary Politics* 16(1):81–100.

Baer, Werner. 1972. "Import substitution and industrialization in Latin America: experiences and interpretations." *Latin American Research Review* 7(1):95–122.

Bagwell, K., and R. W. Staiger. 1999. "An economic theory of GATT." *The American Economic Review* 89(1):215–48.

Bagwell, K., and R. W. Staiger. 2002. *The economics of the world trading system*. Massachusetts Institute of Technology.

Baier, S. L., and J. H. Bergstrand. 2007. "Do free trade agreements actually increase members' international trade?" *Journal of International Economics* 71(1):72–95.

Baldwin, David A. 1971. "The power of positive sanctions." *World Politics* 24(01):19–38.

Baldwin, David Allen. 1985. *Economic statecraft*. Princeton University Press.

Baldwin, R., and D. Taglioni. 2006. "Gravity for dummies and dummies for gravity equations." Technical report National Bureau of Economic Research.

Baldwin, Richard E. 1995. "The eastern enlargement of the European Union." *European Economic Review* 39(3):474–81.

Bank, Nepal Rastra. 2002. *WTO and Nepal*. Nepal Rastra Bank, Research Department, International Finance Division.

Barbieri, Katherine, Omar Keshk, and Brian Pollins. 2008. "Correlates of war project trade data set codebook." *Codebook Version* 2.

Barker, M. B. 2000. "Flying over the judicial hump: A human rights drama featuring Burma, the Commonwealth of Massachusetts, the WTO, and the federal courts." *Law and Policy in International Business* 32:51.

Basch, A. 1944. *Danube Basin and the German economic sphere*. International Library of Sociology and Social Reconstruction.

Bennett, D. S., and T. Nordstrom. 2000. "Foreign policy substitutability and internal economic problems in enduring rivalries." *Journal of Conflict Resolution* 44(1):33–61.

Bhagwati, J. 1998. "Trade linkage and human rights." In *The Uruguay Round and beyond: essays in honor of Arthur Dunkel*, 241. University of Michigan Press.

Blanchard, Emily J., and Shushanik Hakobyan. 2013. "The US generalized system of preferences: In principle and practice." Available at SSRN 2439798.
Bliss, Harry, and Bruce Russett. 1998. "Democratic trading partners: The liberal connection, 1962–1989." *Journal of Politics* 60(04):1126–47.
Blonigen, Bruce A. 2005. "A review of the empirical literature on FDI determinants." *Atlantic Economic Journal* 33(4):383–403.
Bolton, Patrick, and Mathias Dewatripont. 2005. *Contract theory.* MIT Press.
Borchert, I. 2009. "Trade diversion under selective preferential market access." *Canadian Journal of Economics/Revue canadienne d'économique* 42(4):1390–1410.
Bordo, Michael D., Barry Eichengreen, and Douglas A. Irwin. 1999. "Is globalization today really different than globalization a hundred years ago?" Technical report, National Bureau of Economic Research.
Brenton, P. 2003. *Integrating the least developed countries into the world trading system: The current impact of EU Preferences under Everything but Arms.* Vol. 3018. World Bank Publications.
Brenton, P., and M. Manchin. 2003. "Making EU trade agreements work: The role of rules of origin." *The World Economy* 26(5):755–69.
Broz, J. Lawrence, and Seth H. Werfel. 2011. "Exchange rates and industry demands for trade protection." *Economics* 114(3):907–40.
Bruce, Chloë. 2005. *Fraternal friction or fraternal fiction? The gas factor in Russian-Belarusian relations.* Oxford Institute for Energy Studies.
Bueno de Mesquita, B. 1975. "Measuring systemic polarity." *Journal of Conflict Resolution* 19(2):187.
Bulir, Ales, and Alfonso Hamann. 2006. "Volatility of development aid: From the frying pan into the fire?" International Monetary Fund Working Paper.
Busch, M. L., and E. Reinhardt. 2003. "Developing countries and General Agreement on Tariffs and Trade/World Trade Organization dispute settlement." *Journal of World Trade* 37(4):719–36.
Busch, M. L., and E. Reinhardt. 2004. "The WTO dispute settlement mechanism and developing countries." Trade Brief, Swedish International Development and Cooperation Agency.
Busch, M. L., R. Raciborski, and E. Reinhardt. 2009. "Does the rule of law matter? The WTO and US antidumping investigations." Working Paper.
Buss, Terry F., and Adam Gardner. 2005. "Why foreign aid to Haiti failed–and how to do it better next time." In Louis A. Picard, Robert Groselsema, and Terry F. Buss, eds., Foreign Aid and Foreign Policy: Lessons for the Next Half-Century, 173. Routledge.
Büthe, T., and H. V. Milner. 2008a. "The politics of foreign direct investment into developing countries: Increasing FDI Through International Trade Agreements?" *American Journal of Political Science* 52(4):741–62.
Büthe, Tim, and Helen V. Milner. 2008b. "The politics of foreign direct investment into developing countries: Increasing FDI through international trade agreements?" *American Journal of Political Science* 52(4):741–62.
Buwalda, Piet. 1997. *They did not dwell alone: Jewish emigration from the Soviet Union, 1967-1990.* Woodrow Wilson Center Press.
Cain, Frank. 1995. "The US-led trade Embargo on China: The origins of CHINCOM, 1947–52." *The Journal of Strategic Studies* 18(4):33–54.
Carlsson, Jerker, Gloria Somolekae, and Nicolas Van de Walle. 1997. *Foreign aid in Africa: Learning from country experiences.* Nordic Africa Institute.

Carnegie, Allison. 2014. "States held hostage: Political hold-up problems and the effects of international institutions." *American Political Science Review* 108(1): 54–70.

Carothers, Thomas. 2011. *Aiding democracy abroad: The learning curve.* Carnegie Endowment.

Carr, W. 1979. *A history of Germany, 1815-1945.* St. Martin's Press.

Caruana, Leonard, and Hugh Rockoff. 2003. "A Wolfram in sheep's clothing: Economic warfare in Spain, 1940–1944." *The Journal of Economic History* 63(01):100–126.

Chang, Ha-Joon. 2002. *Kicking away the ladder: Development strategy in historical perspective.* Anthem Press.

Charnovitz, Steve. 2006. "Taiwan's WTO membership and its international implications." *Asian Journal of WTO and International Health Law and Policy* 1:401.

Checkel, Jeffrey T. 2005. "International institutions and socialization in Europe: Introduction and framework." *International Organization* 59(04):801–26.

Cheibub, J. A., J. Gandhi, and J. R. Vreeland. 2010. "Democracy and dictatorship revisited." *Public Choice* 143(1):67–101.

Cho, Hui-Wan. 2005. "China-Taiwan tug of war in the WTO." *Asian Survey* 45(5):736–55.

Christensen, Thomas J. 2011. *Worse than a monolith: Alliance politics and problems of coercive diplomacy in Asia.* Princeton University Press.

CIA World Factbook. 2014. *Canada Economy 2014.* CIA.

Cingranelli, D. L., and T. E. Pasquarello. 1985. "Human rights practices and the distribution of US foreign aid to Latin American countries." *American Journal of Political Science* 29:539–63.

Clark, David H., and William Reed. 2005. "The strategic sources of foreign policy substitution." *American Journal of Political Science* 49(3):609–24.

Clark, D. H., T. Nordstrom, and W. Reed. 2008. "Substitution is in the variance: Resources and foreign policy choice." *American Journal of Political Science* 52:763–73.

Clark, D. P., and S. Zarrilli. 1992. "Non-tariff measures and industrial nation imports of GSP-covered products." *Southern Economic Journal* 59:284–93.

Cleveland, S. H. 2001. "Human rights sanctions and the World Trade Organization." In *Environment, human rights and international trade.* Hart.

Clyde and Co. 2013. "New limitations for commodities trade following latest EU sanctions against Iran." Clyde and Co.

Cohn, M. 2000. "World Trade Organization: Elevating property interests above human rights, The." *Georgia Journal of International and Comparative Law* 29:427.

Columbus, Frank. 2003. *Russia in transition* Vol. 2. Nova Science Publishers.

Compa, Lance, and Jeffrey S. Vogt. 2000. "Labor rights in the generalized system of preferences: A 20-year review." *Comparative Labor Law and Policy Journal* 22:199.

Conconi, P., and C. Perroni. 2004. "The economics of special and differential trade regimes." CEPR Discussion Paper.

Conrad, Courtenay Ryals, and Will H. Moore. 2010. "What stops the torture?" *American Journal of Political Science* 54(2):459–76.

Contreras, Carlos Alberto. 2008. *Bankruptcy to NAFTA: Mexico's foreign policy opens to the world, 1982 to 1994.* University of California, Los Angeles.

Cooley, A., and H. Spruyt. 2009. *Contracting states: Sovereign transfers in international relations.* Princeton University Press.

Copeland, Dale C. 1996. "Economic interdependence and war: A theory of trade expectations." *International Security* 20(4):5–41.

Copelovitch, Mark S., and Jon C. W. Pevehouse. 2013. "Ties that bind? Preferential trade agreements and exchange rate policy choice." *International Studies Quarterly* 57(2):385–99.

Cortright, David, and George A. Lopez. 2005. "Bombs, carrots, and sticks." *Arms Control Today* 35:2.

Crawford, G. 2001. *Foreign aid and political reform: A comparative analysis of democracy assistance and political conditionality*. Palgrave Macmillan.

Croix, S. J. La, and C. Grandy. 1997. "The political instability of reciprocal trade and the overthrow of the Hawaiian Kingdom." *The Journal of Economic History* 57(1):161–89.

Dai, Xinyuan. 2002. "Political regimes and international trade: The democratic difference revisited." *American Political Science Review* 96(01):159–65.

Davenport, C. 2000. *Paths to state repression: Human rights violations and contentious politics*. Rowman and Littlefield.

Davis, C. L. 2004. "International institutions and issue linkage: Building support for agricultural trade liberalization." *American Political Science Review* 98(1): 153–69.

Davis, C. L. 2006. "Do WTO rules create a level playing field? Lessons from the experience of Peru and Vietnam." In *Negotiating Trade: Developing countries in the WTO and NAFTA*, 219–256. Cambridge University Press.

Davis, C. L. 2009. "Linkage diplomacy: Economic and security bargaining in the Anglo-Japanese Alliance, 1902-23." *International Security* 33(3):143–79.

Davis, C. L., and S. Meunier. 2011. "Business as usual? Economic responses to political tensions." *American Journal of Political Science* 55(3):628–46.

Davis, Christina. 2014. "Membership conditionality and institutional reform: The case of the OECD." Working Paper.

Davis, Christina L. 2012. *Why adjudicate? Enforcing trade rules in the WTO*. Princeton University Press.

Davis, Christina, and Meredith Wilf. 2011. "Joining the club: Accession to the GATT/WTO." Paper presented at APSA Annual Meeting.

De Benedictis, L., and L. Salvatici. 2011. *The trade impact of European Union Preferential Policies: An analysis through gravity models*. Springer.

De Gortari, Carlos Salinas, Peter Hearn, and Patricia Rosas. 2002. *México: The policy and politics of modernization*. Plaza & Janés.

Democratic Progressive Party. 1999. "DPP White Paper on China Policy for the 21st Century." http://www.dpp.org.tw.

Devault, J. 1996. "Competitive need limits and the US generalized system of preference." *Contemporary Economic Policy* 14(4):58–66.

DiCicco, Jonathan M., and Jack S. Levy. 1999. "Power shifts and problem shifts: the evolution of the power transition research program." *Journal of Conflict Resolution* 43(6):675–704.

Diehl, P. F. 1994. "Substitutes or complements? The effects of alliances on military spending in major power rivalries." *International Interactions* 19(3):159–76.

Dobbins, J. 2008. *Europe's role in nation-building: From the Balkans to the Congo*. Vol. 722. Rand Corp.

Dobson, Alan P. 1988. "The Kennedy administration and economic warfare against communism." *International Affairs* 64:599–616.

Dobson, Alan P. 2005. "The Reagan administration, economic warfare, and starting to close down the cold war." *Diplomatic History* 29(3):531–56.

Domínguez, Jorge I., and Rafael Fernandez De Castro. 2009. *United States and Mexico: Between partnership and conflict*. Routledge.

Dorussen, Han. 2001. "Mixing carrots with sticks: Evaluating the effectiveness of positive incentives." *Journal of Peace Research* 38(2):251–62.

Downes, Alexander B., and Todd S. Sechser. 2012. "The illusion of democratic credibility." *International Organization* 66(03):457–89.

Dreher, A., J. E. Sturm, and J. R. Vreeland. 2009. "Global horse trading: IMF loans for votes in the United Nations Security Council." *European Economic Review* 53(7):742–57.

Dreher, Axel, and Jan-Egbert Sturm. 2012. "Do the IMF and the World Bank influence voting in the UN General Assembly?" *Public Choice* 151(1-2):363–97.

Dreher, Axel, and J. R. Vreeland. 2014. *The political economy of the United Nations Security Council*. Cambridge University Press.

Drezner, Daniel W. 1997. "The hidden hand of economic coercion." *International Organization* 57: 643–59.

Drezner, Daniel W. 1999. *The sanctions paradox: Economic statecraft and international relations*. Number 65. Cambridge University Press.

Drucker, Peter F. 1974. "Management: Tasks, responsibilities, practices." Working paper.

Dumbaugh, K. 2008. "China's foreign policy: What does it mean for U.S. global interests?" Congressional Research Service.

Dunning, T. 2004. "Conditioning the effects of aid: Cold War politics, donor credibility, and democracy in Africa." *International Organization* 58(2):409–23.

Dutt, Pushan, and Daniel Traca. 2010. "Corruption and bilateral trade flows: extortion or evasion?" *The Review of Economics and Statistics* 92(4):843–60.

Eaton, Jonathan, and Samuel Kortum. 2001. "Trade in capital goods." *European Economic Review* 45(7):1195–235.

Eicher, Theo S., and Christian Henn. 2011. "In search of WTO trade effects: Preferential trade agreements promote trade strongly, but unevenly." *Journal of International Economics* 83(2):137–53.

Elliott, K. A., and T. O. Bayard. 2004. "Reciprocity and retaliation in US trade policy." Peterson Institute Press.

Energy Information Administration. 2014. "Russia energy statistics." U.S. Energy Administration.

European Commission. 2014. "Iran." Europa.

Feenstra, R. C. 1996. *US imports, 1972-1994: Data and concordances*. Vol. 5515. National Bureau of Economic Research.

Feldman, David H. 2006. "Bring Iran to heel with EU sanctions." *The Sun*.

Finnemore, Martha, and Kathryn Sikkink. 1998. "International norm dynamics and political change." *International Organization* 52(4):887–917.

Forsberg, Aaron. 1998. "The Politics of GATT expansion: Japanese accession and the domestic political context in Japan and the United States, 1948-1955." *Business and Economic History* 27:185–95.

Forsberg, Aaron. 2000. *America and the Japanese miracle: The Cold War context of Japan's postwar economic revival, 1950-1960*. UNC Press.

Francois, Joseph, Bernard Hoekman and Miriam Manchin. 2006. "Preference erosion and multilateral trade liberalization." *The World Bank Economic Review* 20(2):197–216.

Freedom House. 2006. "Freedom in the world: Political rights and liberties 1972-2005." http://www.freedomhouse.org.
Fudenberg, D., and J. Tirole. 1991. *Game theory*. MIT Press.
GAO. 1994. *International trade: U.S. government policy issues affecting U.S. business activities in China*. U.S. General Accounting Office.
Garrett, Geoffrey. 2000. "The causes of globalization." *Comparative Political Studies* 33(6-7):941–91.
Garver, John W. 1991. "China-India rivalry in Nepal: The clash over Chinese arms sales." *Asian Survey* 31(10):956–75.
Gaubatz, K. T. 1996. "Democratic states and commitment in international relations." *International Organization* 50:109–40.
Geller, D. S. 1993. "Power differentials and war in rival dyads." *International Studies Quarterly* 37(2):173–93.
George, Alexander L. 1991. *Forceful persuasion: Coercive diplomacy as an alternative to war*. U.S. Institute of Peace Press.
George, Alexander L. 1994. "Introduction: The limits of coercive diplomacy." In Alexander L. George, Simons William E., eds. *The limits of coercive diplomacy*. Westview.
George, Alexander L., David Kent Hall, and William E. Simons. 1971. *The limits of coercive diplomacy: Laos, Cuba, Vietnam*. Little, Brown.
Gilderhus, Mark T. 2008. "Creating a Third World: Mexico, Cuba, and the United States during the Castro Era." *The Americas* 65(1):134–35.
Gilley, Bruce, and Maureen Pao. 2001. "China-Taiwan: Defences weaken." *Far Eastern Economic Review* 39:41–45.
Gilman, Hon. Benjamin A. 1994. Introduction of NATO Expansion Act of 1994, H.R. 4210. Congressional Record Online through the Government Printing Office, Congressional Record Volume 140, Number 41.
Giumelli, Francesco. 2013. "How EU sanctions work: a new narrative." Chaillot Paper No. 129.
Gladstone, Cary. 2001. *Afghanistan: history, issues, bibliography*. Nova Science.
Glenny, Misha. 2012. *The Balkans: Nationalism, war, and the Great Powers, 1804-2011*. New and Updated ed. House of Anansi.
Godwin, Paul H. B., Alfred D. Wilhelm, and Karen M. Sutter. 1996. *Taiwan 2020: Developments in Taiwan to 2020: Implications for cross-strait relations and US policy*. Atlantic Council of the United States.
Goldstein, J., and J. Gowa. 2002. "US national power and the post-war trading regime." *World Trade Review* 1(02):153–70.
Goldstein, J. L., D. Rivers, and M. Tomz. 2007. "Institutions in international relations: Understanding the effects of the GATT and the WTO on world trade." *International Organization* 61:37–67.
Goodliffe, J., and D. G. Hawkins. 2006. "Explaining commitment: States and the Convention Against Torture." *Journal of Politics* 68(2):358–71.
Government of Nepal. 2013a. *Nepal Trade and Export Promotion Center*. Nepal Trade and Export Promotion Center.
Government of Nepal. 2013b. "Trade Statistics."
Gowa, J. 1995. *Allies, adversaries, and international trade*. Princeton University Press.
Gowa, J. and E. D. Mansfield. 1993. "Power politics and international trade." *The American Political Science Review* 87(2):408–20.

Gowa, J., and E. D. Mansfield. 2004. "Alliances, imperfect markets, and major-power trade." *International Organization* 58:775–805.
Gowa, J., and S. Y. Kim. 2005. "An exclusive country club: The effects of the GATT on trade, 1950-94." *World Politics* 57(4):453–78.
Graham, James. 2004. "Japan's economic expansion into Manchuria and China in World War Two." *Asian History*. http://www.historyorb.com/.
Grayson, G. 1981. *The politics of Mexican oil*. Vol. 7. University of Pittsburgh Press.
Grieco, Joseph M. 1988. "Anarchy and the limits of cooperation: a realist critique of the newest liberal institutionalism." *International Organization* 42(03):485–507.
Grigoriadis, Theocharis. 2014. "WTO accession and energy markets: An overview of Russia." Working paper.
Grzybowski, Kazimierz. 1973. "Control of US trade with China: An overview." *Law and Contemporary Problems*. 38:175.
Guide to GATT Law and Practice (Analytical Index). 1995. World Trade Organisation.
Guimaraes, P., P. Portugal, and B. de Portugal. 2010. "A simple feasible procedure to fit models with high-dimensional fixed effects." *Stata Journal* 10(4):628.
Gwartney, James, Robert Lawson, and Seth Norton. 2008. *Economic Freedom of the World 2008 Annual Report*. The Fraser Institute.
Haass, Richard N., and Meghan L. O'Sullivan. 2000. "Terms of engagement: Alternatives to." *Survival* 42(2):113–35.
Hafner-Burton, E. M. 2005. "Trading human rights: How preferential trade agreements influence government repression." *International Organization* 59:593–629.
Hafner-Burton, Emilie. 2009. *Forced to be good: Why trade agreements boost human rights*. Cornell University Press.
Hafner-Burton, Emilie. 2013. *Making human rights a reality*. Princeton University Press.
Hafner-Burton, Emilie M. 2012. "International regimes for human rights." *Annual Review of Political Science* 15:265–86.
Head, Keith, and Thierry Mayer. 2013. "Gravity equations: Workhorse, toolkit, and cookbook." Working paper.
Hehn, P. N. 2005. *A low dishonest decade: the Great Powers, Eastern Europe, and the economic origins of World War II, 1930-1941*. Continuum International.
Heptulla, Najma. 1991. *Indo-West Asian relations: The Nehru Era*. Allied.
Heritage Foundation. 1981. "The Soviet Grain Embargo." The Heritage Foundation .
Hertog, Steffen. 2010. *Princes, brokers, and bureaucrats: oil and the state in Saudi Arabia*. Cornell University Press.
Herz, B., and M. Wagner. 2011. "The dark side of the generalized system of preferences." *Review of International Economics* 19(4):763–75.
Heston, A., R. Summers, and B. Aten. 2006. "Penn World Table Version 6.2, Center for International Comparisons of Production, Income and Prices." University of Pennsylvania.
Hirschman, A. O. 1969. *National power and the structure of international trade*. University of California Press.
Hiscox, Michael J. 2009. *Balancing act: The political economy of U.S. trade sanctions*.
Hoeffler, Anke, and Verity Outram. 2011. "Need, merit, or self-interest: what determines the allocation of aid?" *Review of Development Economics* 15(2):237–50.
Hoekman, B., and Ç. Özden. 2005. "Trade preferences and differential treatment of developing countries: a selective survey." *Policy research working paper* 3566. World Bank.

Hoekman, Bernard M., and Petros C. Mavroidis. 2007. *World Trade Organization (WTO): Law, economics, and politics*. Psychology Press.

Holland, M. 2002. *The European Union and the Third World*. Palgrave.

Hose, Robert L., and Jared M. Genser. 2007. "Are EU trade sanctions on Burma compatible with WTO law." *Michigan Journal of International Law* 29:165.

House Hearing. 2011. "Ten years in the WTO: Has China kept its promises?" Congressional-Executive Commission on China.

Howse, R., and M. Mutua. 2000. *Protecting human rights in a global economy: Challenges for the World Trade Organization*. Rights and Democracy, International Centre for Human Rights and Democratic Development.

Hsieh, Pasha L. 2008. *China-Taiwan trade relations: Implications of the WTO and Asian regionalism*. Oxford University Press.

Hsu, David T. 2014. "Manipulating the WTO's lowest tier: The Generalized System of Preferences revisited." Working Paper.

Hudec, R. 2002. "The adequacy of WTO dispute settlement remedies: A developing country perspective." In *Development, Trade, and the WTO: A Handbook*. World Bank.

Hufbauer, Gary Clyde, Jeffrey J. Schott, Kimberly Ann Elliott, and Barbara Oegg. 2007. *Economic sanctions reconsidered*. Peterson Institute for International Economics.

Huth, Paul K. 1999. "Deterrence and international conflict: Empirical findings and theoretical debates." *Annual Review of Political Science* 2(1):25–48.

Ianchovichina, Elena, and Will Martin. 2004. "Impacts of China's accession to the World Trade Organization." *The World Bank Economic Review* 18(1):3–27.

Ikenberry, G. John. 2009. *After victory: Institutions, strategic restraint, and the rebuilding of order after major wars*. Princeton University Press.

International Monetary Fund. 1993. "World economic outlook." *Various Issues*.

Irwin, Douglas A. 1993. "Multilateral and bilateral trade policies in the world trading system: An historical perspective." *New Dimensions in Regional Integration* 90:90.

Ishaq, Mohammed. 1999. *The politics of trade pressure: American-Soviet relations 1980-88*. Ashgate.

Jackson, James K. 2003. *Export-Import Bank: Background and Legislative Issues*. Congressional Research Service, Library of Congress.

Jackson, J. H. 1997. *The world trading system: Law and policy of international economic relations*. MIT Press.

Jensen, Nathan M. 2003. "Democratic governance and multinational corporations: Political regimes and inflows of foreign direct investment." *International Organization* 57(03):587–616.

Jha, Hari Bansh. 2011. "India's economic miracle and its impact on Nepal analysis." *Eurasia Review*.

Johnson, H. G. 1967. *Economic policies toward less developed countries*. Brookings Institution.

Johnston, A. I. 2002. "Treating international institutions as social environments." *International Studies Quarterly* 45(4):487–515.

Jones, Vivian C. 2008. "Generalized System of Preferences: Background and renewal debate." *CRS Report for Congress* RL33663.

Jovanovic, Miroslav N. 2013. *The economics of European integration*. Edward Elgar.

Kaempfer, William H., and Anton D. Lowenberg. 1988. "The theory of international economic sanctions: A public choice approach." *The American Economic Review* 78:786–93.

Kaempfer, William H., Anton D. Lowenberg, and William Mertens. 2004. "International economic sanctions against a dictator." *Economics and Politics* 16(1):29–51.

Kaldor, Nicholas. 1962. "Will underdeveloped countries learn to tax." *Foreign Affairs* 41:410.

Kan, Shirley A. 2013. *China/Taiwan: Evolution of the "One China" policy-key statements from Washington, Beijing, and Taipei*. DTIC Document.

Kan, Shirley A., and Wayne M. Morrison. 2012. *US-Taiwan relationship: Overview of policy issues*. Congressional Research Service.

Kan, Shirley A., and Wayne M. Morrison. 2013. "U.S.-Taiwan relationship: Overview of policy issues." *CRS Report*.

Kastner, Scott L. 2007. "When do conflicting political relations affect international trade?" *Journal of Conflict Resolution* 51(4):664–88.

Keck, A., and A. Lendle. 2012. "New evidence on preference utilization." World Trade Organization Staff Working Paper ERSD-2012-12.

Kelley, Judith. 2004. "International actors on the domestic scene: Membership conditionality and socialization by international institutions." *International Organization* 58:425–57.

Keohane, R. 1984. "0.(1984) After Hegemony." In *Cooperation and discord in the world political economy*. Princeton University Press.

Keohane, Robert Owen, and Joseph S. Nye. 1977. *Power and interdependence: world politics in transition*. Little, Brown.

Khanal, Dilli Raj, and Prakash Kumar Shrestha. 2008. "Trade and investment linkages and coordination in Nepal: Impact on productivity and exports and business perceptions." Technical report.

Kirk, R., and M. Raceanu. 1994. *Romania versus the United States: Diplomacy of the absurd, 1985-1989*. Palgrave Macmillan.

Kissinger, H. 2011. *On China*. Penguin Press.

Knorr, Klaus Eugen, and Frank N. Trager. 1977. *Economic issues and national security*. Vol. 7. University Press of Kansas.

Kono, Daniel Y. 2006. "Optimal obfuscation: Democracy and trade policy transparency." *American Political Science Review* 100(03):369–84.

Kono, Daniel Yuichi. 2008. "Democracy and trade discrimination." *The Journal of Politics* 70(04):942–55.

Kovenock, D., and M. Thursby. 1992. "GATT, dispute settlement and cooperation." *Economics and Politics* 4(2):151–70.

Krasner, S. D. 1976. "State power and the structure of international trade." *World Politics: A Quarterly Journal of International Relations* 28:317–47.

Krasner, Stephen D. 1983. *International regimes*. Cornell University Press.

Kuykendall, R. S. 1953. *The Hawaiian Kingdom: 1854-1874: Twenty critical years*. Vol. 2. University of Hawaii Press.

Kuziemko, I., and E. Werker. 2006. "How much is a seat on the Security Council worth? Foreign aid and bribery at the United Nations." *Journal of Political Economy* 114(5):905–30.

Lacy, Dean, and Emerson Niou. 2004. "A theory of economic sanctions and issue linkage: The roles of preferences, information, and threats." *Journal of Politics* 66(1):25–42.

LaFeber, Walter. 1997. *The clash: a history of US-Japan relations*. WW Norton.

Lai, Brian, and Dan Reiter. 2000. "Democracy, political similarity, and international alliances, 1816-1992." *Journal of Conflict Resolution* 44(2):203–27.
Lake, D. A. 1999. *Entangling relations: American foreign policy in its century*. Princeton University Press.
Lake, David A. 2009. *Hierarchy in international relations*. Cornell University Press.
Lederman, D., and C. Özden. 2004. "US trade preferences: All are not created equal." *Documentos de Trabajo (Banco Central de Chile)* 280:1.
Leeds, B., J. Ritter, S. Mitchell, and A. Long. 2002. "Alliance treaty obligations and provisions, 1815-1944." *International Interactions* 28:237–60.
Legler, Thomas F., Sharon F. Lean, and Dexter S. Boniface. 2007. *Promoting democracy in the Americas*. JHU Press.
Leiken, Robert S. 2001. "With a friend like Fox." *Foreign Affairs* 80:91–104.
Lektzian, D. J., and C. M. Sprecher. 2007. "Sanctions, signals, and militarized conflict." *American Journal of Political Science* 51(2):415–31.
Lensink, and Oliver Morrissey. 2000. "Aid instability as a measure of uncertainty and the positive impact of aid on growth." *The Journal of Development Studies* 36(3):31–49.
Levitz, Philip, and Grigore Pop-Eleches. 2010. "Why no backsliding? The European Union's impact on democracy and governance before and after accession." *Comparative Political Studies* 43(4):457–85.
Lewy, Guenter. 2005. *The Armenian massacres in Ottoman Turkey: a disputed genocide*. University of Utah Press.
Lilley, J. R., and W. L. Willkie. 1994. *Beyond MFN: Trade with China and American interests*. American Enterprise Institute.
Lim, H. 2001. "Trade and human rights: What's at issue?" *Journal of World Trade* 35(2):275–300.
Lin, Teh-chang. 1999. "State versus market: Taiwans trade, investment and aid policies in mainland China and southeast Asia in the post-Deng period." *Journal of Chinese Political Science* 5(2):83–113.
Lindsay, James M. 1986. "Trade sanctions as policy instruments: A re-examination." *International Studies Quarterly* 30:153–73.
Liu, X. 2009. "GATT/WTO promotes trade strongly: Sample selection and model specification." *Review of International Economics* 17(3):428–46.
Long, Andrew G., and Brett Ashley Leeds. 2006. "Trading for security: Military alliances and economic agreements." *Journal of Peace Research* 43(4):433–51.
Lum, T. 2009. *Cambodia: Background and U.S. relations*. DTIC Document.
Lum, Thomas. 2013. "U.S.-Cambodia relations: Issues for the 113th Congress." Congressional Research Service.
Maechling, Charles. 2000. "Pearl Harbor: The first energy war." *History Today* 50(12):41–47.
Maggi, G., 1999. "The role of multilateral institutions in international trade cooperation." *The American Economic Review* 89(1):190–214.
Maggi, G., and A. Rodriguez-Clare. 1998. "The value of trade agreements in the presence of political pressures." *Journal of Political Economy* 106(3):574–601.
Mansfield, E. D., H. V. Milner, and B. P. Rosendorff. 2000. "Free to trade: Democracies, autocracies, and international trade." *American Political Science Review* 94(2):305–21.

Mansfield, E. D., H. V. Milner, and B. P. Rosendorff. 2002. "Why democracies cooperate more: Electoral control and international trade agreements." *International Organization* 56:477–513.

Mansfield, E. D., and J. C. Pevehouse. 2008. "Democratization and the varieties of international organizations." *Journal of Conflict Resolution* 52(2):269.

Mansfield, E. D., and R. Bronson. 1997. "Alliances, preferential trading arrangements, and international trade." *The American Political Science Review* 91(1):94–107.

Mansfield, Edward D., and Helen V. Milner. 2012. *Votes, vetoes, and the political economy of international trade agreements.* Princeton University Press.

Manyin, M. E. 2006. "Vietnam PNTR status and WTO accession: Issues and implications for the United States." DTIC Document.

Manyin, M. E. 2001. *The Vietnam-US bilateral trade agreement.* Congressional Research Service, Library of Congress.

Manyin, M. E. 2008. *US-Vietnam relations: Background and issues for Congress.* DTIC Document.

Marceau, G. 2002. "WTO dispute settlement and human rights." *European Journal of International Law* 13(4):753–814.

Marshall, M. G., K. Jaggers, T. R. Gurr. 2004. *Polity IV Project.* Center for International Development and Conflict Management at the University of Maryland College Park.

Martin, Lisa L. 1992. "Interests, power, and multilateralism." *International Organization* 46:765–65.

Martin, Lisa L. 1993. *Coercive cooperation: Explaining multilateral economic sanctions.* Princeton University Press.

Martin, Lisa L. 1994. "Heterogeneity, linkage and commons problems." *Journal of Theoretical Politics* 6(4):473–93.

Mastel, Greg. 2001. "China, Taiwan, and the World Trade Organization." *Washington Quarterly* 24(3):45–56.

McCornac, Dennis C. 2011. "Vietnams relations with China: A delicate balancing act." *China Research Center* 10(2).

McLaren, J. 1997. "Size, sunk costs, and Judge Bowker's objection to free trade." *The American Economic Review* 87(3):400–420.

Mearsheimer, J. J. 1994. "The false promise of international institutions." *International Security* 19(3):5–49.

Migdalovitz, Carol. 1996. "86065: Greece and Turkey: Current foreign aid issues." A CRS Issue Brief.

Milner, H., and D. Tingley. 2012. "Sailing the water's edge: Where domestic politics meets foreign policy." Working Paper.

Milner, Helen V., and Dustin H. Tingley. 2010. "The political economy of US foreign aid: American legislators and the domestic politics of aid." *Economics and Politics* 22(2):200–232.

Minnes, Gordon. 2006. "The Canadian pulp and paper industry." *The Canadian Encyclopedia.*

Moore, W. H. 1998. "Repression and dissent: Substitution, context, and timing." *American Journal of Political Science* 42:851–73.

Morgan, Dan. 2000. *Merchants of grain.* iUniverse.

Morgan, T., and Anne C. Miers. 1999. "When threats succeed: A formal model of the threat and use of economic sanctions." In *Annual Meeting of the American Political Science Association, Atlanta, GA*, Vol. 264.

Morino, Tomozo. 1991. "China-Japan trade and investment relations." *Proceedings of the Academy of Political Science*, 87–94.

Morris, I. I. 1958. "Foreign policy issues in Japan's 1958 elections." *Pacific Affairs* 31(3):219–40.

Morrison, James W. 1995. "NATO expansion and alternative future security alignments." Technical report DTIC Document.

Morrissey, O. 2004. "Conditionality and aid effectiveness re-evaluated." *The World Economy* 27(2):153–71.

Morrow, James D., Randolph M. Siverson, and Tressa E. Tabares. 1998. "The political determinants of international trade: The major powers, 1907-90." *American Political Science Review* 92:649–61.

Most, B. A., and H. Starr. 1989. *Inquiry, logic, and international politics*. University of South Carolina Press.

Nafey, Abdul. 2007. "Mexico's asymmetrical interdependence: Beyond and after." *India Quarterly: A Journal of International Affairs* 63(1):161–88.

National Economic Council. 2000. "Vietnam bilateral trade agreement: Historic strengthening of the U.S.-Vietnam relationship." The White House.

Nilsson, L. 2002. "Trading relations: is the roadmap from Lomé to Cotonou correct?" *Applied Economics* 34(4):439–52.

Nilsson, L. 2007. "Comparative effects of EU and US trade policies on developing country exports." In *The European Union and Developing Countries: Trade, Aid, and Growth in an Integrating World*, 49–70. Edward Elgar.

Nixon, Richard. 1985. "Superpower summitry." *Foreign Affairs*, pp. 1–11.

Noman, Omar. 1990. *Pakistan: A political and economic history since 1947*. Kegan Paul International.

Nunn, N. 2007. "Relationship-specificity, incomplete contracts, and the pattern of trade." *The Quarterly Journal of Economics* 122(2):569.

Nye, Joseph S. 2011. "The changing nature of coercive power." *World Politics Review*.

OECD. 2011. http://www.oecd.org.

Oh, Jinhwan, and Laxmi Prasad Prasai. 2012. "Does gravity matter? Evidence from Nepals trade pattern." *International Area Studies Review* 15(2):161–75.

Ohno, Izumi, and Kenichi Ohno. 2005. "Fostering true ownership in Vietnam: from donor management to policy autonomy and content." In *True Ownership and Policy Autonomy: Managing Donors and Owning Policies*, 37. GRIPS Development Forum.

O'Leary, James P. 1985. "Economic warfare and strategic economics." *Comparative Strategy* 5(2):179–206.

Orbie, J. 2011. *Promoting labour standards through trade: normative power or regulatory state Europe?* Palgrave Macmillan.

O'Rourke, Kevin H., and Alan M. Taylor. 2006. "Democracy and protectionism." Technical report, National Bureau of Economic Research.

Ouchterlony, John. 1844. *The Chinese War: An account of all the operations of the British forces from the commencement to the Treaty of Nanking*. Saunders and Otley.

Özden, Ç., and E. Reinhardt. 2004. "First do no harm: The effect of trade preferences on developing country exports." Emory University, April.

Özden, Ç., and E. Reinhardt. 2005. "The perversity of preferences: GSP and developing country trade policies, 1976–2000." *Journal of Development Economics* 78(1): 1–21.

Özden, Ç., and G. Sharma. 2006. "Price effects of preferential market access: Caribbean basin initiative and the apparel sector." *The World Bank Economic Review* 20(2):241–59.

Palmer, G., and T. C. Morgan. 2010. *A Theory of Foreign Policy*. Princeton University Press.

Papayoanou, Paul A. 1997. "Economic interdependence and the balance of power." *International Studies Quarterly* 41(1):113–40.

Pape, Robert A. 1997. "Why economic sanctions do not work." *International Security* 22(2):90–136.

Pape, Robert Anthony. 1996. *Bombing to win: Air power and coercion in war*. Cornell University Press.

Pasha, Mustapha Kamal. 1992. "Islamization, civil society, and the politics of transition in Pakistan." In *Religion and Political Conflict in South Asia: India, Pakistan, and Sri Lanka*, 113–32. Praeger.

Path, Kosal. 2011. "The Sino-Vietnamese dispute over territorial claims, 1974–1978: Vietnamese nationalism and its consequences." *International Journal of Asian Studies* 8(2):189–220.

Patterson, G. 1965. "Would tariff preferences help economic development?" *The International Executive* 7(3):1–2.

Pedersen, M. B. 2008. *Promoting human rights in Burma: A critique of Western sanctions policy*. Rowman and Littlefield.

Pelc, Krzysztof J. 2011. "How states ration flexibility: Tariffs, remedies, and exchange rates as policy substitutes." *World Politics* 63(4):618–46.

Pellicer de Brody, Olga. 1972. *México y la Revolución cubana*. El Colegio de México.

Petersmann, E. U. 2000. "From 'negative' to 'positive' integration in the WTO: Time for mainstreaming human rights into WTO law?" *Common Market Law Review* 37(6):1363–82.

Pevehouse, Jon C. 2002. "Democracy from the outside-in? International organizations and democratization." *International Organization* 56(3):515–49.

Philippines Statistics Authority. 2013. "Foreign trade statistics of the Philippines." National Statistics Office.

Poast, P. 2012. "Does issue linkage work? Evidence from European Alliance negotiations, 1815 to 1945." *International Organization* 66(2):277–310.

Poe, S. C., C. N. Tate, and L. C. Keith. 1999. "Repression of the human right to personal integrity revisited: A global cross-national study covering the years 1976–1993." *International Studies Quarterly* 43(2):291–313.

Portela, C. 2012. *European Union sanctions and foreign policy: When and why do they work?* Vol. 64. Routledge.

Powaski, Ronald E. 1991. *Toward an entangling alliance: American isolationism, internationalism, and Europe, 1901-1950*. Vol. 22. Greenwood.

Powell, Robert. 2002. "Bargaining theory and international conflict." *Annual Review of Political Science* 5(1):1–30.

Pradhan, Prasanta Kumar. 2013. "India's relationship with Saudi Arabia: Forging a strategic partnership." *Strategic Analysis* 37(2):231–41.

Pregelj, V. N. 2005. *Normal-Trade-Relations (Most-Favored-Nation) policy of the United States*. CRS Report for Congress.

Prime, Penelope B. 2002. "China joins the WTO: How, why, and what now?" *Business Economics* 37(2):26–32.

Purcell, Susan Kaufman. 1997. "The changing nature of US-Mexican relations." *Journal of Interamerican Studies and World Affairs* 39(1):137–52.
Qureshi, A. H. 1998. "International trade and human rights from the perspective of the WTO." In *International Economic Law with a Human Face*, 159–173. Springer.
Rajamohan, P. G., Dil Bahadur Rahut, Jabin T. Jacob et al. 2008. *Changing paradigm of Indo-Japan relations: Opportunities and challenges*. Indian Council for Research on International Economic Relations.
Rauch, James E. 1999. "Networks versus markets in international trade." *Journal of International Economics* 48(1):7–35.
Rector, C. 2009. *Federations: the political dynamics of cooperation*. Cornell University Press.
Reed, W., D. H. Clark, T. Nordstrom, and W. Hwang. 2008. "War, power, and bargaining." *The Journal of Politics* 70(04):1203–16.
Regan, P. M. 2000. "Substituting policies during US interventions in internal conflicts." *Journal of Conflict Resolution* 44(1):90–106.
Reilly, James. 2012. "China's unilateral sanctions." *The Washington Quarterly* 35(4):121–33.
Rejali, D. 2009. *Torture and democracy*. Princeton University Press.
Resnick, Danielle, and Nicolas Van de Walle. 2013. *Democratic trajectories in Africa: Unravelling the impact of foreign aid*. Oxford University Press.
Rickard, Stephanie J., and Daniel Y. Kono. 2013. "Think globally, buy locally: International agreements and government procurement." *The Review of International Organizations* 9:1–20.
Ritchie, G. 1997. *Wrestling with the elephant: The inside story of the Canada-U.S. trade wars*. Macfarlane Walter and Ross.
Roach, Kent. 2003. *September 11': Consequences for Canada*. McGill-Queen's Press.
Rodrik, D., and R. Zeckhauser. 1988. "The dilemma of government responsiveness." *Journal of Policy Analysis and Management* 7(4):601–20.
Rolph, G. M. 1917. *Something about sugar: Its history, growth, manufacture and distribution*. J. J. Newbegin.
Rose, A. 2009. "The effect of membership in the GATT/WTO on trade: Where do we stand?" In Z. Drabek, ed., *Is the World Trade Organization attractive enough for emerging economies? Critical essays on the multilateral trading system*, 195–216. Palgrave Macmillan.
Rose, A. K. 2004. "Do we really know that the WTO increases trade?" *The American Economic Review* 94(1):98–114.
Rosenfeld, Everett. 2012. "Russia's accession to the WTO: Major commitments, possible implications." ITC.
Rosenthal, Mila. 2006. "The Cambodian Trade Agreement: A human rights race to the top?" In *Human Rights, Trade and Investment Matters*, 20–23. Amnesty International.
Ross, Robert S. 2000. "The 1995–96 Taiwan Strait confrontation: Coercion, credibility, and the use of force." *International Security* 25(2):87–123.
Roth, Stanley. 1998. "Waiver of Jackson-Vanik for Vietnam." State Department, Testimony before the Senate Finance Committee.
Rubinstein, Ariel. 1982. "Perfect equilibrium in a bargaining model." *Econometrica* 50(1):97–109.

Ruggie, John Gerard. 1992. "Multilateralism: the anatomy of an institution." *International Organization* 46:561–598.
Sagebien, Julia, and Demetria Tsourtouras. 1999. "Solidarity and entrepreneurship: The political economy of Mexico-Cuba commercial relations at the end of the twentieth century." In *Cuba in Transition*. Brookings Institution Press.
Salvucci, Richard J. 1991. "The origins and progress of US-Mexican trade, 1825-1884: 'Hoc opus, hic labor est,'" *The Hispanic American Historical Review* 71(4):697–735.
Sapir, A., and L. Lundberg. 1984. "The US Generalized System of Preferences and its impacts." In *The structure and evolution of recent US trade policy*, 195–236. University of Chicago Press.
Sasaki, Hitoshi, and Yuko Koga. 2003. "Trade between Japan and China: Dramatic expansion and structural changes." *Economic Commentary* 3.
Savada, Andrea Matles. 1991. "Nepal: A country study." Library of Congress.
Sayuri, Shimizu. 1995. "Perennial anxiety: Japan-US controversy over recognition of the PRC, 1952–1958." *Journal of American – East Asian Relations* 4:223–48.
Schaller, Michael. 1997. *Altered states: The United States and Japan since the occupation*. Oxford University Press.
Schelling, Thomas C. 1989. "Promises." *Negotiation Journal* 5(2):113–18.
Schelling, Thomas Crombie. 1966. *Arms and influence*. Vol. 190. Yale University Press.
Schimmelfennig, Frank. 2005. "Strategic calculation and international socialization: Membership incentives, party constellations, and sustained compliance in Central and Eastern Europe." *International Organization* 59:827–860.
Schneider, Christina J. 2009. *Conflict, negotiation and European Union enlargement*. Cambridge University Press.
Schultz, Kenneth A. 2001. *Democracy and coercive diplomacy*. Vol. 76. Cambridge University Press.
Sikkink, Kathryn. 2011. *The justice cascade: How human rights prosecutions are changing world politics*. WW Norton.
Simmons, Beth A. 2009. *Mobilizing for human rights: international law in domestic politics*. Cambridge University Press.
Simpson, Matthew T. 2007. "Chopping away at Chapter 11: The Softwood Lumber Agreement's effect on the NAFTA investor-state dispute resolution mechanism." *American University International Law Review* 22(3):479–515.
Singer, J. D. 1988. "Reconstructing the correlates of war dataset on material capabilities of states, 1816–1985." *International Interactions* 14(2):115–32.
Smith, Alastair. 1995. "The success and use of economic sanctions." *International Interactions* 21(3):229–45.
Smith, Gordon B. 1984. *The politics of East-West trade*. Westview Press.
Snyder, Jack, and Erica D. Borghard. 2011. "The cost of empty threats: A penny, not a pound." *American Political Science Review* 105(03):437–56.
Souva, Mark, Dale L. Smith, and Shawn Rowan. 2008. "Promoting trade: The importance of market protecting institutions." *The Journal of Politics* 70(02):383–92.
Spaulding, R. M. 1997. *Osthandel and Ostpolitik: German foreign trade policies in Eastern Europe from Bismarck to Adenauer*. Vol. 1. Berghahn Books.
Staiger, R. W., and G. Tabellini. 1999. "Do GATT rules help governments make domestic commitments?" *Economics and Politics* 11(2):109–44.
Steil, Benn, and Robert E. Litan. 2006. *Financial statecraft: The role of financial markets in American foreign policy*. Yale University Press.

Stevens, C., and J. Kennan. 2005. "Making trade preferences more effective." IDS Briefing, Institute for Development Studies.

Stevenson, Charles. 2012. *America's foreign policy toolkit: Key institutions and processes.* CQ Press.

Stirling, P. 1996. "Use of trade sanctions as an enforcement mechanism for basic human rights: A proposal for addition to the World Trade Organization." *American University International Law Review* 11:1.

Stone Sweet, Alec. 2010. "The European Court of Justice and the judicialization of EU governance." Living Reviews in EU Governance.

Strezhnev, Anton, and Erik Voeten. 2012. "United Nations General Assembly voting data." V4.

Subedi, Surya. 2006. "Dynamics of foreign policy and law: A study of Indo-Nepal relations."

Subedi, Surya P. 2013. "India's new bilateral investment promotion and protection treaty with Nepal: A new trend in state practice." *ICSID Review* 28(2):384–404.

Subramanian, A., and S. Wei. 2007. "The WTO promotes trade, strongly but unevenly." *Journal of International Economics* 72(1):151–75.

Suzumura, Kotaro. 1997. "Japan's accession to the GATT: A teacher by positive or negative examples?" *Hitotsubashi Journal of Economics* 38:101–23.

Tanner, Murray Scot. 2007. *Chinese economic coercion against Taiwan: A tricky weapon to use.* Rand Corp.

Thompson, Alexander. 2006. "Coercion through IOs: The Security Council and the logic of information transmission." *International Organization* 60(1):1.

Tiedemann, Arthur E. 2013. *Sources of Japanese tradition, abridged: Part 2: 1868 to 2000.* Columbia University Press.

Tirole, Jean. 1988. *The theory of industrial organization.* MIT Press.

Tobin, Jennifer L., and Susan Rose-Ackerman. 2011. "When BITs have some bite: The political-economic environment for bilateral investment treaties." *The Review of International Organizations* 6(1):1–32.

Tomz, M. 2007. *Reputation and international cooperation: sovereign debt across three centuries.* Princeton University Press.

Tomz, M., J. L. Goldstein, and D. Rivers. 2007. "Do we really know that the WTO increases trade? Comment." *The American Economic Review* 97(5):2005–18.

Tong, Zhenyuan. 2007. *Cross-strait economic relations in the era of globalization: China's leverage and Taiwan's vulnerability.* Lulu.

Tooze, A. 2006. *The wages of destruction: The making and breaking of the Nazi economy.* Allen Lane.

Travis, Karen F. 1992. "Women in global production and worker rights provisions in US trade laws." *Yale Journal of International Law* 17:173.

Tsoutouras, Demetria, and Julia Sagebien. 1998. *Mexico-Cuba commercial relations in the 1990s.* Saint Mary's University.

UNCTAD. 1998. "Handbook on the GSP scheme of the European Community: Generalized System of Preferences."

United Nations. 2003. *The DOHA development agenda: Perspectives from the ESCAP Region: Papers presented at the "High-level Regional Policy Dialogue on the WTO Negotiating Agenda in Preparation for Cancbun" and the "Regional Seminar on Facilitating the Accession of ESCAP Members to WTO through Regional Cooperation," Bangkok, 10-13 June 2003.* United Nations.

Upadhya, Sanjay. 2012. *Nepal and the geo-strategic rivalry between China and India*. Routledge.
Upreti, B. C. 2003. "India-Nepal relations: Dynamics, issues and problems." *South Asian Survey* 10(2):257–74.
U.S. Census Bureau. 2013. "U.S. trade statistics." U.S. Census Bureau.
U.S. Department of State. 2004. "Refugee admissions program for East Asia." Bureau of Population, Refugees, and Migration.
U.S. GAO. 2008. "U.S. trade preference programs provide important benefits, but a more integrated approach would better ensure programs meet shared goals." Report.
U.S. Government. 1985. "Soviet acquisition of militarily significant Western technology: An Update." Report.
Usa, Ibp. 2009. *US Vietnam economic and political cooperation handbook*. International Business Publications.
USTR. 2002. "U.S.-Cambodian textile agreement links increasing trade with improving workers' rights." USTR.
Uvin, Peter. 1993. "Do as I say, not as I do: The limits of political conditionality." *The European Journal of Development Research* 5(1):63–84.
Uvin, Peter, and Isabelle Biagiotti. 1996. "Global governance and the 'new' political conditionality." *Global Governance* 2(3):377–400.
Vachudova, Milada. 2005. *Europe undivided: Democracy, leverage, and integration after Communism*. Cambridge University Press.
Verdeja, L. 2006. "EU's preferential trade agreements with developing countries revisited." University of Nottingham, School of Economics.
Vermillion, D. I., G. P. Shivakoti, D. L. Vermillion, W. F. Lam, E. Ostrom, U. Pradhan, R. Yoder et al. 2005. "Irrigation sector reform in Asia: from 'participation with patronage' to 'empowerment with accountability.'" In *Asian irrigation in transition: Responding to challenges*, 409–34. Sage.
Vreeland, J. R. 2008. "Political institutions and human rights: Why dictatorships enter into the United Nations Convention against Torture." *International Organization* 62(1):65.
Wallander, C. A. 2000. "Institutional assets and adaptability: NATO after the Cold War." *International Organization* 54(4):705–35.
Wallner, Klaus. 2003. "Specific investments and the EU enlargement." *Journal of Public Economics* 87(5):867–82.
Walmsley, T. L., T. W. Hertel, and E. Ianchovichina. 2006. "Assessing the impact of China's WTO accession on investment." *Pacific Economic Review* 11(3):315–39.
Wan, Ming. 2001. *Human rights in Chinese foreign relations: Defining and defending national interests*. University of Pennsylvania Press.
Wang, Qingxin Ken. 1993. "Recent Japanese economic diplomacy in China: political alignment in a changing world order." *Asian Survey* 33(6):625–41.
Ward, Richard Edmund. 1992. *India's pro-Arab policy: A study in continuity*. Greenwood.
Weeks, Jessica L. 2008. "Autocratic audience costs: Regime type and signaling resolve." *International Organization* 62:35–64.
Weeks, Jessica L. 2012. "Strongmen and straw men: Authoritarian regimes and the initiation of international conflict." *American Political Science Review* 106(02):326–47.

Bibliography

Whang, Taehee. 2011. "Playing to the home crowd? Symbolic use of economic sanctions in the United States." *International Studies Quarterly* 55(3):787–801.
White, Christopher M. 2007. *Creating a Third World: Mexico, Cuba, and the United States during the Castro era*. UNMPress.
Wilson, B. 2007. "Compliance by WTO members with adverse WTO dispute settlement rulings: The record to date." *Journal of International Economic Law* 10(2):397–403.
Wolford, Scott, and Moonhawk Kim. 2012. "Alliances and the high politics of international trade." Working paper.
Womack, Brantly. 2006. *China and Vietnam: The politics of asymmetry*. Cambridge University Press.
Woodrow, Thomas. 2002. "The Sino-Soviet connection." *China Brief* 21.
World Bank. 2011. *World development indicators*. World Bank.
WTO. 2012. http://www.wto.org.
Wu, Chien-Huei. 2012. *WTO and the Greater China: Economic integration and dispute resolution*. Vol. 8. Martinus Nijhoff.
Yamazaki, F. 1996. "Potential erosion of trade preferences in agricultural products." *Food Policy* 21(4):409–17.
Yarbrough, B. V., and R. M. Yarbrough. 1992. *Cooperation and governance in international trade: The strategic organization approach*. Princeton University Press.
Yoshida, Shigeru, Yoshida Ken-Ichi, and Hiroshi Nara. 2007. *Yoshida Shigeru: Last Meiji man*. Rowman and Littlefield.
Zagel, G. M. 2004. "The WTO and trade-related human rights measures: Trade sanctions vs. trade incentives." *Austrian Review of International and European Law* 9: 119–60.

Index

Adair, Marshall F., 151
Afghanistan, invasion by Soviet Union, 92–93, 132
African Growth and Opportunity Act, 53
Albright, Madeline, 133
Alinsky, Saul, 109
American Federation of Labor and Congress of Industrial Organizations (AFL-CIO), 55, 125
Amnesty International, CIRI Index and, 119
Andean Trade Preference Act, 53, 64
Anderson, J., 67, 87
Anti-Comintern Pact, 52
Araral, Eduardo, Jr., 14
Argentina, relations with Soviet Union, 132
Armenia, relations with Turkey, 162
Armenian genocide, 115, 162
Association of Southeast Asian Nations (ASEAN)
  ASEAN-EU Economic Cooperation Agreement, 113–114
  Burma in, 113–114
  overview, 16
Australia, relations with Soviet Union, 132
Austria, annexation by Germany, 51, 53
Austria-Hungary
  Pig War (1906), 22
  Serbia, relations with, 22
Autarky, 49

Bagwell, K., 80
Baldwin, David, 20
Bangladesh
  foreign aid to, 163
  India, relations with, 23
  Nepal, relations with, 90, 94–97
  Saudi Arabia, relations with, 91
  United States, relations with, 57
Barshefsky, Charlene, 56
Bereuter, Doug, 104
Berman, Howard, 28, 135
Bilateral trade agreements, 46–68
  African Growth and Opportunity Act, 53
  Andean Trade Preference Act, 53, 64
  Caribbean Basin Trade and Partnership Act, 53, 64
  coercive diplomacy and, 13
  Cotonou Agreement, 53
  FDI and, 67
  foreign aid and, 67
  Germany, involving, 50–53
  GSP (*See* Generalized System of Preferences (GSP))
  MFN tariff rates and, 54
  overview, 17, 46–47
  preference programs, 53–54, 124–128 (*See also* Generalized System of Preferences (GSP))
  protectionism and, 49
  state similarity and, 46–47
Blanchard, Emily J., 64
Bond, Christopher, 156
Boxer, Barbara, 145
Brazil, relations with United States, 56

Bulgaria
    Germany, relations with, 52
    Serbia, relations with, 22
    Yugoslavia, relations with, 52
Burma
    in ASEAN, 113–114
    embargoes against, 113–114
    European Union, relations with, 113–114
    foreign aid to, 114
    GSP and, 113
    National League for Democracy, 113
    sanctions against, 113–114
    United States, relations with, 114
    in WTO, 114
Bush, George H.W., 134, 137
Bush, George W., 104
Buss, Terry F., 15

Cambodia
    CIRI index and, 148
    coercive diplomacy and, 1
    embargoes against, 146–148
    foreign aid to, 146–148
    human rights in, 146–148
    MFN tariff rates and, 146
    National Assembly, 148
    PNTR with, 146–148
    reduced effectiveness of coercive diplomacy and, 130, 146–148
    tariffs against, 147
    United States, relations with, 130, 146–148
    U.S.-Cambodia Bilateral Textile Trade Agreement, 146
    USTR and, 146–147
    in WTO, 147–148
Canada
    Soviet Union, relations with, 132
    United States, relations with, 24–25
Cardin, Ben, 135–136
Caribbean Basin Trade and Partnership Act, 53, 64
Carlsson, Jerker, 14
Carnegie, Allison, 88
Castro, Fidel, 102
Ceausescu, Nicolae, 149–150
Chamber of Commerce, 57
Charter of Economic Rights, 101
Cheibub, J.A., 62, 122
Chen Shui-Bian, 104–105
China
    Cheng Shin Rubber International Company, 106
    Chinese Academy of Social Sciences, 76–77
    CIRI index and, 142
    coercive diplomacy and, 1
    Communists in, 99–100, 141
    Export-Import Bank and, 140
    GSP and, 62
    human rights in, 136–142
    India, relations with, 7, 94–95
    Japan, relations with, 25–26, 73–75
    MFN tariff rates and, 75, 137–139
    Mongolia, relations with, 24
    Nepal, relations with, 7, 94–95
    Olympics in, 140
    "one China policy," 1
    Opium Wars (1842), 50
    Philippines, relations with, 23–24
    PNTR with, 138–141
    reduced effectiveness of coercive diplomacy and, 130, 136–142
    Russia, relations with, 76–77
    sanctions against, 137
    Sino-Japanese War (1894), 97
    Taiwan, relations with, 5, 91, 103–107
    tariffs against, 75, 137–138
    Tiananmen Square Incident, 75, 137–138
    United Kingdom, relations with, 50
    United States, relations with, 50, 75, 130, 136–142
    USTR and, 141
    Vietnam, relations with, 76
    in WTO, 70, 73–77, 136, 138–142
China Commission (CHINCOM), 137, 139–141
CHINCOM (China Commission), 137, 139–141
Chiquita Bananas, 27
Christensen, Thomas J., 20
CINC. *See* Correlates of War, Composite Index of National Capability (CINC)
Cingranelli, D.L., 122, 125
Cingranelli-Richards (CIRI) Human Rights Project, 119. *See also* CIRI index
CIRI index
    Cambodia and, 148
    China and, 142
    overview, 119
    Romania and, 152
    Russia and, 136
Clinton, Bill, 138, 140, 143
COCOM (Coordinating Committee for Multilateral Export Controls), 131

Index

Coercive diplomacy
  during Cold War, 74
  comparative perspective (*See* Comparative perspective of coercive diplomacy)
  defined, 20–21
  displacement of (*See* Displacement of coercive diplomacy)
  efficacy of coercion, 38–39
  FDI and, 111
  foreign aid and, 14–15, 110
  GATT and, 71–73
  instruments of coercion, 110–112
  international institutions, effect of, 2–4, 11
  international trade and, 4–6
  MFN tariff rates and, 130–131
  model of, 30–45
  model of coercive diplomacy, 30–45 (*See also* Model of coercive diplomacy)
  nature of investment, effect of, 12–15 (*See also* Nature of investment, effect of)
  overview, 1–2
  political hold-up problems, relationship to, 11
  reduced effectiveness of (*See* Reduced effectiveness of coercive diplomacy)
  sanctions and, 9, 11, 14–15, 21
  tariffs and, 110
  theoretical framework of (*See* Theoretical framework of coercive diplomacy)
  WTO and, 71–73
Cold War
  coercive diplomacy during, 74
  Japan and, 98, 100, 108
  Soviet Union and, 62, 132–133
Colombia
  GSP and, 58
  United States, relations with, 58
Commitment strategy, 69–88
  causal mechanism, testing of, 80–88
  contract intensity and, 83–84
  fixed capital investment and, 84–85
  GATT and, 26–27
  hypotheses regarding, 77–78
  inferences, 85–88
  investment, relationship with, 82
  logged imports and, 81–82, 84
  model of, 78–79
  overview, 17, 69–71
  political hold-up problems, reduction of, 77–80
  results of analysis, 80
  robustness checks, 85–88
  state similarity and, 81
  statistical tests of, 77–80
  trade, relationship with, 78
  variables in analysis, 78–79
  WTO enabling commitment, 26–28
Comparative perspective of coercive diplomacy, 89–108. *See also specific country*
  overview, 17–18, 89–91, 107–108
Conditionality, GSP and, 57–58
Constructivism, 11
Contract intensity, commitment strategy and, 83–84
Contract theory, political hold-up problems and, 10
Coordinating Committee for Multilateral Export Controls (COCOM), 131
Correlates of War, Composite Index of National Capability (CINC)
  for Bangladesh, 96
  coercive diplomacy and, 61
  for Cuba, 102
  for India, 94, 96, 99
  for Japan, 99
  for Mexico, 102
  for Nepal, 94, 96
  for Pakistan, 92
  for Saudi Arabia, 92
  for Taiwan, 104
  for United States, 99, 102, 104
Cotonou Agreement, 53
Cox, Christopher, 140
Cuba
  Mexico, relations with, 91, 101–103
  OAS, expulsion from, 102
Cyprus, invasion by Turkey, 162
Czech Republic in NATO, 156–157

Dalai Lama, 24
Davis, Christina L., 13
DeFazio, Peter, 135
Defense Department, 132
Dependence, 21–26
Displacement of coercive diplomacy, 109–128
  European Union, WTO-induced policy substitution in, 112–116
  foreign aid and, 122–124
  GSP and, 118, 124–128
  human rights and, 116–121, 124–128
  hypotheses regarding, 116–118
  instruments of coercion, 110–112
  measurements of, 116–118

Displacement of coercive diplomacy (*cont.*)
  overview, 2–4, 9, 18, 109–110
  preference programs and, 124–128
  statistical model of, 118–121
  statistical tests of WTO-induced policy substitution, 116–128
  worker rights and, 124–128
Dominican Republic
  Dominican Association of Free Zones, 58
  GSP and, 58
  Labor Code, 58
Drucker, Peter, 69
Dulles, John Foster, 99

Eaton, Jonathan, 86
The Economist, 51
Egypt
  foreign aid to, 163
  India, relations with, 93
Eisenhower, Dwight, 99
El Salvador, relations with Mexico, 101
Embargoes
  against Burma, 113–114
  against Cambodia, 146–148
  against Iran, 115
  against Japan, 74, 97
  against Soviet Union, 132–133
  against Spain, 22
  against Taiwan, 105
  against Vietnam, 142
Enforcement mechanisms, 15–16
Eritrea, foreign aid to, 163
European Union
  accession, political hold-up problems at, 156–157
  ASEAN-EU Economic Cooperation Agreement, 113–114
  Burma, relations with, 113–114
  coercive diplomacy and, 1
  Cotonou Agreement, 53
  displacement of coercive diplomacy in, 112–116
  dispute settlement mechanism, 15–16
  GSP and, 61–62
  Iran, relations with, 114–115
  Romania in, 151–152
  Serbia in, 157
  Treaty of Rome (1957), 117
  Turkey, relations with, 115–116
  WTO-induced policy substitution in, 112–116
  Zimbabwe, relations with, 113

Export Control Act of 1949, 97, 131, 137
Export-Import Bank
  China and, 140
  Russia, departure of, 14
  terrorism and, 111

Fang Lizhi, 137
FDI. *See* Foreign direct investment (FDI)
Financial transactions, 14
Finland, relations with Soviet Union, 22
Fixed capital investment, commitment strategy and, 84–85
Foreign aid
  to Bangladesh, 163
  bilateral trade agreements and, 67
  to Burma, 114
  to Cambodia, 146–148
  coercive diplomacy and, 14–15, 110
  displacement of coercive diplomacy and, 122–124
  to Egypt, 163
  to Eritrea, 163
  to Greece, 162
  to India, 163
  to Iran, 162
  to Kenya, 163
  to Pakistan, 162–163
  politicization of, 161–163
  to Turkey, 162
  to Vietnam, 144–145
  WTO and, 122–124
  to Zimbabwe, 113
Foreign direct investment (FDI)
  bilateral trade agreements and, 67
  coercive diplomacy and, 111
  political hold-up problems involving, 10, 49–50
France
  former colonies, relations with, 23
  National Assembly, 115
  Romania, relations with, 52
  Serbia, relations with, 22
  Turkey, relations with, 115–116
Freedom House
  on China, 142
  on human rights, 124
  on Russia, 136
Funderburk, David, 150

Game theory, 19–21. *See also* Model of coercive diplomacy; Theoretical framework of coercive diplomacy

Index

Gandhi, J., 62, 122
Gardner, Adam, 15
General Agreement on Tariffs and Trade (GATT)
   coercive diplomacy and, 71–73
   commitment strategy and, 26–27
   Japan in, 90, 97–100, 108
   Mexico in, 91, 101–103, 107–108
   Nepal in, 95–96
   overview, 7
   termination of, 86, 158
   United States and, 69–70
   WTO (*See* World Trade Organization (WTO))
Generalized System of Preferences (GSP)
   alliance with United States, effect of, 61–62
   Burma and, 113
   China and, 62
   coercive diplomacy and, 55–57
   Colombia and, 58
   conditionality and, 57–58
   democracy, effect of, 62
   descriptive statistics, 62–63
   displacement of coercive diplomacy and, 118, 124–128
   distribution of benefits, 59–60
   Dominican Republic and, 58
   European Union and, 61–62
   human rights and, 124–128
   hypotheses regarding exports, 60–62
   Israel and, 59
   measurement of exports, 60–62
   MFN tariff rates and, 54
   model regarding, 64–68
   OAS and, 61
   OECD and, 55, 61
   overview, 53–60
   Pakistan and, 60
   power, effect of, 61
   Russia and, 62
   Soviet Union and, 62
   state similarity and, 64–68
   statistical tests of coercive diplomacy, 60–68
   terrorism and, 55
   Thailand and, 59–60
   underinvestment and, 57–58
   United States and, 55–68
   USTR and, 55–56, 62–63, 125
   Vietnam and, 144–145
   worker rights and, 124–128
George, Alexander, 89

Germany
   Austria, annexation of, 51, 53
   bilateral trade agreements involving, 50–53
   Bulgaria, relations with, 52
   in European Union, 16
   Greece, relations with, 52
   Hungary, relations with, 52
   Poland, relations with, 52
   Romania, relations with, 52
   Russia, relations with, 14, 48
   state similarity and, 50–53
   Turkey, relations with, 52
   Yugoslavia, relations with, 51–52
Gorbachev, Mikhail, 133–134
Grassley, Chuck, 151
Greece
   foreign aid to, 162
   Germany, relations with, 52
   Serbia, relations with, 162
Group of 77, 101
GSP. *See* Generalized System of Preferences (GSP)
Guatemala
   United States, relations with, 56–57
   U.S./Guatemala Labor Education Project, 56

Hakobyan, Shushanik, 64
Hawaii (Kingdom)
   coercive diplomacy and, 1, 5
   United States, relations with, 1, 5
Head, Keith, 78, 86
Hirschman, A.O., 50–51
Hitler, Adolf, 51
Hold-up problems. *See* Political hold-up problems
Hoyer, Steny, 140
Humanitarian Aid Corridor Act, 162
Human rights
   in Cambodia, 146–148
   in China, 136–142
   displacement of coercive diplomacy and, 116–121, 124–128
   GSP and, 124–128
   OECD and, 117–119
   in Romania, 149–152
   in Soviet Union, 131–135
   in Vietnam, 142–146
   WTO and, 116–120, 124–128
Human Rights Watch, on Vietnam, 145
Humphrey, George M., 100

Hungary
  Germany, relations with, 52
  in NATO, 156–157
Hyde, Henry, 145

IAEA (International Atomic Energy Agency), 115
IMF (International Monetary Fund), 78
India
  Bangladesh, relations with, 23
  China, relations with, 7, 94–95
  Confederation of Indian Industry, 93
  Egypt, relations with, 93
  foreign aid to, 163
  Iraq, relations with, 93
  Israel, relations with, 93
  Japan, relations with, 90, 97–100
  Nepal, relations with, 5, 7, 23, 70, 90, 94–97
  Pakistan, war with, 91
  Peace and Friendship Treaty (1950), 94–95
  protectionism in, 95
  Saudi Arabia, relations with, 90–93
  Soviet Union, relations with, 92–93
  Sri Lanka, relations with, 23
  Syria, relations with, 93
International Atomic Energy Agency (IAEA), 115
International institutions
  coercive diplomacy, effect on, 2–4, 11
  enforcement mechanisms, 15–16
  political hold-up problems in absence of, 47–53
International Military Tribunal for the Far East, 98
International Monetary Fund (IMF), 78
International relations, implications for, 158–160
International trade
  coercive diplomacy and, 4–6
  political hold-up problems and, 5–6
Iran
  embargoes against, 115
  European Union, relations with, 114–115
  foreign aid to, 162
  sanctions against, 114–115
  in WTO, 115
Iraq
  India, relations with, 93
  Kuwait, invasion of, 93

Ishaq, Mohammed, 133–134
Israel
  GSP and, 59
  India, relations with, 93
  United States, relations with, 59
Italy, relations with Yugoslavia, 52

Jackson-Vanik Amendment, 132, 134–136, 143
Japan
  China, relations with, 25–26, 73–75
  Cold War and, 98, 100, 108
  embargoes against, 74, 97
  in GATT, 90, 97–100, 108
  India, relations with, 90, 97–100
  Korea, annexation of, 13, 97–98
  Manchuria, annexation of, 97–98
  MFN tariff rates and, 99
  Russia, relations with, 97, 99
  Russo-Japanese War (1904), 14
  Sino-Japanese War (1894), 97
  Socialists in, 74, 98
  Taiwan, annexation of, 97
  Taiwan, relations with, 74
  United Kingdom, relations with, 13
  United States, relations with, 27, 50, 90, 97–100

Kennan, George, 98
Kenya, foreign aid to, 163
Korea
  annexation by Japan, 13, 97–98
  Korean War, 137
Kortum, Samuel, 86
Kurile Islands, 97
Kuwait, invasion by Iraq, 93
Kyl, John, 104

Lang, Jeffrey, 157
Lantos, Tom, 104, 151
Latin American and Caribbean Economic System, 101
Laughlin, Gregory, 150
Lee Teng-hui, 105
Levin, Sander, 28
Levin-Bereuter Proposal, 140
Libya
  terrorism and, 22
  United States, relations with, 22
Lofgren, Zoe, 144
Logged imports, commitment strategy and, 81–82, 84

Index

Magnitsky Act, 135–136
Manchuria, annexation by Japan, 97–98
Mayer, Thierry, 78, 86
McCain, John, 147
McInnis, Scott, 104
MERCOSUR, 16
Mexico
  Cuba, relations with, 91, 101–103
  El Salvador, relations with, 101
  in GATT, 91, 101–103, 107–108
  Nicaragua, relations with, 101
  tariffs against, 102
  United States, relations with, 5, 46, 91, 101–103
  in WTO, 70
MFN tariff rates. *See* Most favored nation (MFN) tariff rates
Military action, 50
Milner, Helen V., 29
Mobile Transatlantic Oceanic Corporation, 149–150
Model of coercive diplomacy, 30–45
  cost uncertainty in, 42–45
  deviation from WTO commitments in, 39–42
  efficacy of coercion in, 38–39
  extensions of, 39–45
  investment decision in, 36–38
  overview, 30–34
  solution of, 34–39
  state similarity and, 37–38
  WTO membership, effect of, 35–39
Mongolia
  China, relations with, 24
  coercive diplomacy and, 1
Most favored nation (MFN) tariff rates
  bilateral trade agreements and, 54
  Cambodia and, 146
  China and, 75, 137–139
  coercive diplomacy and, 130–131
  GSP and, 54
  Japan and, 99
  Nepal and, 70, 96
  reduced effectiveness of coercive diplomacy and, 153
  Romania and, 149–151
  Soviet Union and, 134–135
  Vietnam and, 142–145
  WTO and, 7, 71, 73
Myanmar. *See* Burma

Nagasaki Flag Incident, 74
National Economic Council, 144
NATO. *See* North Atlantic Treaty Organization (NATO)
Nature of investment, effect of, 12–15
  bilateral trade agreements and, 13
  financial transactions and, 14
  foreign aid and, 14–15
Nehru, Jawaharlal, 98
Neoliberalism, 11
Nepal
  Bangladesh, relations with, 90, 94–97
  China, relations with, 7, 94–95
  coercive diplomacy and, 1
  in GATT, 95–96
  India, relations with, 5, 7, 23, 70, 90, 94–97
  MFN tariff rates and, 70, 96
  Peace and Friendship Treaty (1950), 94–95
  in WTO, 70, 90, 94–97
Neutrality Act, 97
New York Times, 139, 141
Nicaragua
  Contras in, 101
  Mexico, relations with, 101
  Sandinistas in, 101
Nixon, Richard, 132
North American Free Trade Agreement, 15
North Atlantic Treaty Organization (NATO)
  accession, political hold-up problems at, 156–157
  Air Defense Ground Environment, 156
  Czech Republic in, 156–157
  Hungary in, 156–157
  Poland in, 156–157
  political hold-up problems at accession, 156–157
  Romania in, 151–152
  Ukraine in, 157
Nunes, Devin, 134
Nye, Joseph S., 20

OAS. *See* Organization of American States (OAS)
ODP (Orderly Departure Program), 143
OECD. *See* Organization for Economic Cooperation and Development (OECD)
Office of Trade Representative (USTR)
  Cambodia and, 146–147
  China and, 141
  GSP and, 55–56, 62–63, 125
Olympics in China, 140
Opium Wars (1842), 50

Orderly Departure Program (ODP), 143
Organization for Economic Cooperation and
    Development (OECD)
  GSP and, 55, 61
  human rights and, 117–119
Organization of American States (OAS)
  Cuba, expulsion of, 102
  GSP and, 61
Özden, Ç., 54

Pakistan
  foreign aid to, 162–163
  GSP and, 60
  India, war with, 91
  sanctions against, 92
  Saudi Arabia, relations with, 90–93
  United Arab Emirates, relations with, 91
  United States, relations with, 60
Pal, Radhabinod, 98
Pallone, Frank, 151
Pape, Robert Anthony, 20
Pascrell, Bill, 135
Pasquarello, T.E., 122, 125
Pauling, Linus, 46
Peace and Friendship Treaty (1950), 94–95
Pearl Harbor attack, 97
Permanent normal trade relations (PNTR)
  with Cambodia, 146–148
  with China, 138–141
  with Romania, 149–151
  with Russia, 131–135
  with Soviet Union, 131–135
  with Vietnam, 143–144
Perry, William, 157
Philippines
  China, relations with, 23–24
  Department of Agriculture, 24
  Pilipino Banana Growers and Exporters
    Association, 24
Pig War (1906), 22
PNTR. *See* Permanent normal trade relations
    (PNTR)
Poland
  Germany, relations with, 52
  Law on Citizenship, 6
  in NATO, 156–157
  Soviet Union, relations with, 131
  West Germany, relations with, 6
Political hold-up problems
  in absence of international institutions,
    47–53
  at accession, 156–158

autarky, 49
coercive diplomacy, relationship to, 11
commitment strategy reducing, 77–80
contract theory and, 10
FDI, involving, 10, 49–50
international trade and, 5–6
military action, 50
overview, 2–4
between states, 10–11
underinvestment, 48
WTO reducing, 5–9
Portman, Rob, 28
Preference programs
  displacement of coercive diplomacy and,
    124–128
  GSP (*See* Generalized System of Preferences
    (GSP))
  overview, 53–54
Protectionism
  bilateral trade agreements and, 49
  in India, 95
  reduced effectiveness of coercion and,
    152–153
  WTO and, 73

Rauch, James E., 83
Reagan, Ronald, 132, 134
Realism, 11
Red Cross, 75, 138
Reduced effectiveness of coercive diplomacy,
    129–154
  Cambodia and, 130, 146–148
  China and, 130, 136–142
  hypotheses regarding, 130–131
  MFN tariff rates and, 153
  overview, 9, 18, 129–130, 152–154
  protectionism and, 152–153
  Romania and, 130, 149–152
  Russia and, 130–136
  tariffs and, 153
  United States influence and, 130–131
  Vietnam and, 130, 142–146
Regional trade agreements (RTAs), 53
Relationship specificity, 21–26
Resettlement Opportunity for Vietnamese
    Returnees (ROVR), 142
Ridgway, Rozanne, 149
Ritter, Karl, 51
Romania
  CIRI index and, 152
  coercive diplomacy and, 1
  in European Union, 151–152

Index

France, relations with, 52
Germany, relations with, 52
human rights in, 149–152
MFN tariff rates and, 149–151
in NATO, 151–152
PNTR with, 149–151
reduced effectiveness of coercive diplomacy and, 130, 149–152
United States, relations with, 130, 149–152
in WTO, 149, 152
Romanian Americana, 150
Roosevelt, Franklin D., 97
Roth, William, 147
ROVR (Resettlement Opportunity for Vietnamese Returnees), 142
RTAs (Regional trade agreements), 53
Russia. *See also* Soviet Union
China, relations with, 76–77
CIRI index and, 136
coercive diplomacy and, 1
Export-Import Bank, departure from, 14
Gazprom, 76
Germany, relations with, 14, 48
GSP and, 62
Japan, relations with, 97, 99
PNTR with, 135–136
reduced effectiveness of coercive diplomacy and, 130–136
Russo-Japanese War (1904), 14
United States, relations with, 130–136, 135–136
in WTO, 28, 48, 70, 76–77, 135–136
Russo-Japanese War (1904), 14

Salinas de Gortari, Carlos, 103
SALT (Strategic Arms Limitation Talks), 132
Sanctions
against Burma, 113–114
against China, 137
coercive diplomacy and, 9, 11, 14–15, 21
against Iran, 114–115
against Pakistan, 92
against Serbia, 162
against Soviet Union, 131–132
terrorism and, 14
WTO and, 71–72
against Zimbabwe, 113
San Francisco Peace Conference, 98
Saudi Arabia
Bangladesh, relations with, 91
India, relations with, 90–93

Pakistan, relations with, 90–93
United States, relations with, 92
in WTO, 70, 90–93
Scala, Armand A., 150
Schacht, Hjalmar, 51
Schelling, Thomas, 20
Section 301, 69–70
Serbia. *See also* Yugoslavia
Austria-Hungary, relations with, 22
Bulgaria, relations with, 22
in European Union, 157
France, relations with, 22
Greece, relations with, 162
Pig War (1906), 22
sanctions against, 162
Sergei Magnitsky Rule of Law Accountability Act, 135–136
Sharma, G., 54
Shifting of coercive diplomacy. *See* Displacement of coercive diplomacy
Sino-Japanese War (1894), 97
Smith, Christopher, 139, 150
Smoot-Hawley Act, 133
Somolekae, Gloria, 14
Southern Common Market (MERCOSUR), 16
Soviet Union. *See also* Russia
Afghanistan, invasion of, 92–93, 132
Argentina, relations with, 132
Australia, relations with, 132
Canada, relations with, 132
Cold War and, 62, 132–133
embargoes against, 132–133
fall of, 75
Finland, relations with, 22
GSP and, 62
human rights in, 131–135
India, relations with, 92–93
MFN tariff rates and, 134–135
PNTR with, 131–135
Poland, relations with, 131
sanctions against, 131–132
tariffs against, 132–133
United States, relations with, 131–135
Spain
embargoes against, 22
former colonies, relations with, 23
Spratly Islands, 24
Sri Lanka
coercive diplomacy and, 1
India, relations with, 23
Staiger, R.W., 80

State Department
  China and, 141–142
  CIRI Index and, 119
  Japan and, 97
  Russia and, 134
State similarity
  bilateral trade agreements and, 46–47
  commitment strategy and, 81
  Germany and, 50–53
  GSP and, 64–68
  model of coercive diplomacy and, 37–38
Strategic Arms Limitation Talks (SALT), 132
Sunni Muslims, 91
Syria, relations with India, 93

Taiwan
  China, relations with, 5, 91, 103–107
  embargoes against, 105
  Japan, annexation by, 97
  Japan, relations with, 74
  United States, relations with, 91, 103–107
  in WTO, 91, 103–107
Taiwan Relations Act, 103–104
Tariffs
  against Cambodia, 147
  against China, 75, 137–138
  coercive diplomacy and, 110
  GSP and (*See* Generalized System of Preferences (GSP))
  against Mexico, 102
  MFN tariff rates (*See* Most favored nation (MFN) tariff rates)
  reduced effectiveness of coercive diplomacy and, 153
  against Soviet Union, 132–133
  WTO and, 116
Terrorism
  Export-Import Bank and, 111
  GSP and, 55
  Libya and, 22
  sanctions and, 14
Thailand
  GSP and, 59–60
  United States, relations with, 59–60
Theoretical framework of coercive diplomacy, 19–38
  assumptions in, 20–29
  coercive diplomacy defined in, 20–21
  commitment, WTO enabling, 26–28
  dependence in, 21–26
  domestic policy assumptions, 28–29

game theory in, 19–21
  international relations, implications for, 158–160
  model of coercive diplomacy, 30–45 (*See also* Model of coercive diplomacy)
  overview, 17
  relationship specificity in, 21–26
  underinvestment in, 21–26
  welfare, implications for, 160–163
Thomas, Craig, 147
Tiananmen Square Incident, 75, 137–138
Tingley, Dustin H., 29
Trading with the Enemy Act of 1917, 136–137
Treaty of Nanking (1842), 50
Treaty of Rome (1957), 117
Turkey
  Armenia, relations with, 162
  Armenian genocide and, 115, 162
  Cyprus, invasion of, 162
  European Union, relations with, 115–116
  foreign aid to, 162
  France, relations with, 115–116
  Germany, relations with, 52
  Kurds in, 162
  in WTO, 115–116

Ukraine, NATO and, 157
Underinvestment
  conditionality and, 57–58
  GSP and, 57–58
  as political hold-up problem, 48
  in theoretical framework of coercive diplomacy, 21–26
United Arab Emirates, relations with Pakistan, 91
United Kingdom
  China, relations with, 50
  Foreign Office, 52
  former colonies, relations with, 23
  Japan, relations with, 13
  Opium Wars (1842), 50
United Nations
  Charter, 71
  Conference on Trade and Development, 55
  Security Council, 115
United States
  AFL-CIO, 55, 125
  African Growth and Opportunity Act, 53
  Andean Trade Preference Act, 53, 64
  Bangladesh, relations with, 57

Index

Brazil, relations with, 56
Burma, relations with, 114
Cambodia, relations with, 130, 146–148
Canada, relations with, 24–25
Caribbean Basin Trade and Partnership Act, 53, 64
Chamber of Commerce, 57
China, relations with, 50, 75, 130, 136–142
China Commission (CHINCOM), 137, 139–141
Colombia, relations with, 58
Coordinating Committee for Multilateral Export Controls (COCOM), 131
Defense Department, 132
Export Control Act of 1949, 97, 131, 137
Export-Import Bank (*See* Export-Import Bank)
GATT and, 69–70
GSP and, 55–68
Guatemala, relations with, 56–57
Hawaii (Kingdom), relations with, 1, 5
Humanitarian Aid Corridor Act, 162
Israel, relations with, 59
Jackson-Vanik Amendment, 132, 134–136, 143
Japan, relations with, 27, 50, 90, 97–100
Levin-Bereuter Proposal, 140
Libya, relations with, 22
Magnitsky Act, 135–136
Mexico, relations with, 5, 46, 91, 101–103
National Economic Council, 144
Neutrality Act, 97
Orderly Departure Program (ODP), 143
Pakistan, relations with, 60
reduced effectiveness of coercive diplomacy in (*See* Reduced effectiveness of coercive diplomacy)
Resettlement Opportunity for Vietnamese Returnees (ROVR), 142
Romania, relations with, 130, 149–152
Russia, relations with, 130–136, 135–136
Saudi Arabia, relations with, 92
Section 301, 69–70
Smoot-Hawley Act, 133
Soviet Union, relations with, 131–135
State Department (*See* State Department)
Taiwan, relations with, 91, 103–107
Taiwan Relations Act, 103–104
Thailand, relations with, 59–60
Trading with the Enemy Act of 1917, 136–137

U.S.-Cambodia Bilateral Textile Trade Agreement, 146
U.S.-China Business Council, 137
U.S./Guatemala Labor Education Project, 56
USTR (*See* Office of Trade Representative (USTR))
Vietnam, relations with, 130, 142–146
Universal Declaration of Human Rights, 116–117
USTR. *See* Office of Trade Representative (USTR)

Van de Walle, Nicolas, 14
van Wincoop, E., 67, 87
Venezuela, Latin American and Caribbean Economic System and, 101
Vietnam
  China, relations with, 76
  coercive diplomacy and, 1
  embargoes against, 142
  foreign aid to, 144–145
  GSP and, 144–145
  human rights in, 142–146
  MFN tariff rates and, 142–145
  Orderly Departure Program (ODP), 143
  PNTR with, 143–144
  reduced effectiveness of coercive diplomacy and, 130, 142–146
  Resettlement Opportunity for Vietnamese Returnees (ROVR), 142
  United States, relations with, 130, 142–146
  in WTO, 142, 144–146
Vietnam Human Rights Act of 2008, 145
Vreeland, J.R., 62, 122

Wei Jingsheng, 141
Welfare, implications for, 160–163
  domestic actors and, 161
  politicization of other areas, 161–163
Wellstone, Paul, 75, 138, 157
Wen Jaibao, 76
West Germany, relations with Poland, 6
Worker rights
  displacement of coercive diplomacy and, 124–128
  GSP and, 124–128
  WTO and, 124–128
World Bank, 147
World Court, 134

World Trade Organization (WTO)
  accession, political hold-up problems at, 158
  Burma in, 114
  Cambodia in, 147–148
  China in, 70, 73–77, 136, 138–142
  coercive diplomacy and, 71–73
  commitment strategy (*See* Commitment strategy)
  dispute settlement system, 8–9, 26–28
  enforcement mechanism, 26–28
  foreign aid and, 122–124
  Government Procurement Agreement, 114
  human rights and, 116–120, 124–128
  international relations, implications for, 160
  Iran in, 115
  Mexico in, 70
  MFN tariff rates and, 7, 71, 73
  model of coercive diplomacy, effect of WTO membership in, 35–39
  Nepal in, 70, 90, 94–97
  protectionism and, 73
  reduced effectiveness of coercive diplomacy, WTO entry and (*See* Reduced effectiveness of coercive diplomacy)
  reducing political hold-up problems, 5–9
  Romania in, 149, 152
  Russia in, 28, 48, 70, 76–77, 135–136
  sanctions and, 71–72
  Saudi Arabia in, 70, 90–93
  studies regarding, 12
  Taiwan in, 91, 103–107
  tariffs and, 116
  Turkey in, 115–116
  Vietnam in, 142, 144–146
  welfare, implications for, 160–163
  worker rights and, 124–128
  Zimbabwe in, 113
WTO. *See* World Trade Organization (WTO)

Yanukovich, Victor, 157
Yugoslavia. *See also* Serbia
  Bulgaria, relations with, 52
  Germany, relations with, 51–52
  Italy, relations with, 52

Zimbabwe
  European Union, relations with, 113
  foreign aid to, 113
  sanctions against, 113
  in WTO, 113
Zoelick, Robert, 56

For EU product safety concerns, contact us at Calle de José Abascal, 56–1°,
28003 Madrid, Spain or eugpsr@cambridge.org.

 www.ingramcontent.com/pod-product-compliance
Ingram Content Group UK Ltd.
Pitfield, Milton Keynes, MK11 3LW, UK
UKHW011315060825
461487UK00005B/85